The Early Life of
Walt Disney

To Maxwell, my 'little Disney biographer,'
Henry, my 'little historian,'
and Andrea, who made it all happen.

The Early Life of Walt Disney

Andrew Stanley Kiste

WHITE OWL

AN IMPRINT OF PEN & SWORD BOOKS LTD.
YORKSHIRE – PHILADELPHIA

First published in Great Britain in 2021 by
White Owl
An imprint of
Pen & Sword Books Ltd
Yorkshire – Philadelphia

ISBN 978 1 52678 080 5

Typeset by Mac Style
Printed and bound by CPI Group (UK) Ltd
Croydon, CR0 4YY

Pen & Sword Books Limited incorporates the imprints of Atlas,
Archaeology, Aviation, Discovery, Family History, Fiction, History,
Maritime, Military, Military Classics, Politics, Select, Transport,
True Crime, Air World, Frontline Publishing, Leo Cooper, Remember
When, Seaforth Publishing, The Praetorian Press, Wharncliffe
Local History, Wharncliffe Transport, Wharncliffe True Crime
and White Owl.

For a complete list of Pen & Sword titles please contact

PEN & SWORD BOOKS LIMITED
47 Church Street, Barnsley, South Yorkshire, S70 2AS, England
E-mail: enquiries@pen-and-sword.co.uk
Website: www.pen-and-sword.co.uk

Or

PEN AND SWORD BOOKS
1950 Lawrence Rd, Havertown, PA 19083, USA
E-mail: Uspen-and-sword@casematepublishers.com
Website: www.penandswordbooks.com

Contents

Acknowledgements

When I was first approached by White Owl Books to write a biography about Walt Disney, I quickly became overwhelmed. Not only is Walt Disney a historical figure that I admire personally, but millions of people around the world have grown up with 'Uncle Walt' and the work he is famous for playing prominently in their lives. *How do I do justice to this great man?* I asked myself. *How do I tell his story in a way that has never been told before while making it interesting and engaging to a new audience? And how does someone like me, a high school history teacher living in suburban North Carolina, even begin to convey how important this man's story is to me and everyone who adores his work?*

As a result, there is no way I could have successfully undertaken this project without a number of people who have provided me with essential help along the way.

I first want to give thanks to those closest to me: God, who has bestowed me with the gift of writing and storytelling; my wife Andrea, who never gave up hope on me and supported me wholeheartedly in my pursuit of research while working on this project for the last couple of years; and my children, who always got excited about and asked questions regarding 'Daddy's book'.

I also would like to thank the staff at White Owl Books, including Lori Jones, Aileen Pringle, Natasha Weale, and Jonathan Wright, for their interest in the life of Walt Disney. I appreciate their willingness to take a chance on me in tackling this enormous undertaking, as well as their patience in the face of dozens of emails I sent regarding everything from word count and illustrations to cover art and contracts.

I also want to extend a very gracious thank you to Mr Titus Koesters, who produced the drawing of Walt Disney for the cover art. I was very lucky to get to know Titus in 2019 as a sophomore student in my Advanced Placement US History class. Titus is a very humble and extremely talented young man who creates excellent pieces of artwork, and I can't wait to see where his talent takes him in the future.

I also would like to thank everyone with whom I developed relationships during my research trips to Chicago and Missouri during the first half of 2020. Robert Coker and his staff over at the Walt Disney Birthplace and The O-Zell Soda Co. were incredibly helpful in bringing the Chicago of Elias Disney's day to life. Rey Colón was also invaluable in developing the narrative of Elias and Flora's design and construction of the houses on Tripp Avenue, as well as their role in shaping life in the neighbourhood of Hermosa.

The people of Missouri were also wonderful and incredibly helpful in bringing Walt Disney to life for me, going above and beyond to help me, even during the restrictions created by COVID-19. I am forever thankful to Kaye Malins, Director of the Walt Disney Hometown Museum in Marceline, who provided my family and I with a wonderful couple of days in town, touring us around and treating us to a delicious lunch (including Dusty Millers) at Ma Vic's Café. I would also like to thank her for getting us into the Disney farmhouse, an evening I will remember for the rest of my life. I would like to thank Ms Chris Ankeney and her family for allowing us to stay on Manly Howe Taylor's farm, as well as sharing the family's story and photographs with us. Dan Viets, Director of Thank You Walt Disney, Inc. also deserves my gratitude, as he spent his afternoon touring us around Kansas City and showing off the Laugh-O-gram studio building. Finally, thank you to Ms Roberta Long, who invited me to sit on the front porch of her home, the Disneys' Bellefontaine house, while she told me stories about her history in the house. Seeing the garage behind the house was particularly special, allowing me to touch the very building that was built with both Elias and Walt's hands.

I owe a special thanks to Michael Tritt, Chief Marketing Officer, and Lauren Hypse Kovarna, Marketing Manager, of Union Station. While Union Station was closed due to COVID-19 during our trip to Kansas City, Lauren was able to schedule us a tour with Michael, who gave up a few hours to show us around. Lauren was also instrumental in providing me with the photographs of Union Station during the 1920s, allowing my readers to visualise some of the sights and locations that Walt experienced during his young adulthood in Kansas City.

Finally, I would be remiss if I didn't take a moment to express thanks to the amazing help I had in researching this book. When it came to some topics, especially the role of the American Red Cross in the First World War, there was only so far I could get through basic web searches and books. The staff at the library of the University of North Carolina at Greensboro were incredibly helpful in locating the annual reports of the American Red Cross, while Jean Shulman from the American Red Cross was instrumental in providing documents regarding Walt's service in the relief organisation, including the passport application he forged.

Thus, while the story of the young Walt Disney has been a wonderful one to tell, the credit belongs to all of those above. From the bottom of my heart, and from everyone who picks up this book, thank you.

Note

Everything that I have written is factual. Any piece of actual information has come directly from some sort of primary source, whether book, newspaper article, video, telegram, scientific study, or peer-reviewed article. I also use photographs and interviews to flesh out the conversations and thoughts that various individuals had, interspersed with quotes and dialogue pulled from interviews and primary source material. None of this is historically or factually inaccurate, but rather a narrative representation of actual events that happened based on individuals' recollections of specific events.

A select bibliography of sources can be found at the end of this volume.

Cast of Characters

Call, Charles and Henrietta Gross: Walt Disney's maternal grandfather and father to Flora (née Call) Disney.

Cauger, Arthur Vern (A.V.): owner of the Kansas City Slide Company, which later became known as the Kansas City Film Ad Company.

Cottingham, James: Principal of Benton Grammar School in Kansas City.

Crane, William: Civil War veteran who was the previous owner of the farm that Elias purchased north of Marceline, Missouri.

Davis, Virginia: discovered in 1923 at the age of four by Walt Disney; he would later sign her to become the titular character of his Laugh-O-gram animated series, the Alice Comedies. Davis would be a part of the series for a year until her parents disagreed with Walt on salary.

Disney, Arundel Elias and Maria Swan: Walt Disney's paternal great-grandparents, who emigrated from Ireland to Canada in 1834.

Disney, Elias: Walt Disney's father, who was born in Bluevale, Canada and would later move to the U.S. and marry Flora Call.

Disney, Flora (née Call): Walt Disney's mother, who was born in Steuben, Ohio and would later meet Elias Disney in Ellis, Kansas.

Disney, Herbert Arthur: firstborn of Elias and Flora Disney and older brother of Walt Disney.

Disney, Kepple and Francis Best: Walt Disney's paternal great-great-grandparents who abided in County Kilkenny, Ireland.

Disney, Kepple and Mary Richardson: Walt Disney's paternal grandparents, who resided in Bluevale, Canada.

Disney, Lillian (née Bounds): wife of Walt Disney who was originally hired to be an ink-and-paint girl for the Disney Bros. Studio.

Disney, Margaret (née Rogers): wife of Robert Disney and aunt of Walt Disney, who provided her nephew with art supplies, inspiring his passion for illustration, and later, animation.

Disney, Raymond Arnold: second child of Elias and Flora Disney and older brother of Walt Disney.

Disney, Robert: the second son of Kepple and Mary (née Richardson) Disney and younger brother of Elias Disney. Known by his nickname in Marceline as 'Gold Bug' Disney, Robert often migrated around the United States, searching for (and often finding) economic success in real estate.

Disney, Roy Oliver: third child of Elias and Flora Disney, and Walt Disney's older brother who partnered with him in his pursuits as an animator as part of the Disney Bros. Studio.

Disney, Ruth Flora: fifth child of Elias and Flora Disney and younger sister of Walt.

Disney, Walter Elias: fourth child of Elias and Flora Disney and the hero of our story and animation pioneer. Shortened his name to Walt in late 1919 while working at Pesmen-Rubin, his first job as a professional artist.

Dollard, Kathleen: ink-and-paint girl who worked for the Disney Bros. Studio in Los Angeles.

Feld, Milton: general manager of Kansas City's Newman Theater.

Fleischer, Max: creator of 'Out of the Inkwell', an immensely popular animated series during the early days of syndicated animation.

Flickinger, Clem: childhood friend of Walt Disney during his time living in Marceline, Missouri.

Francis, Edna: long-suffering fiancée and later wife of Roy Disney, sister of Roy's friend, Mitch Francis.

Francis, Mitch: Friend of Roy Disney and brother of Roy's wife, Edna Francis.

Freleng, Isador 'Friz': animator from Kansas City who was hired to work for the Disney Bros. Studio in Los Angeles. It was Freleng who replaced Ham Hamilton in 1926.

Gay, Margie: young actress who took over when Dawn O'Day stepped down as the main character in the Alice Comedies. Third actress to play Alice.

Hamilton, Irene: ink-and-paint girl hired by Walt Disney to help produce the Alice Comedies. Sister of Ham Hamilton.

Hamilton, Rollin 'Ham': animator who joined the Disney Bros. Studio in Los Angeles for the production of the Alice Comedies.

Hardwick, Lois: young actress who took over when Margie Gay stepped down as the main character in the Alice Comedies. Fourth and final actress to play Alice.

Harman, Fred: younger brother of Hugh Harman who was hired by Walt to work at Laugh-O-gram. Later moved to Los Angeles to work at Disney Bros. Studio.

Harman, Hugh: friend of Walt whom he met during their time at the Kansas City Film Ad Company. Walt later worked with Harman when they created Kaycee Studios and later hired him to work at Laugh-O-gram. Later moved to Los Angeles to work at the Disney Bros. Studio.

Howell, Harriett Alice: head cook of the canteen at Neufchâteau, France during the First World War. It was here that Walt became close friends with Howell while working as a driver for the canteen.

Ising, Rudolf 'Rudy': early employee of Walt's at Laugh-O-gram in Kansas City. Later moved to Los Angeles to work at the Disney Bros. Studio.

Iwwerks, Ubbe: young artist who became friends with Walt during their time at Pesmen-Rubin in Kansas City. After losing their jobs, Walt and Ubbe would go into business together, creating their own advertising studio, Iwwerks-Disney. Ubbe would become one of Walt's first employees with the start of Laugh-O-gram and the Disney Bros. Studio. Later changed the spelling of his name to Ub Iwerks.

Laemmle, Carl: head of Universal Studio who originally requested that Charles Mintz and the Disney Bros. Studio create a rabbit character, who would ultimately become Oswald the Lucky Rabbit.

Land, Frank S. 'Dad': founder of the Order of DeMolay of Kansas City and sponsor for Walt Disney during his time as a DeMolay in 1920.

Loomis, Ann: ink-and-paint girl who worked for the Disney Bros. Studio in Los Angeles.

Lyon, Red: camera operator who worked for Walt at Laugh-O-gram in Kansas City.

Maas, Russell: friend of Walt Disney whom he met while working in the Chicago Post Office. Maas and Walt conspired together to enlist in the days following the outbreak of the First World War, even though they were underage. Like Walt, Maas would also be accepted into the American Red Cross.

Mace, Leslie: distribution salesman who worked with Walt at Laugh-O-gram in Kansas City.

Martin, Mike: Walt's uncle, married to Flora Disney's sister, Alice. Uncle Mike was a train engineer for the Atchison, Topeka & Santa Fe Railroad and often passed through Marceline, Missouri, allowing young Walt to pilot the train into town.

Maxwell, Carman: animator who worked with Walt Disney at Laugh-O-gram in Kansas City.

McCay, Winsor: animation pioneer, best known for his syndicated comic strip, *Little Nemo*, and his animated film, *Gertie the Dinosaur*.

McCrum, Dr Thomas B.: Kansas City dentist who commissioned two films from Walt in the final days of Laugh-O-gram: *Tommy Tucker's Tooth* and *Clara Cleans Her Teeth*.

Messmer, Otto: co-creator of animated series 'Felix the Cat', a popular character in the early days of syndicated animation.

Mintz, Charles: distributor of the Alice Comedies and Oswald the Lucky Rabbit, who inherited the responsibilities after marrying Margaret Winkler. Mintz is best known for his 'theft' of the rights of Oswald from the Disney Bros. Studio in 1928, as well as most of the Disney staff.

Muybridge, Eadweard: animation pioneer and author of *Animals in Motion*, which inspired Walt and Ubbe to hone their animation skills. Inventor of the zoopraxiscope, which allowed for the illusion of animation of still images.

Newman, Frank: Owner of the Newman Theater, one of the largest and most successful movie palaces in Kansas City, Missouri. It was Newman who first gave Walt the opportunity to screen his work professionally before paid audiences in the form of his Newman Laugh-O-grams.

O'Day, Dawn: young actress who took over when Virginia Davis stepped down as the main character in the Alice Comedies. O'Day performed in only one film for Disney: *Alice's Egg Plant*. Second actress to play Alice.

Orr, Carey: political cartoonist for *The Chicago Tribune* and personal hero to a young Walt Disney.

Pantages, Alexander: owner of Los Angeles chain of theatres and vaudeville houses who agreed to distribute gag reels upon Walt's arrival from Kansas City in late 1923.

Parr, Dr Walter R.: reverend of St. Paul's Congregational Church, located in the Hermosa neighbourhood of Chicago. Parr and his wife Mary were also close friends of Elias and Flora Disney, and the two men agreed to name their next children after each other.

Pesmen, Louis: Walt's first boss, along with Bill Rubin, as a professional artist during his time working at Pesmen-Rubin in Kansas City.

Pfeiffer, Walt: childhood friend of Walt Disney in Kansas City, Missouri. Walt often spent time at the Pfeiffer home and, after encouragement from Pfeiffer's father, the two boys began to perform vaudeville skits. Walt Disney would remember his childhood friend when he did some art work for Pfeiffer's father upon his return to Kansas City after the First World War. Pfeiffer would later join Walt at Laugh-O-gram in Kansas City.

Reynolds, Aletha: artist responsible for inking and tracing cels for the animators at Laugh-O-gram in Kansas City.

Rubin, Bill: Walt's first boss, along with Louis Pesmen, as a professional artist during his time working at Pesmen-Rubin in Kansas City.

Scrogin, Ernest A.: founder and owner of O-Zell, the soda and jelly factory at which Elias Disney worked and owned stock in Chicago. It was later found that Scrogin participated in corrupt business practices.

Sewell, Hazel (née Bounds): sister of Lillian Disney.

Sherwood, Leighton 'Doc': farmer and retired doctor who lived near the Disneys north of Marceline, Missouri. It was Doc Sherwood who would give young Walt his first illustrated commission.

Simpson, Nadine: stenographer and bookkeeper at Laugh-O-gram in Kansas City. Simpson would later have mercy on Walt when he suffered financial difficulty during Laugh-O-gram's final days.

Stalling, Carl: piano player at the Isis Theater and friend of Walt Disney. Stalling originally began working with Walt when the two collaborated on the Song-O-Reel, *Martha: Just a Plain Old-Fashioned Name*. Stalling would later move to Los Angeles where he would produce music for animated shorts for the Walt Disney Studio.

Sullivan, Pat: co-creator of animated series 'Felix the Cat', a popular character in the early days of syndicated animation.

Tague, Lorey: animator who worked with Walt Disney at Laugh-O-gram in Kansas City.

Taylor, Don: childhood friend of Walt Disney and son of Manly Howe and Bertha Taylor.

Taylor, Erastus 'Grandpa' and Elizabeth: neighbours of the Disney family in Marceline, Missouri. 'Grandpa' Taylor often told an enraptured young Walt Disney about his experiences, real and fictional, in the American Civil War.

Taylor, Manly Howe and Bertha (née Phillips): neighbours of the Disney family, just north of Marceline, Missouri. Manly Howe was the son of Erastus 'Grandpa' Taylor, while Bertha Phillips Taylor was the niece of William and Elizabeth Crane. The Taylors often spent time with the Disney family, and their children were playmates to the Disney kids.

Walliman, Otto: animator who worked with Walt Disney at Laugh-O-gram in Kansas City.

Winkler, George: brother of Margaret Winkler who was hired by Charles Mintz to act as an intermediary between the distribution company and the Disney Bros. Studio. While Mintz was the brains behind his corrupt dealings with the Disney Bros. Studio, Winkler was the one who carried out the deeds.

Winkler, Margaret: animation distributor for Pat Sullivan's 'Felix the Cat' and Walt Disney's Alice Comedies. Stepped down as distributor of Disney films after her marriage to Charles Mintz in 1923.

Preface

Walter Elias Disney was an incredible man. He has been described by his numerous biographers as 'an American Original,' 'the Triumph of the American Imagination,' and 'the Illustrated Man,' attributing to his significance as an innovator in the world of animation.

The multitudinous biographies written about Disney tend to focus on his childhood in small-town America, his fondly-remembered Marceline, Missouri. They go on to describe his early years dabbling in film and animation, listing his different ventures including Laugh-O-gram Studios, the Alice Comedies, and Oswald the Lucky Rabbit, before detailing the loss of his first original character and many of his animators to film distributor, Charles Mintz. These books follow Walt, dejected, back west and peer over his shoulder as he creates his famous mouse, leading to the explosion of the Disney Studios as it began to create Mickey Mouse and Silly Symphony cartoons. Readers begin biting their nails in suspense (and quietly judge) as Walt takes the risk to create the first full-length animated film, *Snow White and the Seven Dwarfs*, which is released to universal acclaim in 1937. His biographers trace the growth of his film ventures during and after the Second World War with his well-known films, *Dumbo, Bambi,* and *Cinderella,* which catapulted him into global fame. Never satisfied, Walt began utilising the medium of television, ultimately paying for the financing of his theme park, Disneyland, which would transition Disney entertainment from an evening's escape to a vacation destination. As Walt Disney's fame grew and he became involved in outside ventures like the 1964 New York World's Fair and city planning, his biographers note how his life was sadly cut short due to lung cancer, and how the company began limping along throughout the 1960s and 1970s before bringing us into the present day.

But oftentimes, written biographies, as well as podcasts, blog posts, and even television specials, focus on Walt Disney and his life as a series of incredible events and innovations he experienced, isolating him from the world around him. They focus on his trial-and-error experimentation (and numerous failures) when creating his own animation companies; the success of his Mickey Mouse shorts and feature animation, including the several technological and technical advancements of his studio; and the great success of his Disneyland theme park, a larger-than-life toy for its creator, himself a big kid.

The scores of people who discuss and analyse Walt's life and sing his accolades are at best biographers, but more often, they are Disney fans who have bought into the message and dreams of the things he created. They are often not trained historians, instead simply telling the story of one man without understanding or explaining his place in events unfolding around him. But one man's life doesn't happen in a vacuum, especially that of Walter Elias Disney.

Walt Disney was a real-life version of Forrest Gump: not only did he affect the world around him, leading to memorable fads still a part of the collective memory today, including Davy Crockett coon-skin caps and Ingersoll Mickey Mouse watches, but he was also affected *by* the history that he experienced as well, reacting to many of the most important events of the twentieth century in the imaginative way that only Disney could.

Walt Disney not only influenced American and global culture through the development of his animated shorts and features, television programmes, theme parks and attraction technologies, but he was also a product of American and global culture, which then led him to be a creator of culture. His exposure to vaudeville performance and early films as a child instilled in him a love for performance; the introduction of television into American homes encouraged him to embrace the medium by creating family-friendly programming that helped further create his brand; and his partnership with four very different corporations in 1964 for the New York World's Fair led to the development of new robotics technology and special effects, which would change the entertainment world for decades to come.

Walt Disney was not just a culture-creator, as without his exposure and response to American culture, he would likely have been just another person, not a household name. The world would be one without Disney parks or Mickey Mouse.

It would be a world with less magic, less joy, and fewer dreams.

Part I

Stories [of] my fathers

1801–1890

Chapter One

Heritage

History's greatest figures often break the mould in their families, either overcoming adversity to become remarkable or using the resources they were blessed with to put their own distinct mark on the world. Usually these people are few and far between, with one individual rising to prominence in a family line.

Walt Disney's family of origin, however, is an anomaly: historians have traced his ancestry back 1,000 years, which included nobility and farmers, warriors and pacifists, criminals and the respectable. His story, and that of his family, is a fascinating one, spanning a millennia and both hemispheres. While social class, career choice, and reason for importance have varied immensely over the span of the family's history, the characteristics that defined the Disneys have always remained the same: hard work, a desire for self-improvement, a dream of progress, a strong loyalty to their nation, and a willingness to move to pursue new opportunities when one's luck had run out.

The Disney family can be traced as far back as 1066 to the town of Isigny-sur-Mer in the Duchy of Normandy in northwest France. It was here that a local named Hughes owned the Chateau de Monfreville, having received it from a local bishop. Hughes and his family were surrounded by both flora and fauna at their chateau, enjoying the migration of dozens of bird species including storks, swallows, owls, and cuckoos. Badgers and foxes wandered by on regular intervals, and game for hunting was plentiful. Nearby, cows owned by local farmers were utilised for their dairy products, while agricultural produce grown in enclosures as well as the commons, including apples, provided a steady supply of food and by-products like ciders and vinegars.

In 1066, Edward, King of England, died, and his brother-in-law, Harold, Earl of Essex, was crowned his successor. This didn't sit well with William, Duke of Normandy, who believed he had been given Edward's word that he would be the next king of England. In an effort to secure his right to the throne, William decided to invade England to assert his power. An order was sent around the Duchy of Normandy to all landowners, nobility and knights alike, requiring that they report for duty in fighting for and standing with their duke as the new king of England.

As owner of the Chateau de Monfreville, Hughes, along with his son Robert, was expected to serve as part of the invading army that would be crossing the English Channel to Britain's southern shores. When William's forces were successful in defeating those of the rival claimant at the Battle of Hastings, he rewarded his troops with land in England; as survivors of the war, Hughes and Robert were granted land in Lincolnshire, as well as authority as Normans who had conquered English citizens. To assert their power over the locals, as well as to differentiate themselves from the English, Hughes, Robert, and their family took the surname 'd'Isigny'. This showed that they had hailed from the Norman village and thus were more powerful than their neighbours. Over the next few centuries, the family's surname would be shortened and anglicised, ultimately changing to 'Disney'.

The strong devotion to one's nation was a prevailing theme over the next several centuries, as the Disney family aligned themselves with the British monarchy. War broke out in 1642 when King Charles I, who had been attempting to rule with absolute authority, was challenged by Parliament, which was trying to strip power away from the monarchy. The allegiance that the Disneys had to the Crown made it a no-brainer about which side to support in the English Civil War. Finding it his duty to help the king put down the rebellious supporters of the legislature, known as Parliamentarians, Edward Disney went to war, fighting in the Battle of Edgehill as a Royalist.

When the Royalists were defeated by the Parliamentarians, Edward Disney was captured and taken to nearby Warwick Castle. Because he was a man of wealth, Edward was held in Guy's Tower, where the Parliamentarians held nobility while they awaited execution. Over the approximately six months he was held captive, the young man had much free time, coming to the conclusion that, while he was facing death as an enemy of the state, he was on the correct side. He decided that it was time for him to make his mark on the world as a martyr for the Royalist cause, engraving his name, 'Edward Disney', and the year, '1643', inside an arrow slit set into the room's wall.

Edward's execution didn't come, however: in an effort to raise money to support their fight against Charles and his supporters, the Parliamentarians began ransoming prisoners back to their families. Edward Disney became one of these ransomed captives, returning home to his family.

After the execution of Charles I and the assumption of power by Oliver Cromwell, the Disneys realised that they were on the wrong side of the conflict. Selling their holdings in England in the 1660s, the family moved to County Louth, Ireland, north of Dublin, and then southwest to County Kilkenny a few decades later. It was here that the Disney family once again asserted its noble heritage, renting more than 30 acres of land for the growing family. As a result of this wealth, they often exerted political power, going as far as serving in the mayorship or collecting tolls at various ports throughout Ireland.

In 1801, Kepple Disney and Frances Best Disney welcomed a son, Arundel Elias Disney, to their Kilkenny estate. It was here that young Arundel, who went by the name of Elias, received an upbringing that was fit for his position in society. His father's wealth and status allowed him to receive an education, which in the early nineteenth century was a luxury. In addition, the family had little need for anything, relying on a number of servants who attended to them.

As he grew older, Elias fell in love with a local girl, Maria Swan, thirteen years his junior. While his family weren't too keen on their son marrying Maria, as she came from a family with a lower social status than the Disneys, they recognised that she was of good birth, and thus allowed the union. Elias and Maria were married in 1832, and a son, Kepple, was born on 2 November that same year.

A few years later, Elias and his brother Robert learned of business opportunities in New York City in the USA. The two young men sold their farms and set out for Liverpool, accompanied by their wives and children. In mid-September 1834, Elias Disney and his six accompanying travellers set out for America on a large steamer, *The New Jersey*, arriving in New York City on 3 October.

While Robert and his family decided to remain in New York to take advantage of business opportunities, Elias and Maria continued on to Canada. They had learned that the Canada Company was selling tracts of land in Ontario, promising that the inexpensive land was extremely fertile and ripe for crops. The company also explained in their advertisements that the area around Goderich Township featured full facilities, including roads, businesses to serve the influx of settlers, and infrastructure. Elias purchased a portion of land in Goderich, near Holmesville, situated along the Maitland River, to establish a farm. He acquired it by taking advantage of a Crown Grant that the Canada Company offered, meaning that his family purchased the land directly from the government, rather than from a previous owner. By 1842, he owned two separate lots, totalling 149 acres, where he grew wheat. Upon arrival, he was discouraged to learn that he had been misled: facilities in the area were scarce to none. Goderich Township had very few buildings and no church, and the land that he had purchased had not been cleared as had been promised. As a result, because the area that Elias Disney owned was previously undeveloped, he recognised that an alternative plan was required in order to support his family. He set to work building a gristmill and sawmill along the Maitland River, using the water's currents to drive the mills, and opening them up to the community to patronise.

Frontier life was very different from the nobility and privilege that Elias Disney was used to in Ireland. However, he and Maria quickly learned to adapt to the resources that were abundant in nature to provide for the family. Wild fruit, such as grapes and plums, grew in abundance, while Elias and young Kepple relied on the Maitland for fishing and the forest for wild game. Life on the Canadian frontier was not without its dangers, however: it was not uncommon for the men in the area to fight off packs of wolves who posed a threat to their families or livestock.

When he came of age, Kepple married a local girl, Mary Richardson, whose family had also emigrated from Ireland. Shortly after their marriage in 1858, the newlyweds moved to Bluevale, a small village approximately 50 kilometres from where their parents lived in Holmesville. Within a year, Mary was pregnant with her first child and on 6 February 1859, Elias Disney was born. With the expectation that their family would continue to grow, Kepple established a farm in Bluevale, supplemented by other money-making pursuits. For example, when drilling for oil turned out to be an unsuccessful venture, Kepple was pleased to find that his land bore salt instead, and he established the area's first salt mine.

Over the next eighteen years, Kepple and Mary had seven more children. As the oldest son, Elias recognised the importance of being a leader in his family, taking advantage of the education he received at the local public school and the moral and religious training provided at the Wesleyan Methodist Church and Sunday School. Collectively, this education, as well as the Christian upbringing provided by Kepple and Mary, provided Elias and his siblings with moral and physical fortitude, instilling in them the values of hard work, ethical purity, honesty, and frugality.

While embracing the strict moral upbringing provided by the Wesleyan Methodist Church and the local public school, young Elias took up a hobby he knew would be frowned upon by his conservative family. When he asked Kepple and Mary for permission to learn how to play the fiddle, his parents scoffed at him, explaining that it was an instrument played by the devil himself and that no son of theirs would embrace such an immoral pursuit. In a moment of rebellion, the young man defied his parents, stealing off into the woods where he could practice the fiddle out of sight and earshot of authority. This didn't last long, however. One afternoon, Grandma Maria heard the dancing notes echoing through the forest. Following the sound of the evil music, she discovered her eldest grandson on a log playing the sinful instrument. She rushed forward and snatched it from the boy's hands, and before he could protest, brought it down over his head, leaving the fiddle a pile of smashed parts and shattered wood.

In 1877, Kepple's financial success began to dry up and he began to look elsewhere for opportunities. Mary was pregnant once again, meaning that there would soon be another mouth to feed. Word had arrived that there was still the opportunity to become rich off the goldfields in California and the silver fields in the American West. Together, Kepple, Elias, and second son Robert made their way across the Canadian border into the American Midwest, heading towards the Pacific where the temptation of riches lay.

While riding on a train heading west from Missouri, a representative from the Union Pacific Railroad approached Kepple and his sons, offering them a land grant. Sending for Mary and the rest of the children, Kepple began the process of settling his sons on a section of a few hundred acres of land along Big Creek in the new railroad town of Ellis, Kansas.

Kepple Disney and his family weren't the only people who had begun to settle west of the Mississippi River. In the midst of the American Civil War in 1862, President Abraham Lincoln signed the Homestead Act, with the purpose of 'elevat[ing] the condition of men, to lift artificial burdens from all shoulders and to give everyone an unfettered start and a fair chance in the race of life.' The Act officially opened land in the American West, including land in modern-day Montana, North Dakota, Colorado, and Nebraska. This land was provided to American citizens relatively inexpensively: 160-acre plots were awarded to pioneers for a mere filing fee of $18. In order to keep the land, the homesteaders were required to live on it for five years, farm it, and make improvements such as digging a well or constructing a road. While the Homestead Act was a relative success for Americans – more than 270 million acres were settled over the course of the next 124 years – it forced thousands of Native Americans off the land they had inhabited for generations, impelling them to less desirable plots or even relocating them to reservations.

Unfortunately, Kepple and Mary Disney were not American citizens. As a result, they were unable to take advantage of the cheap land offered by the Homestead Act fifteen years after Lincoln had signed it. However, the major railroad lines, which were spreading west across the continent, offered a solution: their own land grants.

The railroad corporations had no way of making an immediate income and it was also difficult to acquire investors because of the sheer number of different railroad companies. It was their development that was primarily driving the rise of heavy industry in the United States in the second half of the nineteenth century, so the railroad corporations turned to the federal government for assistance.

While the government didn't give them free financial appropriations, it did provide them with land grants, amounting to 20 square miles per mile of track constructed. These land grants could be sectioned off as the companies saw fit and then sold to individuals or families to help raise money to continue building the railways. This was a particularly lucrative opportunity for railroads in the 1870s and 1880s, as huge numbers of people, American and immigrant alike, including Kepple and Mary Disney, began to migrate west looking for cheap land and new opportunities. In 1871 alone, railroad companies in the American West had been granted approximately 130 million acres, which amounted to 7 per cent of the total amount of land owned by the United States at the time.

Life in Ellis, Kansas was not easy for Kepple and his family. As a stop along the Kansas Pacific spur of the Union Pacific Railroad, the town soon became a loading station for cattle being sent east to Chicago that were being driven from the grazing land in Texas and New Mexico. As a result, crime and drunkenness became prevalent among those visiting the town. The citizens of Ellis often participated in debauchery and the other vices the town offered to visiting cattle drivers, such as the booming prostitution industry that existed in the town. Kepple and his sons, except the morally upright Elias, left their conservative nature behind in Canada and gave themselves over to the temptations of Ellis, becoming frequent visitors of both the saloons *and* the prostitutes.

The town was also victim to frequent raids by Native Americans. Angry at having been pushed off the land they had occupied for generations, the Native American tribes believed that the only remaining tactic for getting the white Americans to vacate their land was to attack: negotiations over the previous five decades had failed.

Elias found solace from the temptations of the railroad town in the local church, which did far more than solely providing sermons on Sunday morning. Churches in American frontier towns often served as the social hub of the region, where locals would meet to exchange news and gossip, and social events were hosted including picnics and camp meetings. The centrally-located church in Ellis gave Elias an opportunity to gather with like-minded individuals who were attempting to resist the temptations of the brothel and saloon. It also reinforced the character traits his childhood had instilled in him, making him even more devoted to honest, hard work and a deeply moral lifestyle.

The Disneys were not well-off after settling in Ellis. After paying the Kansas Pacific for their section of land, they also had to buy the tools, animals, seeds, and other materials necessary to start their farm; establishing the farm was of utmost priority, as it was farming that would help the family make money so they could survive. With eleven mouths to feed (Mary had given birth to her ninth child in March 1878, shortly before Kepple had sent for her to join him in Kansas), not much money was left over after the grocery bill.

The landscape in Kansas was very flat, and the environment made up of prairies was covered in shortgrass. As a result, hardwoods and timber cost a premium to purchase, making the construction of a typical home difficult. Taking a cue from their German neighbours who had settled with them in Ellis, the Disney family began to construct a home made out of prairie sod. Kepple and his sons hollowed out the hill sloping down to the banks of Big Creek, stacking rectangular clumps of sod to serve as the structure's walls. The prairie grass that was rooted in these clumps held the dirt together, and the dry summer heat eventually baked the sod into brick. Poles were hewn from a few scattered cottonwood trees that grew along the creek; these served as the trusses for the roof which, after being covered with lighter clumps of earth, prevented the occasional rain from soaking the packed earth floor of the dwelling. Not only did this prairie building style allow for constructing a home in a place devoid of typical building materials, but it was also helpful in guarding against the harsh conditions of the region's climate: the partially underground nature of the structure helped to keep the house cool in the blistering summer heat, while the bricks of earth allowed for insulation against the frigid winter temperatures. However, this crude home was only temporary: once Kepple and Mary had achieved relative success on the farm and had acquired enough money, they soon invested in building a house of stone acquired from a nearby quarry.

Not satisfied working for his father, Elias decided to leave the modest wheat and cattle farm Kepple had established and began looking for work elsewhere. It was time to break away from his past and take advantage of the opportunities that America offered him and any future Disneys, who were willing to dream for a better life in the world.

Chapter Two

Elias and Flora

As Elias Disney began his second decade of life, he left his mother, father, brothers and sisters and decided to join the great march west by joining forces with the expanding railroad industry. He soon found employment in a machine shop for the Kansas Pacific Railroad, utilising the skills he had learned over the years working at Kepple's gristmill and sawmill in Ontario, as well as fixing broken machinery and farming implements on the farm in Ellis.

The Kansas Pacific Railroad was a spur of the Union Pacific Railroad, whose inception began as early as 1838. It was during the early nineteenth century that America had begun its push west across the American plains through the ideology of Manifest Destiny, which stated it was God's intention that the American people conquer the North American continent from the Atlantic to the Pacific. In an effort to facilitate the easy transport of people and supplies west, suggestions were made to construct a transcontinental railroad across North America connecting the two coasts. Congress scoffed at this idea, arguing that building such a railroad would be as silly as constructing one from the Earth to the moon.

Prior to the construction of the major railways, travel through the wilderness was difficult, often conducted by wagon and draught animal. Journeys west usually took several days, weeks, or even months, as the clumsy creatures often found the hills, mountains, forests, and muddy paths difficult to navigate. After the rush of people to California seeking gold and other precious metals in the 1840s and 1850s, advocates for a rail line encouraged prospectors to petition Congress for a railroad that would link them to the east, making travel back and forth easier. A number of debates were held in the legislature over the idea of a transcontinental railroad, stalling after sectionally-motivated arguments occurred over whether the eastern terminus of the railroad would be in the American north or south.

Finally, in 1853, the Congress of the United States signed a bill allowing for geological surveys to begin for a transcontinental railroad stretching between St. Louis, Missouri and California. Two different railroad companies emerged to fulfil the mission of building the railroad: the Central Pacific Railroad, which began building east from Sacramento, California in January 1863, and the Union Pacific Railroad, which began building west from Omaha, Nebraska the following December. While the two railroad companies initially intended to build separate railroads across America, it was soon agreed that the two rail lines would meet and join together to create a single transcontinental line.

On 10 May 1869, the Central Pacific and Union Pacific Railroads met at Promontory Summit in Utah. A ceremony commemorated the momentous accomplishment of America's first transcontinental railroad: as a locomotive on each railroad was pulled towards the joining of the two lines, a ceremonial golden spike was driven to connect the rails together, signifying the completion of the project. The news was immediately telegraphed across the nation as American citizens celebrated the important occasion. Regular service across the Transcontinental Railroad began five days later.

This triumphant project inspired smaller railroad companies to expand and strive for success similar to that achieved by the Central Pacific and Union Pacific Railroads. It also soon became recognised that other areas of the country needed to connect with the transcontinental line, which only stretched from Sacramento to Omaha. As a result, new railroads began to connect to the long line, including the Atchison, Topeka & Santa Fe; the Denver & Rio Grande; and the Missouri, Kansas & Texas Railroads.

Beginning construction in 1855, the Union Pacific Eastern Division officially became a southern railroad line running parallel to the Transcontinental Railroad in 1863. However, five years later, the Eastern Division changed its name to the Kansas Pacific Railroad, creating a major rail line from Kansas City, Kansas in the east to Denver, Colorado in the west. It was from this line that Kepple Disney purchased his land in Ellis.

When young Elias Disney heard the exciting stories of those building the rail line across the American frontier, he soon abandoned the Kansas Pacific machine shop. Instead, he decided to join the construction crews building the new line west from Ellis to its terminus in Denver, where it turned north to connect with the Union Pacific. It was along this route that

Elias began to realize the corruption that big business exerted over the poor and marginalised, including immigrants. While he had gained American citizenship after Kepple and Mary had become naturalised the year before, he observed the poor treatment and conditions experienced by many of the labourers along the railroad. Constructing a new railroad through the plains and mountains could be extremely dangerous, so company leadership often resorted to using immigrants for labour, including the Irish and Germans on the eastern lines and the Chinese on the western lines.

Upon completing the line in Denver, many of the labourers found themselves no longer needed and out of work. Elias, reluctant to return to Kepple's farm in Ellis, decided to purchase himself another fiddle and use his talent to entertain the citizens of Denver by performing outside saloons. Unfortunately, when this didn't bring him success, he decided to return home to Kansas, feeling great discouragement about what his future would hold.

Luckily, fate was on Elias's side. While he resumed working on Kepple's farm, his younger sister Annie began teaching at the Beaver Bank School in Ellis in 1884, serving under the school's headmaster, Charles Call. Call had left his childhood home in the mid-1800s, joining the rush to California to search for gold. However, when his search came up dry, he made his way back east, settling in Ellis in 1879 and opening Beaver Bank School for the growing town's children.

Elias occasionally filled in to teach for his sister, allowing him to get to know Call and the students of the school. He soon became familiar with Call's daughter Flora, an intelligent 16-year-old girl who often performed very well academically, including a score of 99 per cent in her end-of-year examination in her advanced class in 1881. Over the next few years, Elias began spending more time with Charles Call and his family and started to pursue a relationship with Flora.

Flora graduated from high school as Beaver Bank's valedictorian. A few years later, at the school's commencement (similar to a graduation), she gave a speech that was timely for a young girl growing up in an American frontier town: "Neglect not the Gift that is in Thee." The young woman acknowledged that each person was endowed with some sort of gift and that it was their responsibility to foster that gift in order to fulfil their fate.

With his daughter graduated, Charles Call and his wife Henrietta sold their land in Ellis and moved to Akron, Florida. Kepple, who had got to know the Calls through his children's relationship with the family, chose to go along to survey opportunities in the area. Elias, who was smitten with Flora, decided to accompany his father. When Kepple realised that Kansas held more opportunity for his family, his eldest son resolved to stay behind due to his budding romance with Flora Call. Purchasing 80 acres of farmland in nearby Kismet, Elias began to actively court Flora and the two married in the Call family home in Akron on 1 January 1888.

The newlyweds settled on Elias's farmland in Kismet, purchasing an additional 150 acres and several head of cattle. Unfortunately, a disease swept through the herd, and when many of the cows died, Elias realised that raising cattle wasn't for him. The new husband sold his land and the couple moved to Daytona Beach, where they managed the Halifax Hotel during the tourist season of 1888. When the autumn arrived and tourists left the area, the owner of the hotel had no more need for his manager and forced Elias and Flora to vacate their room. This was especially difficult for the couple: Flora was pregnant with her first child and was due in December.

Elias quickly realised that he needed to find work to provide for his growing family. After getting a part-time job as a postal carrier for the town of Kissimmee, he also purchased approximately 160 acres of land on which to attempt growing an orange grove. However, this still did not provide sufficient income.

Later that autumn, Elias Disney enlisted in the Florida militia: a wave of American patriotism had been rising over the previous few years as talk of war with Spain began to circulate around the country. While the Caribbean island of Cuba had been owned by Spain since the fifteenth century, Cubans finally began to agitate for independence in the late 1870s. Cuban exile José Martí began to gather Cubans living in west and south Florida to support his cause. While the United States saw the Spanish treatment of Cubans as abhorrent, the government also saw a potential Cuban revolution as an opportunity to annex the island as a part of the budding American empire in the Western hemisphere. To secure Cuban 'victory', paving the way for American acquisition, the idea of America as the liberator of the Spanish Empire began to circulate around the nation. This was a result of articles published by American newspaper magnates,

Joseph Pulitzer and William Randolph Hearst, during their fierce battle to sell papers, utilising tactics such as sensationalising news stories in an effort to increase subscriptions, becoming known as 'yellow journalism'. Collectively, these ideas persuaded young and old alike to begin enlisting in the U.S. armed forces and local state militias in preparation for war, which would finally break out in 1898.

After spending several weeks training at the militia base, Elias realised that military life wasn't for him: the strict discipline clashed with his personality, while the behaviour and language of his fellow soldiers didn't align with his conservative Methodist morals. Written communication with Flora also revealed that the new mother was struggling to keep the orange grove afloat while also caring for a new-born: Flora had given birth to a son, Herbert Arthur, on 8 December. The young father decided to leave the camp and return home to Kissimmee.

A few days later, a number of U.S. Army policemen arrived at their front door, prepared to arrest the young man who had deserted. Elias, however, refused to go with the officers.

"I didn't desert," he explained. "I volunteered for this outfit, which means I can just as easily *un*-volunteer."

This caught the U.S. Army policemen off guard. "We need your uniform then, sir," they explained.

"You don't get my uniform. I paid for it out of my own money, so it belongs to me," Elias retorted. Not expecting resistance like this and realising the young man was absolutely right, the policemen left the Disney property, letting the deserter off without punishment.

A few weeks later, a record frost landed across central Florida, coating the orange trees on the Disney farm. Elias had hoped that some of the oranges would be spared, and he quickly set out to recover some of his trees. In the midst of his hard work, he began to feel ill, and he was diagnosed with malaria. Fed up with his run of bad luck in Florida, the new father began to look elsewhere for job opportunities.

In 1890, important political and cultural figures in the United States came up with the idea to celebrate the 400th anniversary of Columbus's discovery of America. Inspired by the Paris *Exposition Universelle* held the year before, it was decided that the United States needed to have its own version of an exposition to celebrate the momentous occasion. While it was generally agreed that Washington, D.C. should host the fair, other large cities throughout America realised that hosting the event would bring prestige and increase their stature both in the nation and around the world. St. Louis, Missouri and New York City threw in their hats to host the fair. Cultural leaders in Chicago, who believed that the city best exemplified the American spirit due to their fast comeback after the Great Chicago Fire in 1871, desired that their city play host to the fair. After the American Congress held a vote on 24 February 1890, it was decided that Chicago would be the location for what would become the World's Columbian Exposition of 1893.

Jackson Park, southeast of downtown Chicago and along the shores of Lake Michigan, was the chosen spot where the fairgrounds would be built. Originally designed by Frederick Law Olmstead, who was famous for designing New York's Central Park, Jackson Park was the city's attempt at bringing beauty to the urban district. Unfortunately, the park's location along Lake Michigan led to the growing issue of hills of sand that had blown in from the lake, as well as great whirling cesspools that were a result of the rising tides. The choice to bring Olmstead back to Chicago to serve as the designer of the fairground was an attempt to fix the problems of Jackson Park, as well as to bring in a globally-renowned landscape architect to draw visitors to the fair.

A well-known architectural firm, Burnham & Root, was employed to design the fair's buildings. Classical in nature, the fairground was scattered with edifices sporting soaring columns, high domes, and vast arcades, while fountains, statuary, and small lakes made the industrial exhibition graceful. Soon dubbed 'The White City' due to the pure and classical colour of the buildings, Chicago and the grounds of the World's Columbian Exposition served as a place where sophisticated and advanced culture could be put on display, demonstrating the ability of 1890s America to overcome the temptations and vice of the period.

As he recovered from his bout of malaria, Elias would read the newspaper to keep him busy. He often saw advertisements taken out by the Carpenters and Building Association listing jobs for constructing the temporary buildings in Jackson Park for the exposition. This opportunity created interest in the young man: Chicago would be a new start. He was tired of rural life and the lack of consistent work; he saw how difficult it was for his father to start the farm in Ellis, remembered how he'd been laid off upon reaching Denver while working on the Kansas Pacific, and was incredibly frustrated and slightly depressed over the fate of his orange grove in Kissimmee. A large city in the north offered new opportunities: steady work, a higher standard of living, good schools for Herbert, the chance of an easier life with access to existing infrastructure and new technologies. His younger brother Robert had already established himself in Chicago and was in the process of scoping out land on Chicago's south side to build a hotel near Jackson Park. This meant that it would be slightly easier to become established, as he could draw upon Robert's experience to help acclimatise himself.

Besides, he thought to himself, Chicago won't be an *entirely* new experience. Chicago was far enough east that it had a history and had been exposed to American industrial development. It was the hub of the livestock slaughter and meatpacking industry in the United States, and as such, dozens of rail lines terminated in the city. However, Chicago was also far enough west that the city was newer than places like New York, Philadelphia, and Washington, D.C. As a result, there were a lot of opportunities for work and for making something of himself. From what he understood, there were still open areas of prairie land just north and west of the city, meaning that there was even the possibility for land ownership, as well as utilising some of the skills he had acquired working on his father's land back west. And not only that, but as a growing city, it seemed to be a place that attracted many of the *respectable* immigrants, such as the German population he had got to know in Kansas.

An unexpected family tragedy was a factor in the couple's decision. In 1890, Flora's father, Charles Call, was severely injured in an accident while clearing his Florida land of pine trees, succumbing to his injury a few weeks later. His death made it that much easier for Elias and Flora to leave Florida.

So, in late spring 1890, along with their 18-month-old son, they packed up their things and moved to Chicago to find work at the fairgrounds at the World's Columbian Exposition, which was due to open in three years' time. Convinced that he would finally find a stable job, Elias didn't realise that his chances of employment were slim: contrary to what *The Rights of Labor* had said in its advertisement, there was no abundance of jobs. Later statistics show that for every job opportunity open for construction at the fairgrounds, applicants would be competing with at least ten other men. It was these conditions that the Disneys found themselves walking into, along with more than 25,000 other families.

Part II

I'll name mine after you

Chicago, Illinois, 1890–1906

Chapter Three

The White City

Elias, Flora, and Herbert didn't move to Chicago alone. As the three Disneys made the long trip north from Florida to Chicago, they were accompanied by their unborn second child. Young Flora was only a few months into her pregnancy when the family arrived in Illinois.

Elias wasted no time in finding a new home for their expanding family. Because he recognised the temporary nature of the work that would be offered at the World's Columbian Exposition, he convinced Flora that they should rent, rather than purchase a house. They soon found a home at 3515 Vernon Avenue, south of downtown Chicago, where their second son, Raymond Arnold, was born on 30 December 1890. The location of the property was as much out of necessity for additional space as it was for Elias's new job working at the world's fair: the house sat approximately twenty blocks, or about 2 miles, from the fairgrounds, at the southern edge of Washington Park. As a result, it was fairly easy for him to get back and forth to work every day, either by walking or taking the trams that travelled down the Midway Plaisance, a boulevard surrounded by a greenway connecting Washington Park to Jackson Park, the location of the exposition. As the construction of the fair progressed, Elias found himself walking past the exhibits that would be placed in the Midway Plaisance, including recreations of authentic villages from around the world, a Californian Ostrich Farm restaurant, a tethered balloon which carried passengers 60 metres into the air, and venues for various performances including animal shows and belly dancers. However, it was the World Columbian Exposition's answer to Gustav Eiffel's Tower at Paris's *Exposition Universelle* of 1889 that was most impressive to those travelling through the Midway Plaisance: an 80-metre wheel that bore the name of its designer, George Washington Gale Ferris.

The work constructing the World's Columbian Exposition was certainly not always easy. Compared to what he was likely making in Florida, Elias seemed to be earning more money. His wage equalled to around $1 per day (the equivalent to around $28 in today's money). However, this was well below the national average for carpenters. In fact, carpenters throughout the United States were getting paid an average of $2.52 each day for their work. Unfortunately for Elias and his colleagues preparing the fairgrounds for the Exposition's 1893 opening, the construction managers of the fair's buildings needed a large supply of carpenters and other labourers, which allowed them to pay low wages to their workers. Any employee who expressed dissatisfaction with the necessary long hours or low pay could be quickly dismissed for another candidate waiting in the wings who would be content with the same long hours and low pay. The struggles and frustrations brought about by the poor working conditions and low compensation were compounded by the difficulties of winter. In early 1892, the temperatures averaged −23°C, while the winter of 1893 was even colder. Some organised into labour unions to agitate for better treatment.

A number of industrial conflicts broke out in the Chicago area during the early 1890s, many of which were a direct result of the economic recession. A strike at the Pullman factory in Gary, Indiana occurred when the owner of the company, George Pullman, lowered the wages of his workers. This was incredibly difficult for his employees, as they not only worked for Pullman, but rented their homes and bought their food from him too: Pullman owned the entire town in which his factory was located. As a result, when wages decreased, rent and the cost of food remained steady, putting a strain on the working poor who laboured in Pullman's factories. When the workers threatened to organise, the tycoon outlawed labour unions and laid off 75 per cent of his workforce, replacing them instead with workers who were willing to work for much lower wages.

The workers in Gary were struck hard by their financial strain, and many suffered from homelessness, a lack of food, or an inadequate supply of fuel to heat their homes. It was at this point that a labour organiser, Eugene V. Debs, arrived in Gary, willing to fight for the rights of the workers. Comparing George Pullman to a slaveholder, Debs helped to organise the workers into an official union, encouraging them to strike and urging other members of the American Railway Union around the country to boycott the Pullman railroad cars. As a result of the boycott, rumours began to spread that the American railroad system would cease to transport goods and people, and slow down the transport of mail around the country. The protests soon became violent after Debs ignored an injunction issued by the federal government, forcing it to send troops to occupy Chicago, allowing trains to pass through the city unmolested.

While the strikers lost the battle with George Pullman, their efforts didn't go unnoticed by others around the city and the nation. Laws began to change, forbidding children from working and instead requiring them to enrol in compulsory schooling until the age of 14. Writers of exposés, such as Lincoln Steffens, began touring the big cities. In his book, *The Shame of the Cities*, Steffens called Chicago out for being the most violent and filthiest in the country. As the middle and working classes became wary of the American *laissez-faire* capitalist system, leaders like Debs began to gain followers, advocating for socialist-style governments and placing ownership of the railroads and utilities that were necessary to American livelihoods in the hands of the public.

Debs himself visited Chicago throughout the period of time that he worked with the strikers at the Pullman factory, recognising his responsibility to fight for the industrial workers of the great city, many of whom were immigrants and thus easy to exploit through low wages. He supported Chicago's industrial workers through his organisation, the Industrial Workers of the World, which was often accused by its opponents and industrial leadership as being socialist. He was joined by other labour unions fighting for better working conditions, including the American Federation of Labor, a craft union, and the Knights of Labor, which welcomed all workers, skilled and unskilled alike. While the American Federation of Labor was relatively new compared with the Knights of Labor around the turn of the century, it quickly surpassed the latter in terms of membership due to its appeal to the urban middle classes, particularly native-born white Americans. It was in this political, social and industrial climate that Elias Disney worked in the early 1890s, one which had an impact on his attitudes toward labour and big business for decades to come.

When he took the job as carpenter at the fair, Elias realised that work would only be temporary. As a result, he used the skills learned on the Transcontinental Railroad and honed in Chicago to start making furniture for local markets.

In 1891, using the money he and Flora had saved up from his work at the World's Columbian Exposition and sales from his handmade furniture,

Elias purchased a 7.62m by 38.1m lot in Northwesttown, which also went by the name Kelvyn Grove, a suburb outside Chicago. The couple made the agreement to build the house together: Flora would design the home and Elias would construct it. The neighbourhood was fairly new when Elias and Flora purchased the land; originally settled around 1885, the area became a popular place to live for German, Scottish and Swedish immigrants due to a nearby railroad station, where they could be whisked away to the numerous manufacturing centres around the city. In 1889, the area had been annexed by the city of Chicago, and the neighbourhood was given a new official name: Hermosa.

As the days for the opening of the World's Columbian Exposition drew nearer, the global economy was struck by a downturn. As early as 20 January 1891, important banks were failing in Kansas City, Missouri, which led to apprehension for millions of Americans. Union leaders and labourers at the World's Columbian Exposition used this as an opportunity to leverage better wages and an eight-hour workday. Unwilling to negotiate, the leadership of fair construction, which was headed by Daniel Hudson Burnham, instead hired Italian immigrants to continue construction on a ditch at Jackson Park. In response, on 12 February 1891, more than 2,000 angry workers stormed the worksite armed with sharpened sticks. Two Italian workers were captured by protestors and beaten until police officers arrived to break up the violence.

Labour-induced violence at the fairgrounds also became personal for the Disney family. One morning, while approaching his worksite, Elias saw a small group of recently laid off workers beating up a still-employed carpenter on his way to work; the angry men were frustrated that their victim had retained his job as a result of accepting the low pay of his employer, while they had been fired due to their cooperation with the unions. The man was cowering on the ground, unsuccessfully covering his head and neck while blows and kicks rained down on him from above. Blood splattered and pooled nearby as the well-aimed kicks split open the screaming man's skin. While Elias felt bad for his co-worker, he decided to discreetly continue walking; with his growing family, he needed income from work, no matter how little his boss offered to pay him. Unfortunately, he was spotted, and the group abandoned their first victim and began to follow their second. Not wanting to show he was scared, Elias didn't look back or walk faster. A dark flash exploded across his field of vision as his legs crumpled beneath him and he dropped to the ground. Dazed and lying on the dusty road, Elias's senses drifted as his eyes registered a shovel being dropped alongside him. The dark stain of what he realised was his blood was smeared across the spade, while his ringing ears picked up the sound of yelling and the curses of his attackers. Curling up to protect his vital areas, Elias waited for what felt like eternity until the assault ended as other men on their way to work rushed to his rescue and his assailants scattered. While Elias wanted to project a tough image and decided to continue on to work, his foreman recognised the extent of the man's injuries and sent him home for the day to recover. It is also likely that Elias's boss didn't want the injured man to receive any unwanted attention that could lead to more conflict or attacks on his worksite.

With increased police presence, strikers backed off from violent protest and instead turned to negotiation with exposition officials, beginning talks on 14 February to demand an eight-hour workday, wages adhering to the union pay scale, and the expectation that union labourers would be hired before non-unionised or immigrant workers. When the fair leadership accepted the demand for an eight-hour workday but explained they would consider the others, union leaders threatened to organise unions worldwide to oppose the Exposition.

Unfortunately, the American economy didn't work in the labourers' favour. The job market in Chicago continued to decline, leading to more than 25,000 unemployed wandering the streets. Burnham imposed stricter agreements with subcontractors building the structures in the Jackson Park fairgrounds, setting firm deadlines resulting in a harsh financial penalty for each day a deadline wasn't met. These heightened expectations reinforced the attitude of the fair's construction manager: for over a year, a sign in his office had instructed workers to 'Rush' because the lagging pace at which building was occurring would prevent the Exposition from opening on time.

That same year, 1891, news reached Elias that his father, Kepple Disney, had died in Kansas aged 59, leaving the family farm in Ellis to his wife Mary. It's likely that Elias's grief added to the stress he was under at work.

Throughout 1892, the economy continued to sink as more banks and companies failed and went out of business. Fair executives, already over budget, recognised the need to cut costs, and as a result reduced worker wages and began to lay off employees. Samuel Gompers, American

Federation of Labour founder and president, accused Burnham of discrimination against union workers. In an effort to save face in a period of union tension, the chief of construction instructed a subordinate, superintendent of construction Dion Geraldine, to investigate the allegation. At the same time, to prove to Gompers that he didn't discriminate against the unions, Burnham instructed the various chiefs of the construction departments to fire anyone not efficient or performing poor quality work. These were primarily non-unionised workers, as the American Federation of Labour typically protected skilled workers that performed quality work. Burnham also ordered that all carpentry carried out for the fair and its buildings be completed by employees of contracting businesses chosen specifically by exposition executives. As a result, any carpenters not employed by these companies were immediately out of work, ultimately placating some of the demands made by Gompers and other union leaders.

Labour dissatisfaction continued until spring 1893 when union workers walked off the job, refusing to complete the fair until they received a minimum wage. After threats and counter-threats, Burnham agreed to the minimum wage demand, as well as overtime pay for any extra hours worked.

Unfortunately for all involved, on 3 May 1893 a panic on Wall Street caused stock prices to plummet and banks and companies to close their doors. The Pennsylvania and Reading Railroad went bankrupt, followed closely by the National Cordage Company. By the end of 1893, more than 16,000 businesses and 500 banks had failed, leaving approximately 20 per cent of America's employable population unemployed. The fear of financial instability caused hundreds of thousands of Americans to become more conservative with their finances, leading to low attendance rates in the early days of the World's Columbian Exposition. Luckily for the construction workers preparing for the fair, however, their work was done until demolition was scheduled at the end of the fair's season in October, so many unionised carpenters avoided potential layoffs.

Elias's job as a carpenter for the World's Columbian Exposition was one of the casualties of the recession of 1893. The layoff came as no surprise; winter was traditionally a slow time for carpenters and construction workers due to the cold northern temperatures, resulting in more competition over jobs. However, the consistent work in Jackson Park with wages higher than what he was used to were a blessing to Elias and Flora. In fact, when Flora announced she was pregnant with their third child, Elias was so thrilled with the financial well-being that employment at the fair provided, he petitioned her to name the child Columbus. Flora explained she would think about it.

The World's Columbian Exposition officially opened on 1 May 1893. The pomp and ceremony that surrounded the first day of the fair was bittersweet for Elias: his layoff from the construction crew at the fairgrounds, while expected, was disappointing, but the opportunity to celebrate all his hard work was also rewarding. While the Disneys may not have been a part of the crowd amassing at Jackson Park on that first day, the luck of being in the right place at the right time still afforded them the opportunity to participate in a way that many of the fairgoers would be unable to.

Early in the morning of 1 May, twenty-three black carriages lined up in front of the Lexington Hotel on Michigan Avenue in Chicago. Numerous local, national, and global dignitaries were seated within the vehicles, including the mayor of Chicago; President Grover Cleveland; and the Duke of Veragua, a descendant of Christopher Columbus, and his wife, the Infanta Eulalia of Spain. Behind the carriages were more than 200,000 Chicagoans on foot or in various vehicles, followed by more than 1,500 members of the Columbian Guard (members of the security outfit responsible for keeping peace at the fair). Collectively, this mass of parading humanity turned east and moved past the home of Elias and Flora Disney, making their way down the Avenue of Nations in the Midway Plaisance on the way to Jackson Park where the true opening ceremonies would take place. One can imagine the pride Elias Disney felt, not only as a Chicagoan, but also as someone who had poured himself into constructing the White City, as he watched the grand procession march past while he worked on furniture outside his rented home.

The Disneys' life near the fairgrounds and Midway Plaisance was only temporary, however. Since Elias purchased the lot in Hermosa in 1891, Flora had been hard at work drawing up blueprints for the new home. It would be a two-storey, modelled in the worker's cottage-style typical of Chicago's suburbs. The first floor opened into a hallway with a narrow wooden staircase. To the right was a parlour/living room with large bay windows at the front allowing for natural light. The back of the house had a dining room large enough for a family of five and an equally large kitchen, complete with water pump and cook stove. Upstairs, there were three bedrooms: one big enough for Herb and Ray with a smaller one for the new baby, as well as a spacious master bedroom complete with a rather large closet. While the house was nothing fancy, the fact that the humble Disneys built it with their own hands made it a very special home. Flora completed her plans on 23 November 1892, giving Elias the green light to begin construction in earnest. However, when Flora announced her pregnancy, her husband realised he didn't have as much time to build as originally planned: the current house at Vernon wouldn't be large enough for the growing family.

The new home had a number of features that Elias was particularly proud of. While modelled in the simple steep-gabled worker's cottage-style, the house's wooden siding was painted white and finished with bright blue trim, a popular colour choice for the American Victorian-style mansions that were being built by the wealthy. The house sat at the intersection of Tripp Avenue and Forty-Second Avenue, both of which were the only paved roads in the area. With the paving of roads, the municipal government of Chicago decided to lay better, longer-lasting water and sewer lines due to the difficulty of digging up paved roads, especially at the turn of the century. As a result, the Disneys' house at 1249 Tripp Avenue became the first in the neighbourhood to have both running water and an indoor toilet, which was located in a small closet beneath the stairs to the second floor. This was fairly uncommon: only 43 per cent of homes had inside toilets in the early 1900s.

The house was finally completed in the late spring of 1893 for about $800 and Elias was exhausted; he had been working extra hard in the evenings and during weekends as soon as he'd finished work at Jackson Park. The layoff from the construction crew had been a blessing in disguise; while he was no longer employed, the lack of professional work gave him the opportunity to finish up the house before the arrival of his third child.

This migration from the urban district of Chicago to the suburbs was a common trend with the middle and upper classes in this period. With the arrival of thousands of new immigrants to large metropolitan areas in the United States, those who were wealthy enough left their mansions and homes located on 'the Avenues' along the shores of Lake Michigan and began expanding to newly-developed suburbs north and west of the city. The mansions were converted into multi-family tenement units, while a new type of community of platted, or planned, suburbs allowed the well-to-do and working classes to segregate themselves from what they deemed to be 'undesirables'. These new neighbourhoods created a small-town environment within a short tram ride of the city's entertainments and amenities. It created a community for residents that enriched the culture of the working- and middle-class family, providing shops, better schools and churches, and social life opportunities for the neighbourhoods' homogenous residents. Real estate developers for the suburbs capitalised on the family-oriented nature of the new suburban neighbourhoods when they explained that the laws of the developments forbade saloons, drawing the city's best and 'the right kind of citizens' that respectable Chicagoans would want for their neighbours.

Shortly after the Disneys moved into their new home on 24 June 1893, Flora gave birth to a boy. Elias reminded her about his request to name the baby Columbus. She objected, choosing the name Roy instead. However, the problem of choosing a middle name for the new-born persisted. One day, while sitting with the baby in the front parlour of her new home, Flora noticed a large lumber truck driving down Tripp Avenue outside the bay window, likely dropping off wood for new home construction. The name of the company was painted large across the side of the truck: Oliver Lumber Company. The couple decided that 'Roy Oliver' went together nicely, bringing Elias's desire to give tribute to the Exposition to an end.

The couple quickly found that things weren't as easy with their third child as they had been with the first two. Roy was constantly fussy and often sickly, and it was soon discovered that he was unable to digest milk. When wealthy Aunt Margaret, the wife of Elias's brother Robert, found out, she wrote to a doctor in Boston who had treated her in her youth. The doctor developed a specialised dairy-free formula and sent it to Chicago. It did the trick. Roy quickly began to grow and had fewer digestion issues. However, the lack of natural milk likely led to a decreased immune system, as illness and disease plagued him his entire life.

As if life with a sickly baby wasn't difficult enough for Elias and Flora, there was worry too about Elias's mother, Mary. Unfortunately, it was increasingly difficult for her to maintain the family farm, and on 15 March

1894, it was sold to pay off the debts her husband left behind when he died three years earlier. She soon moved in with Elias's younger brother Kepple, who, at 29, owned his own farm ranching cattle. While Elias was at peace knowing that his mother was being taken care of by the family, his father's death and the loss of the farm likely put some strain on him as he was struggling to care for his own family.

Because of the high unemployment rate in Chicago, Elias was unable to find traditional work and instead turned to something he could do that drew upon his skills of carpentry: he decided to continue making furniture to sell. Members of the community had seen some of the pieces he had crafted and began to commission work. Over the next few years, Elias built tables, chairs, and wardrobes, as well as some specialty pieces. His work was so unique and well-made that local furniture stores noticed and began ordering pieces to sell in their showrooms. At one point, early in the days of the World's Columbian Exposition, he had even been commissioned to produce some pieces for the fair. While a door had closed when he had been laid off from the construction crew at Jackson Park, another had opened for him, one which was much more comfortable and enjoyable for Elias.

This contentment didn't last long, however. The restless bug which had plagued his family soon reared its head for Elias, and he quickly realised he wanted to use his skills for more than just producing furniture. He and Flora had enjoyed designing and building their home on Tripp and decided to try their hand at building a few more houses in the neighbourhood. The couple purchased two lots down the road from their home on which to build houses, 1141 and 1209 Tripp Avenue, which were both within walking distance of the family home at the intersection of Tripp and Keeler. Over the next few years, Elias would build the two houses, which were similar in structure to his house, in the worker's cottage-style with bay windows on the front. However, the draw for potential homebuyers was the added bonus of indoor running water and sewage, just like the Disneys had incorporated into their own home. Elias signed the papers for 1141 Tripp over to George Ramonberg, a 42-year-old German immigrant, who in addition to his wife and two daughters, shared the house with another newlywed couple and a few boarders. Shortly after, Elias sold 1209 Tripp to Harvey Craigmile, a railway engineer, and his wife Ethel. Ramonberg, a millwright, and

Craigmile were exactly the type of people Elias wanted to sell his houses to: honest, hard-working family men who were employed in Chicago's burgeoning industrial sector.

Building homes in the neighbourhood meant that Elias and Flora were more involved in the life of the local community and had become well-known by those living around them. Shortly after Roy was born, they joined the congregation of the Hermosa Congregational Church, which met a few blocks away from the Disney home at 1042 North Forty-Third Avenue. It was led by the Reverend H. W. Chamberlain, who strengthened the influence that the church had in the neighbourhood. As the congregation grew and the church established programmes drawing more people from the area, Chamberlain recognised a need to erect a new building. A lot was chosen at 2255 Forty-Second Avenue and a Building Committee was established. Elias's experience of building homes in the neighbourhood caught Reverend Chamberlain's eye and he requested that the carpenter sit on the committee.

Chamberlain stepped down from his post now that his work expanding the church's influence in Hermosa had been accomplished. He moved to Honolulu, placing his flock in the hands of a young pastor, Dr Walter R. Parr. Recognising the piety of Elias and Flora, and their commitment to both the church and the neighbourhood, Parr and his wife Mary quickly became friends with the Disneys, who were given additional responsibilities in the life of the church. Elias became a deacon and occasionally filled in at the pulpit when Parr was out of town, while Flora became the church treasurer and organist.

In early 1900, Parr and the Building Committee decided it was time to begin constructing the new church building. With a change in location, a new name for the church was decided on. It was now called St. Paul's Congregational. An elaborate ceremony was planned for the ground-breaking to represent the symbolism and importance of the church's involvement in the community. On the day of the ceremony, 19 May 1900, Reverend Parr arrived at the site early. He began walking the lot, armed with a tape measure and wooden spikes, and began to mark out the external boundaries of the church building. At around 5.00 pm, members of the congregation, Sunday school, Christian Endeavor programme, and other citizens of the neighbourhood began to arrive, many carrying digging implements including shovels, rakes, picks and spades. Some men accompanied their families, pushing their small children in wheelbarrows that would be used to haul away dirt as the ground-breaking commenced. Elias and Flora stood alongside Parr and his wife, greeting everyone who had come to help mark the occasion.

Small groups of people stood around talking while awaiting the arrival of the congregant bringing the plough that would be used in the ceremony. One of the women from the church, Jennie Bradshaw, a member of the church's Finance Committee, wandered from group to group distributing small badges marking the event. Shaped like sickles, the badges labelled those at the ground-breaking as 'Reapers', with a reference to Luke 10:2 below, explaining that 'the harvest is great but the laborers are few'. On the reverse side, a question was posed to the wearer of the badges: 'Will you be one?'

Around 6.00 pm, the plough arrived and some of the men set to work attaching a rope to the front. The congregation gathered around Reverend Parr with members of the Building Committee and church leadership standing nearby. After a brief prayer by Parr, the church choir and orchestra led the mass in singing *I Love Thy Church, O God*. As the last note died out, the reverend cleared his throat and began to address the crowd.

"Tonight we will commemorate this sacred ground for St. Paul's Congregational Church," he explained. "This ceremony is symbolical of the united effort that has brought the church to its present strength and that will make it still stronger and of greater usefulness in the future. The dragging of this plough through this soil by all members of the congregation pulling on the rope is symbolical of that which the church will accomplish in Hermosa and all of Chicago. Without the congregation of St. Paul's working in harmony in the future, the church will fail of its mission."

Parr looked around the flock of sheep – his sheep – and picked up the rope off the ground, holding it in the air. "I ask of you, men, women and children, to take hold of this rope as we break ground for this, our new church."

A swarm of young boys quickly ran forward and grabbed the rope as other members of the church began filing toward the plough. The eager youths immediately began pulling the rope so that the plough was flipped and began dragging across the field on its side. A few of the men ran towards the boys and stopped them, one moving forward to reset the plough in its furrow. The boys' parents, as well as other members of the church, found a spot on the rope, sinking into a solemn state of worship, recognising the gravity of the moment.

Reverend Parr situated himself behind the plough, ready to take the handles when the time came. Dr H.J. Patton and John Ferrier, members of St. Paul's Building Committee, hitched themselves to the front of the plough as one would a horse. Ferrier joked with Patton that he would only "consent to be yoked in with the doctor on condition that the latter would not shy at white bits of paper or get his feet mixed up in the traces." The small group of men chuckled at this, including Elias, who hitched himself to the plough in front of Patton and Ferrier; it was Elias's yoke which was attached to the rope that the congregants would pull.

"You aren't going to run away either, are you Disney?" Ferrier called. This gave the men another laugh.

After checking with the three yoked men, Reverend Parr gave the signal to his flock to begin pulling the rope as he pushed his hands down onto the handles of the plough. Immediately, the farming tool leapt into the air as the scores began to pull on the rope. Parr attempted to wrestle the steel-bladed plough back down into the dirt, but to no avail. One of the members, John Keeney, recognised the reverend's trouble and brought the pulling to a halt. Picking up the plough from where it sat, he walked it back to its original furrow and showed Parr what he did wrong: instead of pushing down on the handles, Parr instead needed to pull up on them to ensure that the blade cut the ground. The order was given and once again the members of the church began pulling the rope, with Ferrier, Patton and Elias digging in their heels as the symbolic workhorses.

As it quickly became evident that this attempt would be successful in breaking ground for the new church building, the choir began leading the congregants in singing the Doxology. Observers from the neighbourhood stood on the street ringing their bicycle bells and cheering, while one member blew into a tin horn in celebration. At the end of the first furrow, Reverend Parr gave Keeney control of the plough, acknowledging that he was "not a success as a ploughman." Joining his wife and Flora, the reverend watched as Keeney and his congregation completed four circuits around the staked perimeter of the new church building.

After the fourth pass, the celebrants let go of the rope and the Building Committee unhitched themselves from the front of the plough. A team of horses was hitched to the front of the plough and the members of the church, including Parr, grabbed the shovels and began to dig out the furrows, emptying the dirt and sod into the wheelbarrows. The work at 2255 Forty-Second Avenue continued past sundown. After an hour of digging, the work ceased, followed by singing and refreshments. After another word of prayer and encouragement, Parr dismissed his flock.

Over the next few months, Elias and Flora would become increasingly close to the Parrs as a result of Elias's role on the Building Committee. Parr often consulted his older friend on matters of construction and carpentry, and Elias visited the building site almost daily while checking on the worksites of the houses he was building in the neighbourhood.

The couples became even closer when, in early 1901, both Mary Parr and Flora announced that they were pregnant. Mary and her husband were ecstatic: the young couple was preparing for their second child close on the heels of Ilene, their daughter who was just shy of 2. Elias and Flora, on the other hand, were just as surprised: they hadn't planned on having any more children after Roy was born in 1893. However, Elias quickly put aside his feelings of shock in favour of anticipation. While visiting with each other on one occasion, Elias and Parr made an agreement: if their wives bore sons, they would name them after each other.

Reverend Walter Parr didn't keep his end of the bargain – at least not at first. Mary gave birth to a second daughter, who was given the name Bernice. The couple's first son was born in 1902 and was named Charles. It wasn't until the Parrs' fourth child was born in 1904 that the reverend remembered his deal with his friend and gave the baby the middle name of Elias.

But Elias never forgot his promise. On 5 December 1901, Flora gave birth to a son in the upstairs bedroom of their home on Tripp Avenue. His parents named him Walter Elias Disney.

Chapter Four

Moral Oblivion

N ow that Flora and Elias were the parents of four boys ranging in age from a new-born to a 13-year-old, Elias needed stable work. In addition to continuing to create and sell furniture to area showrooms, Elias recognised that he had a budding talent in carpentry. Noting the success of selling his first two spec houses on Tripp, Elias decided to continue his new trade. Over the next few years he would build additional houses in the area, including two one-and-a-half storied frame cottages located at 1676 and 1678 North Costello Avenue, respectively.

Even though he was certainly busy with work, 1249 Tripp Avenue was a hub of activity as well. Young Walter was a well-behaved baby, and healthy too; he didn't experience any of the same lactose intolerance that his older brother Roy had as an infant. Walter quickly became the pride of the family, doted on by his mother and brothers. Roy especially took a fancy to his younger brother: he was often seen pushing Walter up and down Tripp Avenue in a stroller. Not only did he shower his brother with affection, but he also occasionally purchased toys and small gifts for him with his own money.

When his older brothers went off to school at nearby Nixon Elementary School, located a few blocks away, Walter spent time with Flora and visited his father's building sites. However, a few days after his second birthday on 9 December 1903, Flora gave birth to her fifth and final child. A daughter had finally become part of the family: Ruth Flora Disney.

As Walter and Ruth grew, they became playmates while their older brothers were at school. While he loved his children, Elias became more of an authority figure for them.

His increasing piety and devotion at St. Paul's Congregational caused him to exert an increasingly moral strictness over his family. Perhaps in response to the vices and behaviours of his extended family in Canada and Kansas in his youth, Elias became wary of the temptations that an increasingly ethnically- and economically-diverse Chicago offered. He resisted all vices, never indulging in alcohol or a smoke. He had grown up with an understanding of the importance of hard work and honesty, and wanted to impart those qualities to his children.

This sternness often took the form of retribution for his sons if they crossed the line. Even as a toddler, Walter was strong-willed. After committing a wrong, he would often run from his father, wise enough to ensure that a piece of furniture, like a chair in the dining room, was always between him and his father. When Elias attempted to reason with the boy, Walter would argue back, leading to a clashing of wills. Unfortunately for the exasperated father, these instances often ended up becoming a sort of game of keep-away, where it became difficult for Elias to reach his son to punish him. These situations often ended in Flora coming to the rescue by scooping up her child and teasing her husband to get him out of his frustrated mood.

Elias didn't miss any opportunity to mete out discipline to his other sons, however. After committing disobedient acts, or not exemplifying honesty and a good character, Elias would send the offender up to his bedroom. Roy, in particular, remembered a time that he stood beside the window of his room which looked into the backyard, watching as Elias cut a switch off the apple tree in the yard's back corner, before bringing the small branch upstairs to punish his son with a light, yet painful, beating of the backside. In another instance, during one evening around the dinner table, it came to light that Raymond had stolen transfers from a tram conductor on his way to school. Transfers allowed someone who had paid to ride on a public conveyance to get off and board another one to continue their route without having to pay another fare. As a result of his lack of practising good, honest character, Raymond was immediately sent up to his bedroom to await Elias's punishment.

Elias's method of discipline was not unheard of at the time. In fact, many fathers and authority figures believed the maxim, 'spare the rod and spoil the child'. Elias simply believed that levying punishment was a way to improve the moral character of his sons, something done out of love in the moment. As a contractor in the construction and carpentry business, there were no lack of examples to show what vice and the immoral city could do to a person.

While Chicago was certainly a hub of capitalist greatness, as exemplified by the scores of new innovations being implemented, including elevators, the skyscraper, electric lights, and horseless trams, many of these new technologies served as a draw for immigrants and American migrants alike. This was greater magnified by the important presence of the railroad in the lakeside city: as of 1892, one-twenty-fifth of all railroad mileage in the world terminated in Chicago. Serving as both a method of import and export from the city, the railroads spurred the growth of a number of important industries, including meatpacking and steel and iron manufacturing. The factories needed labourers who would be paid low wages; these jobs were often reserved for unskilled and immigrant workers, all of whom descended on Chicago.

The city quickly became a cultural melting pot: Germans, Swedes, Italians, Polish, Irish, and Eastern Europeans all found work and new life in America's second largest city. While many of these new arrivals stayed in the centre near their place of work, some were able to afford to move out to the suburbs, settling in neighbourhoods like Humboldt Park and Hermosa. The teeming masses arriving in Chicago caused the city to grow exponentially in the years the Disneys lived there. Shortly after Flora and Elias arrived from Florida, Chicago had approximately one million citizens. Ten years later, when Walter was born, the population had almost doubled. Chicago quickly became overcrowded, leading to problems like pollution, homelessness, and illness. Corrupt politicians preyed on the ignorance of immigrants' understanding of the American political system, buying votes with promises for housing and jobs. Enterprising entrepreneurs took advantage of the larger population to cater to the needs and desires of the stressed-out immigrants by opening saloons, gambling houses, and brothels, while police officers accepted bribes to look the other way.

The prevalence of saloons and brothels began to creep into middle-class society. Temperance organisations, which aimed at limiting the consumption of alcohol, began to spring up throughout America, including large cities like Chicago. Any kind of liquor, they argued, led to 'moral oblivion', and had adverse effects on the family. When a husband imbibed alcohol, he was using money that could have been spent on his family. Drinking alcohol also served as a gateway to other activities and behaviours. A popular political cartoon from earlier in the century entitled *A Drunkard's Progress* argued that simply having a friendly drink with an associate could lead one towards violence, crime, social ostracisation and, ultimately, death by suicide. While this was obviously a biased and hyperbolic image meant to show the evils of vice and the potential effects it could have on the American family, the prevalence of alcohol did lead to a growth in other activities deemed questionable and immoral to 'respectable' Chicago society. Organised crime skyrocketed. Graft and political manipulation became prevalent. Brothels emerged in the Levee, Chicago's red-light district, which catered for all levels of Chicago society. Many attributed the lack of morals that seemed to have taken over downtown to the large influx of immigrants to the region.

Unfortunately, Elias began to consider that even his humble neighbourhood in Hermosa wasn't safe from the corruption and vice in the downtown district a little less than 10 miles away. Immigrant families had begun to move into houses on Tripp Avenue: many good Irish, Swedes and Poles lived on their street. They were well-behaved now, but God forbid they attracted other immigrants who were immoral or corrupted by the city's temptations.

As more people began to move to Hermosa, things became rougher and more 'dangerous'. Elias despaired when saloons began to open on street corners near the Disney home. Kids and teenagers began to run around the neighbourhood unattended. The worried father reached out to the local police, but while they promised they would clean up the area, nothing seemed to happen. Privately, he complained to Flora that the police were corrupt and probably accepting bribes to look the other way when mischief occurred.

This trend was not just confined to Hermosa, however. Chicago in the early decades of the twentieth century was notorious for its prominent crimes and vices, which were often attributed to the abundant immigrant population, as well as severe overcrowding. In the late nineteenth and early twentieth century, immigrants from Central and Eastern Europe made the journey from New York to Chicago, looking for work in the nation's largest industrial metropolis. Chicago at the turn of the century boasted scores of industrial and manufacturing jobs, including those in steel, meatpacking, railroad, and printing. The youth of Chicago were difficult to rein in to the city's public schools: those who weren't working in factories or selling newspapers on street corners often received what was known as a 'street education' in petty crime by spending time with other youths or unemployed adults. Reformer Jane Addams recognised that many of the problems caused by the immigrant population were attributed to their inability to assimilate into American culture; in an effort to help these 'poor huddled masses,' she established Hull House, a settlement house that provided services including Americanisation classes and job training for new immigrants living in inner-city Chicago. Addams' efforts didn't change the nativist attitudes that many Americans felt, especially those living in the vicinity of the immigrants. Stereotypes, discrimination, and racism continued, as well as scapegoating for the city's problems, drawing further the line between native-born Americans and the European immigrants.

The last straw for Elias Disney in Chicago began in mid-1903. On the evening of 4 July, four young men, between the ages of 18 and 21, entered the building of the Clybourn Junction station for the Chicago and Northwestern Railway and demanded money. One of the employees of the station, L.W. Lathrop, was shot in the ensuing scuffle, but the young men escaped with $70. Around a week later, the same young men entered a saloon. When the proprietor and a patron named Otto Bauder were ordered to put their hands up, Bauder fled. One of the youths shot him and he succumbed to his injury. This time, the gang escaped with $50. Two more saloons were robbed by the young men over the course of the following week.

A few weeks later, on 30 August, the young men entered a street railway car barn at the intersection of Sixty-Fifth and State streets, disguising themselves by wearing underwear on their heads. Recognising that some of the street railway employees were totalling up the day's fares, one of the bandits shot through the window while another took a sledgehammer and rammed down the door. One of the bullets hit Frank Stewart while his two co-workers, William Edmund and Henry Biehl, were also hit by stray bullets and were severely injured. A fourth employee, James Johnson, had been asleep in an adjoining room and rushed to the murder scene, when he too was struck down. One of the murderers swept up the pile of cash from the table at which Stewart, Edmund, and Biehl had been counting it, and fled with over $2,500.

While the Chicago Police had simply chalked the saloon robberies up to petty thieves, they were made painfully aware of what they were up against with the car barn robbery and murders. Herman Schuettler, the captain of Chicago's Sheffield Avenue police station, began investigating the crimes, and learned from an informant where he might find the car barn bandits.

Schuettler dispatched two of his detectives, John Quinn and William Blaul, to Greenberg's Saloon, located at the corner of Robey and Addison Streets in northwest Chicago, to capture one of the thugs in the gang. Upon entering the saloon, the detectives found a sole figure sitting at the bar with his back to them. He looked into the mirror across from him and saw the two detectives creeping up on him. Quickly turning around, he pulled a revolver out of his pocket and shot at the detectives, killing Quinn. When the young man tried shooting at the other detective, his revolver failed; Blaul tackled the youth and held him to the floor until backup arrived and then brought him down to the police station.

The young man was Gustave Marx, one of the four who had been responsible for the string of saloon robberies in July and the car barn robbery and murders at the end of August. He quickly confessed to his crimes, naming his co-conspirators as Peter Neidermeier, Harvey Van Dine, and Emil Roeski.

The other three criminals soon found out about their friend's arrest and went on the run towards Indiana, attempting to escape from Chicago before they could be tracked down by the police. They found refuge in a dugout south of the city, hiding until they ran out of supplies in late November, when they sneaked out to a local grocer. A schoolteacher, Henry Reichers, noticed the boys when Neidermeier pulled a thick roll of dollar bills out of his pocket to pay for their food. On closer inspection, he recognised the three young men by their descriptions in the newspaper and alerted the authorities, who quickly dispatched eight detectives to the location that Reichers identified. However, when the detectives arrived, Neidermeier, Van Dine, and Roeski had already left. Luckily, fresh snow had fallen and they were able to follow the trio's tracks to another shelter nearby. The detectives surrounded the building and called for the youths to come out, but rather than obey, the young gangsters began to fire their weapons at the detectives outside, killing one and injuring another.

In the ensuing chaos, the three young men were able to escape. However, Van Dine had been shot through the cheek, while Roeski was shot in the hip. A disagreement broke out over where they should flee to; Roeski left Neidermeier and Van Dine behind and continued to stumble 8 miles to nearby Aetna, where he could catch a train on the Wabash line out of Illinois. Van Dine and Neidermeier made their way to a nearby train that was sitting at a station, and climbed into the locomotive, ordering the engineer and brakeman to uncouple the engine from the rest of the cars. The brakeman mistakenly thought that Neidermeier was drunk and grabbed his wrist to push the revolver away; he was immediately shot dead. This convinced the engineer, who started the engine flying down the tracks away from the pursuing police. However, one of the detectives had phoned ahead to the railway authorities, and the train was routed to a side track. The criminals ordered the engineer to reverse the engine until it was back on the main line, at which point they jumped off the train and began running through a cornfield to escape.

As the police arrived at the stopped locomotive, a nearby group of farmers on a rabbit hunt heard the commotion and joined in the chase. Finding themselves at a dead end upon reaching a frozen marsh, Neidermeier and Van Dine piled up dead cornstalks to hide behind. This barricade was no match for the farmers, who fired into the cornstalks with their shotguns; small rounds of buckshot hit the two young men, who looked at each other and stepped out from behind the stalks with their hands raised.

"Don't shoot," Harvey Van Dine called out. "We surrender." The farmers kept their guns trained on the murderous youths until the police arrived, led by railway secret service officer Captain William Briggs, who made the arrest.

"We surrendered because you are not the police and because we want to see our mothers again," Neidermeier commented to the farmers as he and his partner were led away into the waiting police van.

A few minutes before the capture of Van Dine and Neidermeier and a mile away, the police arrived at the Aetna train station. They had received a tip that 'a breathless man in his shirt sleeves and covered with blood' had run into a house and asked for a coat. When he was refused, he found the train station nearby. Cleaning himself up in the washroom, the odd-acting young man lay down on a bench in the station's waiting room and fell asleep. When the police arrived at the train station, they found Emil Roeski, sound asleep, exhausted from his escape and from the loss of blood from his hip wound.

Over the next few months, trials would occur for all four boys, who quickly became known as 'The Car Barn Bandits' by the media. Peter Neidermeier, Harvey Van Dine, Gustav Marx, and Emil Roeski were all found guilty of multiple counts of murder, including that of two police officers, and sentenced to death by hanging on 22 April 1904. However, Roeski's sentence was later commuted to life imprisonment at Joliet State Prison when it was determined that it couldn't be proven he had fired the shot that killed Otto Bauder in the first robbery on 4 July. A failed breakout attempt occurred in late November 1904 when Roeski's brother, Herman, tried passing tools through the bars to Emil. However, the attempt was discovered and Herman Roeski joined his brother as a convict.

The story of the young gangsters was prevalent in the news throughout 1903 and 1904, as well as filling the thoughts and discussions of Chicago citizens. A number of copycat gangs began to spring up, consisting of young men who perpetrated their own robberies and murders. This trend continued to increase throughout the early 1900s as the economy of Chicago took a slight downturn, leading to an increase in crime. Unfortunately for Elias, this also meant that the housing market dried up, once again putting him out of work.

Elias Disney was especially fearful of the increase in the boy gangs and their crimes. Many of the robberies and murders carried out at the saloons by Neidermeier and company occurred less than 3 miles from the Disney home on Tripp Avenue. In fact, some members of the gang, including Emil Roeski, attended St. Paul's Congregational, the church at which Elias and Flora served as deacon and treasurer. Because the boys were the same age as Herbert and Raymond, Elias often saw his sons spending time around the accused murderers and worried for his boys' morality.

In February 1906, Sophia Van Dine, mother of the late boy criminal, wrote a series of articles for *The Chicago Tribune* explaining why so many Chicago youths had joined gangs and turned to a life of vice, theft and murder. Mrs Van Dine had devoted her life to helping troubled boys after the death of her son at the hands of the law, hoping to save them from a similar fate. She explained that it was 'the responsibility on the part of normal minded men and women' to save the delinquents, whom she labelled 'feeble-minded' and developmentally 'dwarfed'. She further explained that due to these boys' inability to discern what was morally acceptable behaviour, many of them had been corrupted by their own fathers, who were either absent or also prone to vice and violence, and lived a life of alcoholism or abused their wives and children. A solution, she offered, was isolation, separating these young men from the rest of society thus preventing them from a life of crime, as well as making it impossible for them to procreate and create 'perhaps a greater degree the faults of the parents'.

What was most troubling to Elias, however, was the argument that Mrs Van Dine made in an article published on the morning of 6 February. The feeble-mindedness of young men, she explained, prevented them from recognising the criminal faults of those around them. Chicago's youth spent time together on street corners, in abandoned buildings and homes, in saloons and pool halls. What began as vice and inappropriate language, eventually turned into petty theft before blossoming into holdups, armed violence, and ultimately murder. The prevalence of this crime in the area surrounding the Disney home on Tripp Avenue was a concern to the Disney patriarch: his two oldest sons, Herbert and Raymond, aged 18 and 16 respectively at the time of Mrs Van Dine's article, were the same age as the Car Barn Bandits when they began their rampage of crime, and had, on occasion, spent time with the boys through their association with the family's church.

Fearful that his sons could potentially turn down a similar path due to the influence of other young men in the neighbourhood, Elias decided that the temptations of city life were too much for his family. He determined to find a more rural place where his children would learn what it meant to live a life of honest, hard work and diligence. While the years following the change from Big City Chicago to Main Street, USA would be major for the Disney children, Walt would fondly remember them as some of the best years of his young life.

Part III

Things of importance

Marceline, Missouri, 1906–1911

Chapter Five

Smalltown Folks

"Where will we go?" Elias wondered to himself. It was obvious that the morality of America's cities had gone downhill over the sixteen years they had lived in Chicago, with the increase of organised crime, prostitution, gambling, and alcoholism. This was *not* the environment that he had intended for raising four sons and a daughter.

The family patriarch thought back to his own youth working on the farms in Canada and Kansas. It was here that he learned the importance of determination, hard work, honesty and community. In an era of economic difficulty in the wake of the recent recession, it was these characteristics he sought to instil in his young family.

Together, Elias and Flora began to scour rural America, contacting landowners, real estate companies, and their expansive network of family and friends, looking for opportunities to purchase land on which they could farm. While Steamboat Springs, Colorado and Citronella, Alabama were high on their list, it was the advice given to him by his younger brother, Robert, that he decided to follow.

For years, businessman Robert Disney had been interested in real estate speculation. After leaving the family homestead in Kansas, Robert had been lured by the prospects of wealth in Chicago, which was vying to be the location for the 1893 World's Columbian Exposition. Recognising that hundreds of thousands would be visiting the Great White City to experience all the fair had to offer, in March 1892 he placed an ad in *The Chicago Tribune* offering to pay between $80 and $120 per square foot of land on Chicago's South Side for the purpose of building a hotel.

Foreseeing that the hotel business in Chicago would dwindle after the conclusion of the fair, Robert began to look elsewhere for a business opportunity that would enrich him. His attention settled on an opportunity for land development along the shores of Lake Michigan, receiving a deed of land in exchange for services performed in lieu of financial payment from land 'developer', Captain George Wellington Streeter. Unfortunately for Robert, the land he received from Streeter, as well as adjacent tracts, quickly became the subject of one of Chicago's biggest controversies in the last years of the nineteenth century.

In 1886, George Wellington Streeter, captain of the small yacht, *Rutan*, plied the waters between Chicago and Milwaukee transporting passengers. He stumbled across a 1755 map that identified land owned by the British and later the United States government under the terms of the organisation of the Northwest Territory as part of the conditions of the Treaty of Paris. Streeter realised that the land beneath the surface of Lake Michigan was unclaimed territory. Leaving the *Rutan* anchored offshore in a stretch of the lake used to dump garbage and ashes near Superior Street in northern Chicago, the captain awaited a storm that would wreck the ship and put his plan into action. Luckily for the con-artist, a storm soon came along, the large waves of Lake Michigan in fact grounding the small craft on a sandbar.

Over the next few weeks, as debris from the storm began to be cleared from the shores of Lake Michigan, Streeter strategically placed logs and tree branches from the storm between his grounded boat and the shore. This dammed sand, as well as the floating garbage and dumped ashes, as the currents flowed parallel to the beach, creating a dry path. Claiming squatters' rights, Streeter established ownership of his makeshift island and the growing land around it, converting the *Rutan* into a small house and moving into it with his wife.

As the land claimed by Captain Streeter began to grow to an area of 156 acres, he had the area surveyed and platted into 1,900 prime lots for sale to those interested in owning property along the lakeshore, while earning $150 per month from those who instead decided to rent shanties rather than purchase land outright. The captain was able to sell 300 lots, including some to Robert and Margaret Disney, making more than $200,000 from land sales before those who had original claims to the shoreline, such as N.K. Fairbank, went to local law enforcement to argue against Streeter's claims to the land and selling it off.

To legitimise his claims, Streeter petitioned the United States government to annex the land, which he had set up as a new state called the District of Lake Michigan. He offered the United States four options: either the land could be annexed as part of the state of Illinois;

added to the territory of Alaska; established as a completely new state; or rejected by the United States and instead become an independent territory similar to Puerto Rico. In an effort to make his offer even more appealing, the captain created his own government, establishing posts including treasurers and judges, and wrote his own constitution. One aspect of this founding document was particularly appealing, as it offered citizenship and voting rights to all women aged 18 and older, something not approved for American women until the Nineteenth Amendment to the U.S. Constitution was passed more than twenty years later.

Both the United States and the state of Illinois rejected Streeter's offer, and police officers were sent to the District of Lake Michigan in 1893, arresting the captain and tearing down the shanties that had been erected along the shore. The arrested man, even while sitting in jail, insisted that the Chicago police were corrupt and had been paid to arrest him, even though he hadn't committed any crime. The Streeter debacle eventually ended when the city of Chicago filled in the lake surrounding the District of Lake Michigan to build Lincoln Park and Lake Shore Drive along the coast, ultimately erasing Streeter's claim to the land.

With Robert's newest land development opportunity literally buried by the city of Chicago, the investor instead turned to Marceline, Missouri, a small town along the Santa Fe Railroad, which was slowly becoming an important farming community. While the area was originally known as Bucksnort and had been a rural collection of privately owned farms, the town of Marceline became established as a division point along the railroad in 1888, named for the wife of one of the directors of the Santa Fe Route. During the 1800s, railroads established waypoints every 160 kilometres for trains to refuel and resupply; because of the prevalence of creeks flowing in the area, as well as the discovery of coal nearby, Marceline was established as a prime location for the waypoint of the railroad which stretched between Chicago and Kansas City, Missouri. Recognising it was essential to create buy-in from the families owning farms in the Bucksnort area, the railroad company began to build an infrastructure to support the traffic that a waypoint along the Santa Fe would bring. A wooden two-storey station was constructed along the tracks, featuring a dining hall and overnight accommodations for railroad workers. After coal was discovered, the Marceline Coal and Mining Company was established and Mine No. 1 was opened, creating a number of jobs for men in the area. The main roads through town were graded and paved, a downtown began to be erected, and within a few years, a power plant was built a few hundred metres from the train station, bringing electricity to the town.

However, in order for Marceline to grow, it was essential that it attracted families and not just men to work on the rail line or in the coal mine. E.P. Ripley, president of the Atchison, Topeka & Santa Fe Railroad, decided that outdoor leisure space was needed and donated a few acres of land to the town for the establishment of a park. Named in his honour, Ripley Park featured a large pond, green space, and a gazebo for community concerts and events. The downtown area that developed along Kansas Avenue, the town's main street, soon opened an opera house, department store, banks, a school, boarding houses, and a hotel, all of which not only provided services for those passing through town by way of the train, but also for those who lived near the mines or on nearby farms.

When Robert Disney heard through his network of investors in Chicago that the Santa Fe line would be built through northern Missouri, he purchased 400 acres of land and sold some of it to the Santa Fe Railroad, increasing its premium to make a profit for himself. The remaining acreage, located northwest of downtown Marceline, he kept for himself, establishing a row crop farm which primarily grew corn to be loaded onto the train at the local depot and sent around the country. The enterprising capitalist wasn't a country boy, however: Robert and his wife Margaret lived in Kansas City, approximately 200 kilometres to the southwest, while employing local help to manage the farm in his absence.

Robert and Margaret weren't distant investors who were solely interested in making a buck off the labour of the local population, however. The couple often visited town, taking the Santa Fe before transferring to a horse-drawn buggy that took them to their land a few kilometres away. It was obvious to the citizens of Marceline that Robert and Margaret were wealthy out-of-towners; Robert often wandered downtown in fancy suits lined with accessories such as golden pocket napkins and watch chains, an expensive cigar hanging from his lips, earning him the nickname 'Gold Bug Disney'. His attitude towards locals was not one of derision, however; recognising the importance of the people of Marceline for his farm's success, as well as remembering his own small-town agricultural roots in Goderich and Ellis, Robert was kind to those in town, helping its inhabitants when he could.

Thus, when Elias mentioned to Robert that he and Flora were looking for somewhere to move their family that would align with their values of community and hard work, Robert heartily recommended the small town of Marceline. When Elias agreed that Marceline would be perfect for his family, Robert purchased the farm of the recently deceased William Crane from Crane's wife, who had moved to New York to live with family after her husband's death. Crane had received his farmland in northern Missouri as payment for serving in New York's 94th Infantry during the American Civil War and had been living on the land for twenty-seven years before his death. Robert Disney, in turn, sold it to Elias for $125 per acre to make the transition into town easier for his brother's family. The property measured approximately 45 acres and featured a two-storey white clapboard farmhouse, a small red barn, animal pens and pastures, and fields full of crops including sorghum, corn, and two orchards growing Wolf River apple trees.

Elias was eager to move his family out of Chicago. He purchased four train tickets for Flora, Roy, Walter and Ruth and sent them with a few of the family's belongings to Marceline to get settled on the farm. He, Herbert and Raymond stayed to settle their affairs in Chicago before bringing the rest of the family's possessions by rail freight later.

As the train pulled into Marceline, plumes of steam issued from the locomotive causing dust that had settled on the bricked train platform to jump into the air in spinning clouds. Roy helped his mother with the family's bags, which were loaded onto a handcart on the platform. He and Flora each took the hand of one of the younger children and stepped from the train into the shadow of the two-storey wooden station Marceline had erected for trains and passengers passing through town.

As they walked around to the front of the station, Flora explained to her children that Mr James Coffman, a local resident, would be picking them up and taking them to their new farm. Flora maintained a brave face for her children – she was secretly worried about her role as a mother raising a small family on the farm and hoped she could adequately prepare things before Elias's arrival with her two older sons.

The sun hovered in the sky; while it was an early spring day with moderate temperatures, the sun's rays beat down on the family accustomed to wearing heavy and layered clothing necessary for living in the north. Flora motioned her children to an area across the street from the station, shaded by a towering grain elevator. Walter and Ruth held hands as they followed their mother, while Roy, pushing the handcart stacked with trunks, followed close behind.

The family didn't have to wait long, as a few minutes later, an old horse was seen as it clip-clopped down the bricked lane pulling a cart driven by a grizzled man about Elias's age. The man brought the animal to a stop in front of the family. The two adults exchanged pleasantries while Roy began to load the trunks and bags onto the back of the cart. Mr Coffman helped Flora onto the cart, then lifted Walter and Ruth to their mother, who got the two settled for the ride to their new home. Over the next few minutes, as the horse-drawn buggy slowly made its way north to the family's new home, young Walter was enraptured by the rural landscape, a marked contrast from urban Chicago: Missouri's rolling green hills were crowned by bright blue skies, alternating lots featuring houses, cattle pastures, and row crops on either side of the road.

The small farmhouse was perfect for the Disney family. On the first floor, a kitchen and parlour served as the area in which the family entertained. A small bedroom off the parlour was used by Herbert and Raymond, who at the ages of 17 and 15, were often employed labouring on the family farm as well as other farms in the area, and needed an easy exit from the house at all hours of the day due to the nature of their work. The top floor featured three bedrooms, including a small room for Elias and Flora, and two equally-sized rooms at the front of the house: one which Roy and Walter shared and another across the hall for Ruth alone, which she enjoyed as the benefit of being the only girl in the family. While the house didn't have electricity or running water when the Disneys moved in – Flora had to get water from a handpump in the kitchen – one luxury Elias insisted on having was a telephone. Life in Chicago had shown him the benefits of emerging technologies and he was always looking for new opportunities, wanting to stay ahead of the curve to potentially open financial doors for him. Recognising the benefit of closets in the Tripp house in Chicago, Elias was pleased that his new home featured the storage space in each of the bedrooms. He was willing to spend a little bit more on the mortgage for a house with closets (the extra rooms led to increased taxes on a house than those without). However, one thing that the family particularly missed, especially in the winter months, was a bathroom. While they'd had a small water closet beneath the stairs in their Chicago house, the Marceline farmhouse instead had an outhouse set a distance away from the home to protect the water supply from contamination.

While Flora got things settled at the farmhouse over the next few weeks, Elias wrapped things up in Chicago. The sale of the family home that he and his wife had built on Tripp was finalised, and the deed was transferred to a young family of German immigrants that had recently moved to Hermosa. Raymond and Herbert helped their father pack up the last of the family's belongings and pick out a team of draught horses at the city's stockyards before loading everything onto a boxcar and taking the Santa Fe to Marceline.

Life in a small, rural town was quite different for the Disneys. The five children, who were between the ages of 3 and 17, certainly learned the ethics their father sought to instil in them through life in an agricultural community, rather than those gleaned in the big city. With a population of only 5,000, Marceline had a sense of community, which was exemplified by the interdependence that existed between its citizens.

Remembering the importance of neighbours to one's existence from his time in Ellis, Elias quickly invested his family in the life of the town. Many of the citizens, who had emigrated from Europe to work in the coal mines, passed the time playing instruments as this was a low-cost leisure time activity. These musical coal miners organised themselves into bands, such the Marceline Town Band, to perform at the weekends in the gazebo at Ripley Park. Over time, the band incorporated men who worked on area farms and for the Santa Fe Railroad, and Elias soon contributed his talent as a fiddler to these performances. Neighbours also often helped each other out in annual agricultural activities, such as barn raising and harvests. Fathers who either owned their own farms or worked in the region's other major industries often hired out their children to the town's farmers to help with work; for example, both Herbert and Raymond worked on a number of farms as part of threshing crews, including the Disney farm and the Taylor farm, located just down the road.

Even young Walter, at the age of 6, was expected to help with agricultural labour: when he wasn't leading a horse around the millstone to crush sorghum on his father's farm, he was partnered up with neighbour boy, Patrick Shermuly, to take water to those working on the threshing crews. Young Walter wasn't very interested in work, however. Like one of his literary heroes, Tom Sawyer, the boy often convinced others to take on more jobs so he could hang back or relax. Another of Walter's chores was herding pigs on the Disney farm. One day, when he realised that the animals were stubborn and wouldn't move in the direction he desired, he mounted the back of one of the largest sows, called Porker, and rode it like a horse to influence the rest of the hogs to move towards the pen. This didn't quite go the way the boy intended: the sow instead moved towards the farm's pond, thick with mud, and reared, throwing Walt into the mud. While his intentions of herding the pigs had failed, the boy had discovered a new pastime, deciding to play with the livestock rather than fulfil the duties assigned by his father.

Walter's chores taking care of the farm's animals led to him developing endearing relationships with the livestock. While Porker always threw the boy off her back and into the mud when he tried to ride her, she recognised him as one of her regular playmates. On one occasion, when Walter and Ruth developed chickenpox, Porker came up onto the farmhouse's porch and began oinking and pawing at the front door. Flora, who had been keeping an eye on Ruth as she sat against the flue of the stove where the heat could help break her fever, went upstairs to Walter and Roy's room where the sick little boy was resting in bed. When Walter learned that his hefty friend was waiting to play on the porch, the boy smiled.

Walter also fell in love with a small piglet, whom he called Skinny. The piglet was the runt and unable to make it through the pack of his brothers and sisters to feed at his mother, so Walter, feeling sympathy for the creature, began to feed it with a bottle. A bond was forged between the boy and piglet, who began to follow Walter around the farm like a puppy.

Living in a small farming community also meant that one quickly got to know the neighbours. Across the street from the Disney farm lived Erastus Taylor, whom everyone in town called 'Grandpa Taylor', and his wife, Elizabeth. The Taylors were one of the founding families of Marceline, purchasing land from the Burlington Railroad in 1867, more than twenty years before the town's incorporation. Taylor was also integral to the town's development, donating land for the area's first cemetery and building the town's first school, which he taught at in addition to farming his 80 acres of land.

The proximity of the Taylor property to the farm that had previously belonged to William Crane exemplified the nature of small-town life:

Crane's niece, Bertha Phillips, had married Erastus's son, Manly Howe Taylor. Erastus Taylor was also childhood friends with Crane's brother-in-law, Josiah Phillips, Bertha's father. As a result, while Erastus and William Crane weren't directly related, the link between their respective families created a bond upon which they learned to rely on each other. Thus, when Elias and his family moved onto the old Crane farm, the Disneys became an adopted part of the Crane/Taylor microcosm north of Marceline.

Over the next few years, young Walter spent some time across the street at Grandpa Taylor's home. The old man loved to tell stories of his exploits serving as a private in Company H of the 6th Regiment of the Minnesota volunteers during the American Civil War. Crane had enlisted in February 1864, where he joined his company at Fort Ridgely in southwest Minnesota. Union troops were stationed there to hold back Native Americans, who, a few years earlier, had attacked the fort. In June, the regiment moved south to Helena, Arkansas, where they occupied the previously held Confederate state. The warmer weather in Arkansas led to a wave of smallpox infection throughout Minnesota's 6th Regiment, claiming the lives of 165 officers and troops. Erastus caught the illness and was transported to Jefferson Barracks in St. Louis, Missouri, where he convalesced until May 1865, missing the Confederate surrender and the end of the war. After being released from the hospital, his service was used to secure Union occupation of the south, before being released from U.S. military service a few months later on 19 August 1865.

While Grandpa Taylor told magnificent stories of 'his experiences' in the Civil War that enraptured the imagination of young Walter, the boy soon realised that it was impossible for the old man to have fought in every battle or to have met every general that he described. However, the art of storytelling wasn't lost on Walter, who recognised the importance of Taylor including vivid details and colourful characters.

Erastus's son, Manly Howe Taylor, lived approximately one kilometre west of the Disney farm with his wife and five children, on the farm that Josiah Phillips had established upon his arrival in Bucksnort more than twenty years earlier. Manly Howe's children were about the same age as the Disneys', creating instant playmates for Walter and Ruth, as well as new peers for Raymond, Herbert, and Roy. The Disneys also became close friends with the Flickingers and Rensimers, whose young sons, Clem and Will respectively, became close friends of Walter and Roy.

But having peers wasn't all that was important to the older Disney boys. Living in a small midwestern agricultural community gave them the opportunity to court country girls and farmers' daughters. Roy, in particular, had fallen for Fleta Rogers who, as a teacher in one of the local schools, was discouraged to marry. As a result, her interest in a relationship with Roy was casual, rather than serious. While Rogers enjoyed spending time with Roy because he was a 'nice boy', she had an undeniable attraction for his older brother Raymond and made every effort possible to be noticed by him. Because Fleta's family lived on the main road downtown, she and her friends, who had selected their best dresses and had perfectly coiffed their hair, would often sit on the front porch on Saturday nights waiting for Herbert and Raymond, who often attended social events in town. As the two brothers walked by in their dapper suitcoats, white flannel trousers, and tall straw hats, the girls would rush to the balcony of the porch and call to the boys. The two eldest Disneys would stop and lean against the gate leading into the Rogers' yard, making small talk and occasionally a courteous but flirtatious comment to the girls. After a few minutes, they would politely tip their hats at the young women, bid them a good evening, and continue on their way. Regardless of the evening's temperature, Miss Fleta Rogers would always collapse onto the porch swing, flushed and breathless that Raymond Disney had noticed and spoken to her.

Fleta Rogers wasn't the only girl in town who was interested in gaining his attention: 17-year-old Raymond was quite the ladies' man and often used his suave charm to get dates with the local girls. Ray often took them dancing or to enjoy time on the shores of the pond at Ripley Park. However, his casual nature with the girls only interested them for a little while before they realised he wasn't interested in commitment and found more steady guys instead.

Physical distance and limitations on transportation weren't hindrances to the Disney's extended family during their time in Marceline. The fact that the town was a division point along the Santa Fe Railroad actually made it easier for members of the Disney kin to drop by on occasion.

As the youngest boy, Walter was often spoiled by his visiting family. One example is when Grandma Mary Richardson Disney, Elias's mother, came to town to visit. Walter and Grandma Mary were kindred spirits, as both enjoyed causing mischief and Mary took advantage of that. During one of her numerous trips to Marceline, Mary took the boy into town, walking along the country roads during the fair weather. As they were passing a small house with a garden in the front yard, Mary spotted some turnips that looked especially tasty.

"Walter, crawl under that fence and fetch me some turnips," she prodded. Eager to please his favourite grandmother, the boy quickly climbed into the garden, unearthing the turnips the woman pointed to. Scrambling back under the fence, he handed the dirt-covered vegetables to Mary, who promptly wrapped them in her apron, not only to aid in carrying them home but also to hide them from suspicious eyes.

Upon arriving home, Walter and Mary found Elias in the kitchen. Walter proudly boasted to his father about his feat of retrieving the turnips for his grandmother. For a moment, Elias didn't say anything. A frown creased his face, which became increasingly redder. Looking down at his young son, Elias began to teach the boy that theft was morally and religiously wrong.

"Thou shalt not steal," the father finished.

"Oh, Elias, stop," his mother said sharply. Her son's eyes snapped from the boy to the old woman. "You're making such a fuss over a few turnips. They had plenty more. There's no need to get so heated." Taking the boy's hand, Mary turned and walked out of the kitchen, leaving her son even angrier.

Leading the boy into the front parlour, Mary took out a small tin pillbox and removed a round, red pellet. Walter loved these pellets as they were sweet and melted in his mouth. The boy made sure to go out of his way to do things for Grandma Mary so she would reward him with these tasty sweets.

One day, when Mary was rewarding her grandson with one of the pellets, Flora happened to be in the room and, horrified, chastised her mother-in-law for giving the boy the tablet. While Walter had thought he was being rewarded with sweets, it turned out that his grandmother was giving him Cascarettes, a popular patent laxative covered in sugar to make the medicine easier to stomach. Grandma Mary defended herself, explaining that giving her grandson laxatives not only reinforced the boy's good behaviour, but they might also benefit his digestion.

Grandma Disney didn't always enlist her grandchildren in making light-hearted trouble. She was also an incredibly affectionate and nurturing woman. Every evening during her stay, while Flora was cleaning up after dinner and Elias went out to finish the evening farm chores, Mary would take a volume of *Grimm's Fairy Tales* or the stories of Hans Christian Andersen down from the fireplace mantle, while Roy, Walter and Ruth would gather around her on the floor. Over the next few minutes, she would enthusiastically spin tales, occasionally using voices and acting out bits of the stories, holding her grandchildren spellbound. Walter, Roy and Ruth loved this evening tradition so much that Flora continued the practice after Grandma Disney returned home, albeit not as dynamically as her mother-in-law.

While some Disney relatives rode the train into town, others *drove* the train into Marceline. Young Walt's Uncle Mike Martin, married to Flora's older sister Alice, worked as a locomotive engineer for the Atchison, Topeka & Santa Fe Railroad, particularly the stretch between Fort Madison, Iowa and Kansas City, Missouri. As Martin approached Marceline on his way to Kansas City, he would blow a distinct pattern on the locomotive's whistle to signal to his sister- and brother-in-law and their kids that he was in town. As a young boy growing up in a town centred on the railroad, Walter was fascinated by trains and raced about 1.5 kilometres east where the Santa Fe crossed a railroad trestle. The little boy scrambled up the rocky hill where the train driven by his uncle waited, and the sooty engineer would scoop up his nephew into the cab of the train. To his delight, young Walter Disney would sit on his uncle's lap, tooting the train's whistle the last few kilometres into town before it stopped at the Marceline station to be restocked before continuing on its way south to Kansas City.

It took time for passengers and cargo to be unloaded from Uncle Mike's train and for its stores of coal, sand and water to be refilled for the next leg of its journey. Rather than hanging out in the train yard or having a meal at the train station's restaurant, Martin would hitch a ride to the Disney farm, where Flora and Elias were waiting for him with a cool drink. The adults would sit on the porch swing, while Walter and Roy sat on the porch steps with a paper bag of hard candies their uncle had brought them and listen to Uncle Mike and Elias take turns spinning tales of their time driving for and building the railroad, respectively. Elias related to his sons how, during his time building the Union Pacific, Buffalo Bill Cody, who would later become famous for creating a Western-themed circus, would shoot buffalo for the purpose of providing meat for Elias's work crew. Uncle Mike also liked to tell the boys stories about important battles of the Civil War, as well as the American tall tale of Casey Jones, based on a real-life railroad engineer named Jonathan Luther Jones, who had died a few years before when the passenger train he was driving had collided with the rear of a freight train in Mississippi. Jones had been well-known for his heroic yet failed attempt at stopping his train prior to the fatal crash, making his way into American legend for slowing the train from 121 kilometres per hour to 51, sparing the lives of everyone else onboard.

If one can attribute Mike Martin's stories and work along the Atchison, Topeka & Santa Fe Railroad to Walter's love of trains throughout his life, another close family member is responsible for instilling an interest in art in the boy. Uncle Robert and his wife, Aunt Margaret, often visited Marceline, not only to see his brother, but to check on his land 4 kilometres west of Elias's farm. On one occasion, Margaret brought her nephew a Big Chief tablet of paper and a box of crayons. Throughout her stay, she would often find the boy on his stomach in the parlour, drawing pictures of people and animals. While she doted on the boy to build his self-esteem, many of her compliments regarding his drawing were genuine; while many children Walter's age were drawing stick figures, the young artist was instead concentrating on a more realistic and natural form.

The high praise from Aunt Margaret inspired the boy to continue drawing when he wasn't expected to help on Elias's farm. As he was part of a large family, this gave Walter an opportunity to draw and improve his depiction of people. But like an avid reader, the budding artist began to look for other things to inspire him, such as advertisements and newspapers. Elias read a weekly newspaper, *The Appeal to Reason*, a socialist publication from Girard, Kansas. Flipping through the paper, the boy discovered that it featured political cartoons and regular comic strips, which served as new models to draw.

Walter also used his experience living on his father's farm to sketch his favourite animals, such as Skinny, Porker, and Martha (a hen). Elias made sure it was understood that the pursuit of drawing did not interfere with farm chores, and was a hobby that would only take place in the boy's spare time. Walter obeyed his father, but that didn't stop him from getting in trouble. One day, while Elias, Flora and Roy had taken the buggy into town with a load of apples to sell and Herbert and Raymond were off working in the fields, Walter and Ruth were wandering around the property when they came across a barrel sitting against the north side of the house. The curious siblings lifted the top off the barrel to find it full of black pitch.

Walter picked a stick up off the ground and stuck it in the barrel, examining the pitch that had been left on the tip.

"Oh!" he exclaimed. "This would be great to paint with!" The boy looked around for a surface to paint on, but nothing presented itself. Deflated, the boy looked longingly back at the barrel and noticed the broad exterior wall of the farmhouse covered in white clapboard siding. "Ruth, let's paint on the house."

"Will it come off?" Ruth asked. "I don't think father will be very happy."

"Sure, it will come off," her older brother said derisively. "Get a stick."

As the little girl picked up a stick from beneath a nearby tree, the aspiring artist dipped his makeshift paintbrush into the tar and began to draw pictures onto the side of the house. For the next few minutes, he created an imaginary world on the blank wooden canvas full of houses with smoke erupting from the chimneys and small, smiling people standing nearby. Two years younger than her brother, Ruth drew zigzags below and beside the boy's town. After a while, the siblings stepped back from their works of art, sticks in hand, and admired their handiwork in the warm sunlight.

"We should probably start cleaning up before Mother and Father get back," Walter suggested. Ruth ran inside to get a rag to scrub off their work, but the pair quickly realised that the tar had begun to dry and harden and wasn't coming off the clapboard siding. The pair was still trying to scrub the tar off the house when they heard the sound of hooves coming up the road. Peeking around the corner of the house, Walter felt a sense of panic rise as he saw his father, mother and brother riding in the buggy past the front of the farmhouse. The boy would be unable to hide his work from his father; the barn in which the family stabled the horses and parked the buggy was on the north end of the property.

Sure enough, when Elias discovered what his two youngest children had been up to, he wasn't happy. Snatching his own stick off the ground, he disciplined both of his children before marching into the house. Over the course of the next few days, Walter's father became angrier as he realised he was unable to scrub nor chip the tar drawings off the side of the house. Eventually he gave up, hoping that others in the town wouldn't see his children's handiwork due to its placement on the north side of the house.

To prevent a similar event from taking place, Elias encouraged his son to take his Big Chief drawing pad into the farmyard if he wanted to draw outdoors. When he got tired of drawing his father's livestock, Walter would carry his art supplies to nearby farms to sketch the neighbours' animals. The boy would stretch in the grass on his belly or perch himself on a fencepost. At one farm in particular, the young artist enjoyed sketching a chestnut-coloured Morgan stallion who gracefully grazed in the pasture.

One day, while sketching the strong horse, a shadow fell over Walter and the boy started as he felt a strong hand on his shoulder. He turned around to find the owner of the farm, Leighton Sherwood, standing behind him. While Sherwood was now a farmer north of Marceline, the elderly man had spent his career as a physician throughout the American Midwest, earning him the nickname 'Doc' around town.

"Not bad, Walter," the old man said, looking over the drawing, a smile spreading across his bare, ruddy-complexed face.

"Do you really like it?" the boy asked.

"I sure do," Sherwood stated. The smile disappeared as a thoughtful look crossed his face. "Say, you wouldn't be interested in selling that picture, would you? Ole Rupert there is my favourite horse and I sure would like to have it."

Young Walter was amazed. "Sell it? You can have it!"

But Doc simply shook his head, pulling the boy's hand toward him and placing a shiny quarter into the palm. After a short talk with the farmer, Walter climbed down off the fence and, tucking his drawing pad under his arm, ran home clutching the quarter in his hand. He could feel a small bulge in his pocket that he'd forgotten about: a buckeye that he carried everywhere he went because his friends told him it would bring good luck. Maybe his friends had been right.

It was the first time Walter Disney was paid for creating art, but it certainly wouldn't be the last.

Chapter Six

Country Boy

While his days in Marceline, Missouri certainly had an impact on Walter Disney's passion for trains and his career path towards creating art, it also inspired a love for nostalgia, community, and small-town Americana that would later be exemplified in his animated shorts, films, and theme parks.

After hearing Uncle Mike's stories about life on the Santa Fe Railroad and getting to ride on his uncle's lap in the locomotive, Walter began to spend as much time as possible near the railroad and train yard. He, Roy and some of the boys living on neighbouring farms, including Clem Flickinger and Don Taylor, would run down to the tracks into town and walk up and down the line, balancing on the steel rails. At times, they would lie down on their bellies in the gravel or on the wooden ties and put their ears to the rails to listen for vibrations of an approaching train. The nearby railroad trestles became a playground for the boys, who enjoyed climbing up the wooden support beams, laying across them and watching a train steam by overhead. On sunny days, Walter and Roy would sneak down to the train yards south of town where the sand and coal chutes towered over the locomotives being serviced. If no one was around, the boys climbed up the ladders running along the sides of the chutes and stood in the small sheds perched atop the structures, surveying the countryside and town laid out around them.

One afternoon in 1909, while hanging around the trainyards with Clem and Don, the boys came across a train in the process of being serviced before continuing its journey along the Santa Fe. Don and Clem recognised that their friend didn't seem to be afraid of anything and always gave into adventure and taking risks, so they dared Walter to give the train whistle a toot. He waited in the shadows of a nearby building until the engineer and trainmen had stepped away, then quickly climbed into the cab of the locomotive. From his elevated perspective above the tracks, the daring boy could see the area around him in case the engineer returned, but the rumbling and hissing sounds emitting from the idling steam engine muted any potential crunching of gravel if an adult should make his way back to the train. Glancing over at his friends who were still in hiding, he plastered a goofy grin on his face and reached for the cord attached to the whistle. Hesitating for a moment, he realised that he still had a chance to back out. But giving up was not something Walter Disney did. As he yanked down on the cord, a long, loud whistle escaped from the locomotive. The boy didn't wait to see the reaction of the trainyard employees as he leapt from the train and onto the gravel. As soon as his feet hit the ground, he sprinted to where Clem and Don were hiding, and together, the three boys, giggling and cheering, made their escape back into downtown Marceline.

Walter's exploits spending time along the tracks and in the trainyard weren't an isolated incident among the boys of Marceline: nearly every young boy aspired to work for the railroad when they got older. Because the town was so important to the operation of the Santa Fe Railroad, the life of its citizens and the local economy centred around providing goods and services that either serviced the trains and rail line or benefited from the trains passing through.

Another local haunt of the youths of Marceline, including Walter and his friends, was the slagheap at Coalmine No. 1 of the Marceline Coal and Mining Company. While the No. 1 mine was one of several on the outskirts of town, this was the closest to the Disney farm. Walter would often lie in the window seat of his bedroom, gazing over the roof of Grandpa Taylor's house across the street, where he could see the top of the slagheap and mineshaft in the distance. It soon became an object of his imagination, and he secretly claimed it as his own private mountain. He was willing to share 'his mountain' with others; he and Clem spent numerous summer afternoons climbing the slagheap, and on one occasion they even got to ride the elevator down into the mine, the cool underground air embracing the sweaty boys who desired an escape from the dry midwestern summer heat.

Life in a small rural Missouri town presented scores of opportunities to an adventurous young Walter Disney. On special occasions, Clem Flickinger's father would hitch up his buggy and drive Walter and his friends down to the nearby Yellow Creek, approximately 5 kilometres west of the Disney farm, where they would spend the day fishing and swimming. It was here that Walter spent many of his summer days in Marceline, catching catfish and bowheads from the wooden bridge, enjoying a picnic on the banks of the stream and, at times, even stripping off his clothes to swim in the water with his friends. Yellow Creek offered entertainment in the winter as well, as many of the nearby children would venture to skate on the frozen ice until dark when someone would light a bonfire to keep the group warm before they trudged back to their respective homes.

On days that Walter knew his father expected him to work on the farm, the boy would find his own entertainment closer to home. On especially hot days, after spending hours working in the energy-draining sun, he would run across the field to a grove of trees on the southwest edge of the property where a soaring 20-year-old cottonwood tree stood. It was here that the young dreamer would lie amidst the tall grasses at its base, watching the meadowlarks, woodpeckers, and swallows flittering in the fields and branches of the tree. The boy also started to notice the multitude of insects that crawled along the tree's trunk and amongst the roots poking out of the ground, bringing his Big Chief drawing pad from Aunt Margaret with him to sketch the creatures. The cottonwood became known as his 'Dreaming Tree' under which his studies of wildlife would become known as 'Belly Botany'. Ruth often accompanied her big brother to his Dreaming Tree, and together the two would race around the trunk, climb high into the branches, and lie in the grass watching the clouds race overhead.

When the boy wasn't spending time alone beneath his Dreaming Tree, he was combining his mischievous spirit with creativity to develop a new characteristic: becoming a performer. One afternoon, while crawling through the lofts of the barn north of the farmhouse, Walter and Ruth discovered some burlap bags. Upon closer inspection, they realised a barn cat was inside, which escaped from its hiding place when it heard the kids draw nearer. But this sight gave the boy an idea: *What if he created a tent from this burlap bag for the barn cats to live in? This tent could be shaped almost like a circus tent. Wouldn't an animal circus be funny? What if he dressed up the farm animals as circus performers and charged his friends to see a show?*

So, the boy set to work, cutting the burlap sacks apart and sewing them together, using sticks to hold the inside up like a miniature circus tent.

He raided his and Ruth's dresser drawers, removing some clothes that he thought would look most humorous on the animals, and dressed some up, leaving them in a pen in the barn. Running around to the surrounding farms, Walter and Ruth gathered up their friends, touting a performance of the 'Disney Circus' later that day. As their friends showed up at the appointed time, Walter collected the 'admission' of 10 cents from each one before having them sit in the grass in front of the barn door. A few minutes later, Walter was leading the barn cats, dogs, and even pigs out of the structure, dressed in his shirts and Ruth's dresses.

"What kind of circus is this?" Clem Flickinger called out. "You can't teach a cat much of anything!"

Flora heard the ruckus from the house and walked to the barn, putting an end to her son's show. She ordered the aspiring showman to return his friends' money and asked both Walter and Ruth to take their clothes off the animals. One can imagine, however, with a predisposition to humour and mischief herself, a small smile playing across Flora's lips as she turned around to return to the farmhouse.

Life in a turn-of-the-century town also provided several new opportunities for socialising and entertainment. During the first decade of the twentieth century, downtown Marceline sported a number of independently owned businesses, such as jewellers, restaurants, and department stores, as well as banks and theatres.

As moving pictures and live performance became more popular, small theatres began to move into Marceline to provide entertainment pursuits for working- and middle-class families and individuals. By the time the Disney family moved out of town in 1911, Marceline sported a couple of theatres and an opera house. The Disneys took advantage of these entertainment opportunities on occasion, and it was the magic of these performances that inspired the young Walter Disney to pursue a career in the arts. Cater's Opera House, owned and managed by local businessman, Dr R.M. Cater, was located at the corner of Kansas Avenue and Howell Street, and primarily showcased travelling vaudeville troupes and performances accompanied by a small orchestra.

It was at Cater's that young Walter experienced his first live theatre performance: a production of *Peter Pan*. So excited was he to see the show that had been advertised around downtown Marceline on plastered broadsides for several weeks that he decided to raid his piggy bank for enough change to purchase his own admission. Starring in the titular role was Maude Adams, one of America's best-known stage actresses who had first portrayed Peter Pan on Broadway in 1905. The popularity of the play in New York led to a nationwide off-Broadway tour, including a short-lived stop in Marceline. The boy perched on the edge of his seat during the battles between Peter Pan and Captain Hook and participated enthusiastically when Adams encouraged the audience to clap in unison to revive an unconscious Tinker Bell. It was the immersion of the audience in the story and the attention to detail in a fantasy world that interested the boy and led to his fondly recalling the production years later.

The nickel theatres in Marceline also provided a multitude of diversions to the population of the rural town, including most of the area's children. These theatres filled their programmes with films rented from distributors, including adaptations of historical events and great works of literature. Located in a simple storefront, one of the town's theatres, the Aerodome, showed films projected on a bedsheet to audiences seated in folding chairs. After being released from school one day in 1910, 8-year-old Walter convinced 6-year-old Ruth to join him in seeing a film at the theatre on their way home, paying for her admission. The programme was a 'Passion Film', depicting scenes from the life, crucifixion, and resurrection of Christ. Just like his experience watching *Peter Pan*, Walter was transfixed by the black and white images flickering across the screen, hardly noticing the sound of the film speeding through the projector in the back of the room. When the short film ended, Walter and Ruth exited the theatre onto Kansas Avenue. At first, Walter believed that his eyes were having a hard time adjusting to the darkness he had experienced in the Aerodome over the past 20 minutes. However, he quickly realised it had become dark and the streetlights had come on throughout Marceline's downtown. Walter took Ruth's hand and together the siblings made their way home, worried about the punishment their father would levy because of their tardiness. After their 2.25 kilometre walk home, the children found Elias and Flora more relieved than angry, escaping a punishment for their transgression – this time.

In rare instances, the entire family would make the trip south to enjoy an evening in town. Shortly after arriving in Marceline, Elias treated his wife and children to a meal at the newly-opened Allen Hotel, located at the intersection of Kansas Avenue and Ritchie Avenue, south of Ripley

Park. While the hotel typically catered to those arriving in town via the railroad, a small restaurant operated off the lobby that sold meals to travellers and locals alike. It was a rare treat to eat at a restaurant when the economic life of a farming family was unpredictable, but somehow Elias was able to find enough money to enjoy an evening at the Allen with the family. Everything was going well until Ruth bumped the table, knocking her plate of food all over her lap and onto the floor.

"Consarnit, Ruth!" Elias cursed. His oldest sons snorted; their father's propriety forbid him to swear, resulting in him developing his own curses. However, Elias didn't notice his sons. He was too focused on the crying girl in the chair across from him and the fact that the spilled meal was a waste of his hard-earned money, as the restaurant wouldn't replace the food that now lay all over the floor and stained his daughter's dress.

The ruined dress, however, was easy for Flora to replace as she often sewed clothes for her children. When she needed something more specialised than she was able to make, she shopped at Murray's Department Store, located around the corner from the Allen Hotel, fronting on Kansas Avenue. Flora often took Walter to Murray's, Marceline's largest department and dry goods store, where she purchased pairs of overalls for him to wear while completing his work on the Disney farm.

In Chicago, the life the family experienced had been fraught with crime, vice, noise, filth, overcrowding, and an overabundance of businesses and services that had the potential to spoil the Disney children and overcomplicate life. But in Marceline, life moved at a much slower pace and offered opportunities for personal growth and more appreciation of the things – and people – that mattered.

Small-town community also led neighbours to become an extension of one's family, resulting in spending weekends and holidays together. On Sunday afternoons, after Ruth returned from the girls' Sunday School class at Marceline's First Baptist Church, Elias and Flora would load the children onto the buggy and make their way a kilometre west to the farm owned by Manly Howe Taylor. There, the two families, joined by the Rensimer family, would spend the afternoon together enjoying a meal and playing music. The three families relaxed and enjoyed an afternoon of hymns, folk tunes, and classical pieces, as Will Rensimer and Elias played their violins, Ches Rensimer the mandolin, and Winifred Taylor the piano. It was understood that the smaller children (Walter, Ruth, and Ken

Taylor) would sit quietly in the corner and listen to the others play music and sing, as both Elias and Manly Howe adhered to the belief of the day that Sunday was for rest and not play. As the afternoons progressed, the children would become restless and squirmy, and Bertha Taylor and Flora finally allowed them to play quiet indoor games such as Old Maid and mumble-peg.

Community organisations also helped to draw neighbours together. Several ladies from Marceline and its rural outskirts set up the Rural Home Circle, a social club where members would read poetry, sew, and quilt together, organise events, and discuss community issues. Flora attended the Rural Home Circle during its monthly meetings, joined by her friends and neighbours, Bertha Taylor and her daughter Winifred, as well as Grandpa Taylor's wife, Elizabeth, and Emma Phillips, sister of the late William Crane.

Community was essential to the success of small agricultural towns throughout America at the start of the twentieth century. Without neighbours coming together, crops wouldn't have been harvested, barns wouldn't have been built, and families would have lived in relative isolation. Instead, as a result of midwestern farm towns being made up of migrants from all over the country, one's neighbours quickly became adopted members of one's family, garnering an extended network of honour, respect, and a sharing of talents and time.

While Walter Disney was born in Chicago and spent his first five years there, the role Marceline and its people played in his life stuck with him forever: he considered Marceline, not Chicago, his hometown. Years later, when attending a ceremony in Marceline, he explained to a group of schoolchildren that "my best memories are the years I spent here. You children are lucky to live here."

It wasn't the trees that he climbed, the animals that he played with, or the chores that he completed that were of such importance to the young Walter Disney. It was the community – the places and people – that made such an impression on the boy's life.

Chapter Seven

Hard Knocks

As the first decade of the twentieth century came to a close, the hard times that often come with farming finally caught up with the Disney family. While these struggles had been befalling farmers west of the Mississippi River for years, Elias's experience working alongside labour unions at the World's Exposition in Chicago made the challenge feel personal. Elias Disney counted himself as a disciple of Eugene Debs and American socialism, as well as William Jennings Bryan, an advocate of Prairie Populism, which attempted to advocate better conditions for farmers who'd felt victimised by the banking system and railroads, and ignored by the federal government.

Beginning in the days following the American Civil War, as the Transcontinental Railroad began its crawl to the west coast of North America, land grants began to be awarded or sold to those looking for new economic opportunities. While thousands took advantage of the land being given by the U.S. government under the Homestead Act, others, including immigrants like Kepple and Mary Disney, purchased land being sold for fundraising purposes from the various railroad lines expanding in the west. While some farmers lived in the area that would become Marceline prior to 1888, when the Atchison, Topeka & Santa Fe established the town as a division point, it brought an influx of individuals looking to purchase cheap land from the railroad to begin their own farms.

As more and more families established farms and began to grow crops throughout the west, including Marceline, the value of these crops began to decrease. With the railroad being the primary mode of transporting goods to markets in America's largest cities, managers of the lines began to increase their fares, further reducing the profit turned by individual farmers. This resulted in the agricultural community often breaking even every year, or in some unfortunate seasons, losing money due to droughts or other environmental disasters.

When his farm took a hit due to the low value of apples nationwide in 1909, Elias devised a plan to hold on to some fruit until prices increased. He sent enough apples to market to pay off some debts, but saved the majority of his harvest. Enlisting the help of Herbert and Raymond, Elias removed his supply of autumn's apple harvest from the family barn late in the season and brought them out into the orchard. The three men spent countless hours spreading straw on the ground between the rows of apple trees, and then piling the fruit into waist-high pyramids on top of the straw. After the piles were complete, they layered straw on top of the fruit, then covered the layers with earth, providing natural refrigeration and protection from the elements and pests.

Sure enough, as winter progressed, the price of fresh fruit dropped. Elias would go to the orchard a few days a week, sometimes in blistering cold and wind, and unearth his fruit, which had remained fresh due to the ground that had frozen over top of the piles.

While this plan was fairly ingenious, Elias also realised that it wasn't sustainable to provide the income his family needed year after year. Taking a page from the teachings of Debs and the Populists, he decided to appeal to the greater agricultural community throughout Marceline to affect change for those in the region. At first, he attempted to become involved in state politics, running for a place in the Missouri state legislature as a socialist candidate. Unfortunately, like the federal government, the state government of Missouri didn't have much interest in smaller groups outside of its standard two-party system.

Instead, Elias decided to appeal to those in his more immediate sphere of influence: his fellow farmers in Marceline. Looking for a centralised location to meet with his neighbours, he convinced the Knights of Pythias, a fraternal order that had a lodge located above Zurcher's Jewelers on the corner of Kansas Avenue and Ritchie Avenue, to allow him to hold an event for his fellow apple growers in the area. In an effort to show his fellow struggling farmers how good life could be if not for the 'evil capitalists' that took advantage of them, he went by the store of Ed Hayden, a local grocer, and purchased several kilograms of oysters.

The farmers attending Elias's dinner were impressed with the delicious oysters. Many of them had only heard of the delicacy, but due to the struggles of living in an agricultural community, they had never eaten food of this calibre. As the meal concluded, Elias surveyed the room and noticed smiles on the faces of many of his peers. He figured that, with their bellies full, this was the best time to make his appeal.

Walking to the front of the room, the farmer utilised the skills he had employed as a guest preacher at the family church in Chicago, requesting that the farmers unionise and collectivise their efforts as part of a Marceline chapter of the Society of Equity. This organisation, he explained, was a sort of union for farmers, which would fight against the injustices perpetrated by the railroads and bankers. The Society would provide grain elevators and cold storage warehouses in town so that all farmers could hold their surplus crops until prices stabilised, much like he had done the previous winter with his own bumper crop of apples. This plan would also give the farmers of Marceline the opportunity to carry weight to the negotiating table: when railroads set their rates too high, the farmers would simply hold their harvests in the community storehouses. When the railroads weren't making money due to a lack of agricultural fares, they would be forced to lower their prices, making farmers the primary beneficiaries.

As he spoke, Elias was disheartened to find the smiles falling from the faces of his audience. The attention of many began to wander, and a few actually got up from their tables and left. As he cleaned up later that evening after his audience had left, the man who desired justice for other farmers reflected on what had gone wrong. He eventually realised that the town existed *because* of the railroad. Yes, railroad prices were unfair for Marceline farmers, but if not for the Santa Fe extension, none of the farmers would have the land that had been in their families for decades. The railroad brought business into town, and many of Marceline's industries, such as the coal mines and newly-established oil fields, directly serviced the railroad, making the farmers' relationship with the Santa Fe Railroad both positive and negative. If they came together to unionise against the railroad, Elias realised, they would literally be severing the hand that was feeding them.

After his attempt to improve the family's financial well-being through creating an alliance with his fellow farmers fell through, Elias instead began to expect the rest of the family to help carry the weight and contribute more. While he already expected his four sons to work on the farm for free, he also asked that they do odd jobs around town to help offset the income lost due to the farm's struggles.

Roy often visited town to do small jobs and took his little brother along with him to help. One sunny afternoon, the two took a job at the local undertaker's to wash Mr Hutchenson's hearse. Unfortunately for Roy, he did most of the work: while he scrubbed the buggy free of dust, Walter lay in the back, his hands crossed over his chest, pretending to be a corpse. Whenever someone walked by or stopped to speak with Roy, the boy would quickly sit up; while some were startled, others knew of young Walter and his antics and were unsurprised at his trick.

Roy also took inspiration from his father's work on the family farm to dive into his own venture of making money. After talking Elias into giving him an acre of land, Roy planted rows of popcorn, working the field on his own. Over the summer months, he spent time in the field ploughing, sowing, watering, weeding, and finally harvesting the hard kernels. After packaging them in small bags he had saved from confectionery, the young man went downtown to the train station and sold his harvest to passengers milling around the platform or waiting for the train while it got serviced.

In addition to fulfilling her duties as a rural wife and mother, Flora also used her creative and culinary skills to help make additional money for the family. To offset expenses, Flora maintained her own vegetable garden. During seasons when she harvested a surplus, she would often sell the produce to neighbours and townspeople; she was particularly known for her excellent grated horseradish that was used in coleslaw and other midwestern recipes.

Flora Disney was also renowned throughout town for the butter that she churned. After purchasing sweet cream from the Marceline Creamery Company, the industrious woman would spend several days churning and methodically adding ingredients to ensure that her product was as creamy as possible, a perfect balance between sweet and salty. After moulding the butter, she would load up the family buggy and ride to the grocer's, where she would trade the butter for groceries, as well as money to supplement the family's income.

People came from the countryside and even from out of town to purchase Flora Disney's sweet cream butter. Elias quickly recognised the value of his wife's butter and forbid his children from partaking in their mother's creation to ensure there would be more to sell. Pitying her children and tapping into her streak of mischief that had been passed on to her youngest son, Flora began to butter the underside of her children's bread before passing it to them at mealtime to subvert her husband's demands.

In an effort to make more money, Elias leased an additional 40 acres of land from his brother Robert, agreeing to allow 19-year-old Herbert and 17-year-old Raymond to work a piece of the land for some income. After a season of hard work in 1907, the two enterprising young men found that they'd earned $175 from the sale of their produce. The boys put most of the money away, deciding to treat themselves with a mere $20 each by purchasing a gold watch and watch chain from Zurcher's, the new jewellery store that had opened just a few years earlier.

The boys proudly wore their watches and chains on their breasts all the way home, but when Elias saw what he considered to be their extravagant purchases, he was disgusted. He clearly made it known to his sons that buying the accessories was irresponsible when times were as hard as they were.

"And what are you going to do with the rest of your income?" the elder Disney asked, half-sarcastically.

"Well," Herb began, looking at his brother. "We would like to purchase a heifer and a colt to help make our tract of land more sustainable."

"*Land o' Goshen!*" Elias sighed loudly. He went on to explain that, as members of the Disney family who were working on land that he'd leased from Robert and partook of the family's resources, such as food and shelter, that their income was meant to help offset the debts incurred by the farm. As he spoke, Herbert and Raymond's faces slowly transitioned from submissive to stony and indignant, but their father was too busy preaching about the family's need to work together for survival to notice.

Over the course of the evening and the next day while working in the fields, Herbert and Raymond became more and more frustrated with the conversation they'd had with their father, and his inability or unwillingness to see them as men who had earned their income through hard work, and no longer as boys. While on their lunch break that afternoon, Herbert unhitched the horse from the plough and rode into town, withdrawing all the funds from his and Raymond's bank accounts. After enjoying a delicious meal that Flora prepared that evening, the two boys feigned exhaustion and excused themselves to bed. Once the house fell silent, the brothers gathered some of their belongings, raised their bedroom window, and stepped out onto the porch.

While they likely felt a twinge of guilt leaving their mother and other siblings behind, their frustration with Elias and his unrelenting expectations clouded their remorse, and together, the two hustled into town and to the Santa Fe train station. Using some of their earnings from their patch of farmland, they each purchased a ticket for the 9.30pm train to Chicago, riding the night train north, away from Marceline, never to return to live at the Disney farm.

Elias saw his eldest sons' departure as a betrayal of the worst kind, but rather than unleash his fury on the rest of the family, he poured himself into the farm even more, picking up the slack left by Herbert and Raymond's vacancies. Roy attended classes at Park School, located west of downtown Marceline, helping out with chores before and after school and on the weekends. It was decided by Elias and Flora alike that, due to the closeness in age between their two youngest children, and because extra help was needed now on the farm, they would keep Walter out of school until Ruth reached an age to be old enough to enrol at Park School. Thus, over the next year, he helped out with farm chores, continuing to mill the sorghum and tend to the livestock. Flora, not wanting her youngest son to fall behind, began giving Walter lessons, particularly in how to read, to prepare him for the rigours of public education.

It was decided that Walter and Ruth would be enrolled at Park School in the autumn of 1908. Over the next couple of years, Walter began to realise that education was not his strong suit: he was more accustomed to dreaming and doodling than learning, going so far as drawing on the pages of his *McGuffey's Eclectic Reader* and carving *W.D.* into his wooden desk, not once but twice. When his teacher, Miss Brown, attempted to refocus his attentions, she found the boy to be 'ornery', refusing to participate in his assignments.

While the academic side of school didn't appeal to Walter, the artistic side was right up his alley. After the popularity of Maude Adams' performance in *Peter Pan* at Cater's Opera House, Park School decided to put on its own production. Walter auditioned and was granted the lead part of the play's protagonist. Even at a young age, Walter Disney wanted to bring the story to life and to immerse his audience in the action. Determining to make himself fly like his character, he convinced Roy to build a hoist and tackle mechanism that would allow him to soar over the audience.

It was during his time at Park School that Walter also discovered his first love and 'dream girl': Mrs Eugenia Moorman, the young wife of Marceline's superintendent of education. Walter was not a shy boy, but he had a difficult time understanding how to get the attention of his object of affection. Luckily for him, when Elias and Flora went out of town for an evening, they asked Mrs Moorman to be Walter and Ruth's babysitter. He was even more surprised at his luck that evening, as she was putting him to bed.

"Are you afraid of sleeping alone in the dark?" the maternal young woman asked the young boy.

The boy assured her that he was.

Not wanting her charge to throw a fit and hoping his parents would allow her to babysit again, Mrs Moorman crawled into bed with the boy, who didn't know much more than the fact that people in love slept in the same bed.

There was one thing Walter hadn't accounted for: his bedwetting problem.

When he awoke several hours later in a panic to find wet sheets, he found the other half of his bed empty. He was never quite sure whether Mrs Moorman left the bed because of his incontinence or for some other reason.

With love often came loss. On 20 January 1909, Erastus 'Grandpa' Taylor passed away. Not only did 7-year-old Walter lose the man whom he loved listening to and learning from, but the Taylor-Phillips-Crane family, into which the Disneys had been adopted, lost its patriarch. Young Walter felt the empty ache of loss every day as he opened his front door to see Grandpa Taylor's small house across the street, its clapboard siding, plate glass windows, and beautiful white screen door less charming without Grandpa Taylor hobbling around the yard or sitting in his chair. The house sat empty now, as Elizabeth Taylor had moved out of the home she'd built with her husband after his passing and into the home of her son Winfield, who lived nearby.

Several months later, Walter was awakened in the middle of the night to yelling outside his bedroom window. Groggily opening his eyes, he noticed a flickering orange light on the wall near his bedroom door. The brass bed that Walter shared with Roy creaked as the boy's older brother slid out from under the covers and crept to the window. As Roy pulled the curtains back from the window, he gasped. Walter hopped out of bed and ran to his brother's side, crawling up into the dormer's window seat so he could see out. Across the street from the Disney home, a violent blaze had engulfed Grandpa Taylor's home, a horse-drawn fire engine and bucket brigade doing its best to extinguish the flames. The boys noticed the slim figure of their father attempting to help, but over the course of the next few minutes, it became obvious that their work was futile as the roof collapsed inward and the grass nearby sizzled.

"It's like the whole world is on fire," Walter commented. While it is obvious that this was the observation of a small boy learning to process trauma in the totality of his world, figuratively he wasn't too far off: the idyllic life of the boy who had fully embraced the charm and simplicity of small-town community was about to be stolen from him much in the same way his elderly friend and the visual reminder of him had been.

While Elias had experienced some success on the farm during the family's years in Marceline, he lacked capability as a farmer and was often looked down on by his peers because of his ineptitude. This, combined with his lack of help due to Herb and Ray's departure, made it difficult to keep up with the work farming required. Near the end of the decade, a drought plagued the area, not only withholding rainwater from the fields, but even causing the family well, from which Elias drew irrigation water, to begin to dry up.

Illness began to sweep through the Disney farm as well, when some of his livestock began to develop maladies, and Elias's overworking himself led to him developing diphtheria. In his incredibly weakened state, at times requiring hospitalisation, Elias was unable to complete the work necessary to turn a profit on the farm, leaving many tasks to Flora, Roy and Walter, none of whom had the knowledge required to make the family venture successful. The final straw was the ultimate collapse of crop prices, the problem which Elias had fought so hard to prevent at his downtown oyster dinner at the Knights of Pythias lodge just a few years earlier.

After much discussion, it was decided by Elias and Flora that it was time to sell the farm and once again move on to new opportunities elsewhere. Robert, who had been living in Kansas City with his wife Margaret, had seemed to find success in the economy of the city, and encouraged his older brother to join him. In an attempt to clear the family's assets in Marceline, Elias determined to hold an auction of the animals and farming equipment. Walter and Roy were enlisted to wander the countryside and into town, putting up signs advertising the auction, as well as the different items that would be for sale. A pre-auction sale took place for the Disneys' neighbours, and some of the draught animals were sold, causing Walter especially to be heartbroken. Collecting their possessions, the family vacated the farm in 1910, moving into a smaller home at 508 Kansas Avenue, much closer to downtown Marceline; rather than immediately leave for Kansas City, it was decided the family would remain in town until the end of the school year. Luckily for Walter, the family's new home was next door to the Moormans.

One afternoon, while parked along Kansas Avenue to sell hay from the farm, the sound of a high-pitched whinnying caught Roy and Walter's attention. The boys looked across the street to where the noise was coming from to find a small colt tied to a hitching post. It had been born on the family farm and on recognising the Disney boys, it had begun crying. Walter, tender-hearted as he was towards his animals, ran across the street to embrace the pony's head, and Roy eventually had to pull his little brother off the animal and lead him away before things got more out of hand.

The boys climbed onto the buggy for the ride home, their old horse Charlie standing quietly munching from a feed bag. As they made their way north along Kansas Avenue towards home, something spooked their horse and he began to run. The buggy was old, and as a result, the handbrake no longer worked. Roy did everything he could to try to slow Charlie down, pulling on the reins and calling out commands, while Walter held on tightly to avoid falling off the cart.

"We need to jump off before we crash, Walter!" Roy called to his brother.

"No!" Walter yelled back, holding onto the handrail of the cart with an iron grip.

"Alright," Roy called. "Take this," he ordered, handing his brother one of the reins, while he held the other. The elder brother's stomach dropped as he realised they were coming to the crest of one of the largest hills in town; if he couldn't get Charlie to stop, this wouldn't end well. Leaning to the left as far as he could without falling off the buggy, Roy pulled on the left rein, steering the horse towards a copse of trees. Charlie dodged the trees, but the cart wasn't so lucky and it crashed into them, jerking the horse to a stop. Residents of nearby houses heard the commotion and came running into their yards to help the boys. Luckily, neither boy was injured and the cart, nor the horse, sustained much damage.

With the decision having been made to move to Kansas City, the Disneys didn't go through their grief alone: the Taylor-Phillips-Crane family that had adopted them as one of their own shared in the sadness of losing those they had come to love over the last five years. Manly Howe Taylor even promised to look after the farm after the family's departure until it was possible to sell in November 1911. Flora attended her last meeting of the Rural Home Circle on 15 May 1911 and was so distraught at leaving her friends, she failed in her club responsibility of preparing to share current events in the life of her family. As per club minutes recorded at the end of the meeting, it was discussed and unanimously passed by the club's twenty-one members that a 'souvenir tea spoon' would be presented to Flora as a parting gift on her departure for Kansas City.

At the conclusion of the school year, Elias, Flora, Roy, Walter and Ruth said their goodbyes to the charming rural town they had come to love so much and the people that they loved more, loaded their belongings at the same train station along the Santa Fe Railroad that they had arrived on, and moved along to their next adventure. As the train pulled away from the platform and began gaining speed, charging towards the southwest, both Elias and Walter looked out of the window as their dreams drifted away behind them: the former, leaving behind his hope to establish himself as a small-town farmer raising his children with small-town morals, while his youngest son left behind the town that had brought him so much life. Little did the boy know that his next home, Kansas City, Missouri, would be even more instrumental in creating the man he would become.

Part IV

It was tough

Kansas City, Missouri, 1911–1917

Chapter Eight

The Paper Route

While much of Missouri life related to agriculture, there was one factor in particular that impacted the lives of nearly every Missourian during the second half of the nineteenth and the early twentieth centuries: the railroad.

With the expansion of the railroads throughout Missouri, massive population growth occurred, both in small agricultural communities such as Marceline and large metropolitan areas like St. Louis, and from small towns on the Mississippi such as Hannibal to cities along the Missouri River like Kansas City. Nearly every town established throughout the state during the last few decades of the 1800s was situated along one of the major rail lines, providing service to locomotives and passengers, identical to those provided along the Santa Fe in Marceline.

The presence of the railroad in these towns often led to the arrival of major industries to the area. For example, with Kansas City serving as a major hub for almost a dozen different railroad lines in the 1870s, it soon became a railhead for cattle drives, where herders known as cowboys pushed many thousand head of cattle from the south to the railroad before the animals were slaughtered and shipped to major cities in the east. Armour and Company, a meat packing business with a branch location in Kansas City, thrived as a result of the booming cattle industry in the area, with an increase in production of canned beef from approximately 779,000 units in 1880 to more than 4 million units a mere five years later. The success of companies like Armour led to improvements in Kansas City's own stockyards, located along the Missouri River in an area known as the West Bottoms. From the establishment of the yards in 1871 until 1901, the number of animals slaughtered in Kansas City tripled, with numerous new companies springing up to challenge the success of Armour and Company.

During the 1870s, a devastating plague of grasshoppers destroyed millions of dollars' worth of crops throughout the Midwest United States.

With their fortunes literally devoured, farmers and their families were particularly attracted to the opportunities that industry and transportation infrastructure offered in Kansas City, choosing to descend on the riverside metropolis rather than take their chances in the fields. As a result of this influx of migration, during the last decade of the nineteenth century, the population of Kansas City increased from approximately 132,000 to 164,000, becoming the second largest city in the United States west of the Mississippi River, second only to San Francisco, California.

With this growth came more industry. By 1900, almost forty rail lines stretched across and through the city, serving as the primary mode of transportation for livestock, grains, and other agricultural products. The city developed elevators and grist mills to store and process grains, sawmills to cut lumber, and infrastructure to support the hundreds of trains that passed through town every week.

Kansas City was soon a bustling hub of industry, business, and transportation, with trains chugging down iron rails, horse-drawn wagons sharing the streets with early automobiles, and the occasional riverboat sloshing through the murky waters of the Missouri River. Industry spewed smoke and steam into the air, while the influx of people moving to the city, native-born American and immigrant alike, caused pollution on the ground.

As early as the 1880s, William Rockhill Nelson, the new owner and editor of *The Kansas City Star*, began pressing for city beautification and civic improvements. This campaign gained more momentum as the City Beautiful Movement swept the United States, calling for better city planning, architecture, parks, and pollution controls to improve the lives of middle-class urban dwellers. Joining forces with landscape architect George E. Kessler, Nelson began planning for open spaces and vast parks for his growing city, with a new boulevard system spearheaded by Kessler and costing approximately $40 million to be completed in 1910. By 1920, Kansas City boasted almost 2,000 acres of parks, 700 acres of parkways, and 90 miles of boulevards.

These grand improvements further encouraged migration to Kansas City, but rather than low-skilled industrial labourers, immigrants, or failed farmers looking for new opportunities, the bustling business hub attracted middle-class Americans who were impressed by the opportunity for investment, the beautiful green spaces, and the growing suburbs that began to spread outward from the city's downtown. More leisure time activities were drawn to the area to entertain these middle-class masses, including vaudeville halls, theatres showing moving pictures, and amusement parks.

As a result, when the train carrying the Disney family pulled up to the platform of Union Depot in Kansas City's West Bottoms neighbourhood in June 1911, Walter's new home was about as different from what he was used to as possible. Stepping off the train, the three children even noticed that the air was different: while the fresh breeze often smelled of sweet grass in Marceline, the stagnant air of Kansas City's West Bottoms was sour with the stench of slaughtered livestock not too far away.

Uncle Robert had sent a buggy to carry the family and its possessions southeast to the opposite side of the city, where they had rented a small house located at 2706 East 31st Street. Flora was disgusted by the new residence and was happy that they were only renting temporarily. While she had become used to having an outhouse at their Marceline farmhouse, the act of using one in the backyard in Kansas City offered much less privacy due to the urban nature of their new home. Flora was also frustrated that the house was located along a busy street, and as a result, the tram line often passed the home. She made sure that her husband knew of her frustrations over the lack of privacy, complaining that those riding the trams could see into her front parlour. Elias's response to his wife's complaints was to install a set of curtains.

Shortly after getting settled in their home, Elias and Roy journeyed downtown on 1 July to the red brick building that housed *The Kansas City Star*, answering an advertisement for the opportunity to purchase a paper route. Delivery Route No. 145 served approximately 700 subscribers located within the boundaries of 27th Street in the north, 31st Street in the south, Prospect Avenue in the west and Indiana Avenue in the east, a total of twenty-four residential blocks. While many of the subscribers received both *The Morning Times* and *The Kansas City Evening Star*, the route included an additional 176 subscribers who received the Sunday edition.

At first, the *Star* wasn't keen on giving 51-year-old Elias ownership of the paper route: they believed he was too old, and as a result, would be unable to fulfil the duties of the job. They were, however, willing to sell the paper route to 17-year-old Roy. Elias forked out over $2,100 to purchase the rights to the route, and in return received a contract and map of the route.

Having left Marceline without many possessions and after losing his investment on the failing farm, Elias didn't have sufficient capital to hire delivery boys or newsies to sell the papers. Instead, he expected his two youngest sons to contribute to the family business. Every day, Roy and 9-year-old Walter would pull themselves out of bed at 3.30 am and meet the horse-drawn wagon that delivered the papers to their home. The brothers would take a stack of papers and begin to distribute them across the route, which luckily included the Disney home that acted as a base to pick up additional papers throughout the morning.

Walter and Roy were meticulous about how they positioned the newspapers, as per their father's commands. Elias, already in middle age, had become frustrated and disappointed due to the numerous failures he had experienced in his various careers as a hotel owner, railroad machinist, construction worker, residential contractor, and farmer. Not wanting to experience the embarrassment of failure as the de facto owner of the paper route, he was sure to instil in his sons how to properly leave the *Star* for its paying customers.

Elias wanted to ensure that his customers recognised the difference in service provided by his family. While delivery boys often rolled newspapers and flung them into yards from the seat of a bicycle, Elias refused to allow his sons to do this. Instead, he expected the personal service of hand-delivering the newspaper to each door so that customers didn't have to leave the comfort of their homes to retrieve their papers. Elias also expected that his two delivery boys protect their product from the elements: any newspaper wasted was one he would have to reimburse the *Star* for later. Instead, he instructed Walter and Roy to place a stone or a brick on top of the folded paper on windy days, and inside the customer's screen door to protect it from getting wet on rainy days. Because of the importance placed on community and one's neighbours at the turn of the century, everyone knew where the newspaper delivery boys lived. If young Walter did something wrong or he forgot to secure a paper or accidently missed a house, his father heard about it and discipline was levied. While it frustrated Roy to still be physically disciplined by his father at the age of 18, he was even more exasperated that their father expected him and his little brother to work for free. The boys each received a monthly allowance ($3 for Roy and 50 cents for Walter), but when it came to working as newspaper delivery boys, their hard work earned them room and board.

Once the route was completed, Walter and Roy returned home where they enjoyed breakfast from Flora. The rest of their morning and afternoon was spent revelling in the numerous pursuits the city had to offer. At times, Roy would pay for Walter and Ruth to ride the tram to Electric Park, located near the intersection of 46th Street and The Paseo, along Brush Creek. Electric Park had originally been opened in 1899 north of Kansas City by the Heim Brothers as a method of selling more beer produced by their brewery in the East Bottoms. When this park became successful, the brothers decided to move it to a location with more land south of the city. The amusement park was incredibly popular with Kansas Citians, giving visitors the opportunity to bathe in a large lake, ride a roller coaster, explore a fun house, and take in shows. The park took on new life after dark, when more than 100,000 lights illuminated the grounds and its numerous attractions. While the brothers' second amusement park was prohibited by city government from selling beer, there were scores of other examples of moral turpitude the Disney children were exposed to, such as dance halls and women's exposed skin. While there was little Elias could do about Roy partaking in the fun of Electric Park, he was furious to learn that his two youngest children were running around there and forbade them to pass through its gates. As a result, when Walter was in the mood for enjoying the sights and sounds of the park, he would take the tram south to stand with his face between the bars of the fence, watching the action inside.

Roy also engaged his siblings in entertainment closer to home. He often threw horseshoes with Walter and Ruth in the backyard or taught them how to play tennis, and on rainy days they played a hand of pinochle in the parlour. On special occasions, the trio would go to a nearby theatre to enjoy a movie at Roy's expense or get a bag of candies from the drugstore.

In the autumn of 1911, Elias and Flora enrolled their children in school: Roy started his senior year at the Manual Training High School, while Walter and Ruth began second grade at Benton Grammar School. The boys' daily responsibilities on their father's newspaper route continued, and as the *Star* transitioned its newspaper delivery system from cart and buggy to automobile, the papers were dropped off at the Disney residence at 2.30 am, requiring the boys to get up even earlier. Over the next few hours, Walter and Roy would wander the neighbourhood, delivering papers, before stopping at home for a quick breakfast and rushing off to school.

Once again, as at Park School in Marceline, Walter wasn't an ideal student at Benton Grammar. Much of his time was spent daydreaming or doodling in the margins of his textbooks. Likely due to his lack of sleep, the boy had a difficult time concentrating and instead spent hours honing his hobby of artistic representation. Much to his teacher's chagrin, his assignments and drawings were often fantastical. In one instance, when expected to illustrate a field of flowers, the creative boy instead decided to represent the flowers with human faces instead of buds and arms ending with hands instead of leaves.

With the dismissal from school every day, Walter quickly made his way home where he met Roy to organise the evening edition of the paper before once again making his way through the neighbourhood to deliver 635 individual copies of the *Evening Star*. After a dinner kept warm by Flora, the boys did some schoolwork followed by some quiet reading time when Walter enjoyed a novel by Twain or Dickens, before an early bedtime to do it all again the next day. Unfortunately, he was so busy he didn't have time for playing or spending time with the other kids in the neighbourhood. To compensate for his lack of playtime, Walter would often find himself in the dimness of dawn playing for a few minutes with the toys that children along the paper route left on their porches before continuing on to the next house.

As 1911 transitioned into 1912, the paper route only became more difficult for 10-year-old Walter as a series of blizzards made their way across the American Midwest, dumping more than 170 cm of snow on Kansas City. Even the hope of an early spring was dashed, with more than 100 cm falling in the month of March 1912 alone. Ever the hard worker and recognising the importance of income to support his family, Elias's expectations for the paper route didn't diminish during this severe winter. Walter and Roy continued to rise well before dawn, bundling themselves up as best they could, making their way through knee-high accumulations, the night-time winds often whipping by, making their eyes water and their faces chapped. At times, Walter would have to climb over snowdrifts higher than himself to get to the front door of a subscriber's home, often falling through the thin layer of packed snow down to his waist, crumbles of snow making their way up his trouser legs and down into his shoes.

Luckily for him, his route included a series of apartment buildings, which allowed him a chance to thaw out in the steam-heated lobbies and hallways. Walter would often stop to sit next to a radiator in the apartments to warm himself before venturing back into the cold, inevitably dozing off before snapping awake in a panic that he had slept through the rest of his route.

With the paper route being the family's primary method of income, Flora took it upon herself to utilise her skills as homemaker to once again make some additional money. Maintaining her contacts in Marceline, Flora imported cream from the Marceline Creamery Company on a weekly basis. Elias would pick up the cream from the Railway Exchange office in downtown Kansas City, and Flora would spend days turning the cream into her famous butter. Elias also sent for fresh eggs from a Marceline farmer, an expensive luxury for urban dwellers in the early 1900s.

Elias thought it would be odd for a grown man to be delivering newspapers, which is why he consistently used his two sons as delivery boys. However, his pride and hard work ethic made him feel guilty that he wasn't doing anything to make money for the family himself. Once Flora finished turning the cream into butter, he would load it and the fresh eggs onto a cart and travel throughout the neighbourhood, selling the farm-fresh products to his neighbours.

On rare occasions, Elias would have a flare-up from his past illnesses of malaria or diphtheria, rendering him unable to make the deliveries. Instead, Flora would take Walter out of school for the day, as he was more familiar with the newspaper route than she, and together they would push the cart through the streets to sell to those who subscribed to their farm products subscription service. Walter loved and respected his 43-year-old mother very much and didn't want her to exert herself, offering to push the cart down the street as his mother delivered the goods. Flora, however, insisted in pushing the cart herself, much to the boy's chagrin.

As Roy and Walter conducted their studies in the big city throughout the 1911–1912 school year, they began to find themselves slowly drifting apart, developing new hobbies and friendships with large groups of kids, opportunities that weren't available in the small rural community of Marceline. One thing in particular that appealed to Roy was the prevalence of girls in Kansas City. While he had enjoyed a steady relationship with Fleta Rogers in Marceline, the large number of city girls allowed Roy to become more social in the world of eligible bachelorhood. This also meant there were more young men to compete with. Using his allowance, as well as money he'd earned conducting odd jobs, he purchased nice outfits and ties to impress the young ladies in his social circle. Always looking up to his older brother, Walter would often don one of his brother's new ties and wear it to school to show off to his friends. He would inevitably spill his lunch, which was often chilli and beans, on the tie. Before meeting Roy on the curb to deliver the afternoon edition, Walter would quickly put the tie back, being careful to hang it up exactly the way Roy had placed it. Unfortunately for the eligible bachelor, he would put the tie on for his next date, only to realise too late that it was still covered in chilli and beans. Needless to say that the conversations with his little brother later that night were not terribly pleasant for Walter.

Roy finished his studies at the Manual Training High School in the spring of 1912. The young man had grown as tall as his father and sported a similar slim physique. But while Elias was becoming frail due to his numerous illnesses and ailments and had just experienced his fiftieth birthday, Roy was instead a strapping specimen. He was frustrated that Elias refused to pay him for his efforts on the paper route, even though it was technically owned by him. One evening, as the boys lay alongside each other in bed, Roy propped himself up on his elbow and shook his dozing brother awake.

"Hey, kid," Roy muttered. Walter stirred, his eyes fluttering open to look at his brother who was hovering over him. "I'm running away to work in the harvest fields. I need you to stay here and work the route. And don't put up with father's beatings anymore."

Halfway between the worlds of sleeping and waking, young Walter begged his brother and best friend not to leave. Convinced that if he remained awake he would be able to stop his brother from leaving at the appointed time, he did all he could to keep his eyes open. Hours later, when his door opened and Elias called for his two sons to get up for the route, Walter realised that Roy was no longer in bed next to him; instead, a mannequin constructed of rolled up bedsheets and clothes was fashioned to resemble his slumbering brother.

After sending Walter out onto the route alone, Elias and Flora sat and discussed the departure of their third son. Flora wept, wiping her tears on the corner of her apron, as Elias furiously paced the floor of the kitchen, throwing curses upon the name of Roy Disney. It was decided that additional boys from the neighbourhood would be hired to help Walter on the route, but unconsciously, the bitter ire of the father was turned upon his youngest son, hoping to shape him into the man he had been unable to become himself.

Chapter Nine

The Performing Butch

L ife without Roy nearby was a new challenge for the young Walter Disney. While Elias was the strict disciplinarian and thought that holding the highest expectations of his children would make them good, productive people, Roy was kind and compassionate; while Elias was tight with his money to ensure that the family's needs were met, Roy instead often spent his money on his little brother and sister by purchasing them treats or small gifts, or occasionally taking them to Electric Park or the movies. Without his best friend and hero, Walter soon found himself distracted by his daily life, which included school, work, and new friends.

Shortly after Roy's departure, Flora decided that she'd had enough of their rented home and convinced Elias that the family needed to purchase a more permanent place. Recognising the importance of owning a home close to the paper route, the family moved a half kilometre east to 3028 Bellefontaine Avenue, a small two-storey house with white wood slat siding, and a large porch spanning the front of the house held up by heavy wooden pillars.

Living in a quiet neighbourhood rather than along a busy street, Walter and Ruth soon found it easier to develop a social life with the neighbouring kids. A short distance away on 41st Avenue lived the Pfeiffers: Mr and Mrs Pfeiffer and their two children, Kitty and Walt, who was the same age as Walter Disney. The two boys quickly became friends, and Walter found himself spending his free time at Walt Pfeiffer's house rather than at his own. The Pfeiffers were everything that Elias was not: fun-loving, musical, mischievous, and creative. Walter Disney and Walt Pfeiffer soon realised something else they had in common other than their names: their love of performance and joking around. The two boys soon started coming up with vaudeville acts in the Pfeiffers' back yard, caricaturising themselves as a pair of Dutchmen, complete with heavy Dutch accents. These impromptu comedy acts were often performed in front of the Pfeiffer family, accompanied by Walt's sister Kitty playing the piano.

Walter quickly became an unofficial part of the Pfeiffer family, spending all the time he had while not in school or delivering his father's papers at their house, attempting to fill the hole left by Roy's departure with his new friend. Walter and Walt were even inseparable during illness; one winter, when Walt Pfeiffer had come down with a case of the mumps and was bedridden, his artistic best friend sat at his side, giving him drawing lessons.

Over the next few years, Walter's penchant for performance often found its way into the classroom to stave off his boredom, much to the delight of his classmates. The most popular shtick was one Walter called 'Fun in the Photograph Gallery': completely silent, the little actor would pose his classmates into a number of ridiculous gestures, then step behind a prop camera to mime taking their photograph. Instead of producing a photo, however, the camera would produce a stream of water, squirting the unsuspecting subject. As the good sport he was, however, Walter would always finish his performance by drawing a caricature of his subject to take with them.

Walter's tendency to act as the class clown also drew the attention of the staff at Benton, which they occasionally used for their benefit. One year, on the birthday of Abraham Lincoln, fifth-grade Walter dressed as the Great Emancipator, donning Elias's long church coat, wearing a makeshift stovepipe hat, pasting crepe paper to his chin to create a bushy beard, and smearing shoe polish across his face to give himself a moustache. As he strode into class that morning, he loudly began to give 'The Gettysburg Address' in the character of Lincoln, enthralling his classmates but frustrating his teacher. When Benton principal James Cottingham learned of this, he decided to embarrass the boy by giving him the biggest audience possible to perform before: the entire school. Cottingham paraded Walter from classroom to classroom to perform the speech, but his ultimate goal of punishing the boy failed: Walter loved the attention, and all the students loved him.

Not all of Walter's teachers were harsh towards him. In seventh grade, the boy had the pleasure of sitting in the classroom of Miss Daisy Beck. Beck was sympathetic to the boy's situation, delivering papers before school: the warmth of the classroom as the day progressed often lulled the delivery boy, who had been awake since 2.00 am, to sleep. The compassionate teacher often let him sleep, recognising that he would not accomplish much more if he were awake and exhausted. She also noticed the boy's artistic talent and bribed him by explaining that if he finished his classwork, he could spend the remaining class time drawing. This motivated Walter, who quickly completed his arithmetic so he could doodle instead. Miss Beck was also Walter's track coach while attending Benton, and under her tutelage, he earned a medal in the 80-pound relay event.

After a brief stint working on Uncle Will Disney's farm in Ellis, Kansas, followed by working as a news butcher selling refreshments on the railroad, Roy returned to Kansas City in 1913, living in his own apartment and finding a job at the First National Bank of Kansas City. It was here that the young man became fast friends with another teller, Mitch Francis. One afternoon Francis told Roy about a dance at a local social club, suggesting that they accompany Francis's two younger sisters to the dance. Roy was not a great dancer, but not wanting to disappoint his new friend, he agreed. Later that evening, Roy showed up at the club in a suit and tie, careful to make sure that neither was covered with chilli or beans. Francis arrived with his two sisters, and the dancing began: Roy was paired off with Edna Francis, and the two had a wonderful evening. After the success of the dance, Roy and Edna began spending more time together and it soon became obvious the two would eventually marry.

Walter was ecstatic that his big brother had moved back to Kansas City and did all he could to spend time with Roy. But Roy wasn't a kid any longer: with a career and a girl, the boy's childhood friend had become a man. Walter's naivety didn't stop him from looking for Roy throughout the neighbourhood when the elder Disney took Edna out. The couple often spent time at a local drugstore soda fountain. After making his rounds, Walter wandered into the establishment to find his brother on his date. Tactlessly, the pre-teen youngster marched up to his brother and asked him for a quarter to purchase drawing paper. Embarrassed and trying to cover up his frustration, Roy pulled some coins from his pocket to satisfy the boy.

It soon became obvious that Roy was now living in a different world to Walter's. Instead, Walter and Walt Pfeiffer began to hone their vaudevillian performances by attending shows at nearby theatres for inspiration. Walter had picked up additional jobs to supplement his allowance from the paper route, such as selling newspapers on a nearby corner, sweeping out a candy shop, and delivering medicine for a local druggist, all to help pay for his admission to the shows. It was clear to the two boys that they could do the same type of comedy acts they saw on stage, and due to their youth, they could create a unique appeal. They decided they would enter a variety competition to test out their hypothesis. This would have to be done secretly, however: Elias felt that vaudeville was crude, immoral and corrupted one's character, and as a result forbade his youngest children from attending such shows.

On the night of the competition, Walter, feigning illness and going to bed early, sneaked out of his window and met Pfeiffer on the pavement outside the house, and together the two boys walked to the nearby vaudeville hall. Somehow, Roy had heard that Walter would be performing that evening and suggested to Elias and Flora that they enjoy an adult evening at the Agnes Theater, not revealing that their youngest son would be performing.

As Elias entered the vaudeville hall, he was disgusted and embarrassed that he was accompanied by Flora and Ruth, who was too young to stay home alone for the evening. The smell of tobacco and alcohol hovered in the air while the raucous laughter and dirty jokes of inebriated men filled the room. Roy led the family in and found a place to sit with a good view of the stage.

The family sat through a variety of acts, Elias becoming more agitated as the evening progressed, uncomfortable with the impolite humour onstage and the behaviour of its audience. As Elias was beginning to gather the family to leave, the announcer on the stage introduced the next act, 'The Two Bad Walts'. Elias froze in his tracks, his eyes glued to the stage. As the curtain parted, he saw his youngest son on stage dressed as Charlie Chaplin, wearing oversized shoes, his father's long church coat, a shoe polish moustache, and holding a cane. Not wanting to draw attention to himself by storming out of the hall, Elias sank down into his seat to watch his son's performance in grim embarrassment as Walter and Pfeiffer chased each other across the stage in the slapstick manner characteristic of the Chaplin films. As the act continued, however, Elias found himself with a mirthful smile spread across his face: not only were some of the jokes clever, but some of them were even funny.

When the act was finished, Elias motioned to the family and they stood up and left. Walter, clueless that his parents and siblings had seen his performance, sneaked back home at the conclusion of the evening 25 cents richer: he and Pfeiffer won fourth place, earning themselves a cash prize.

Elias, who had been amused by the comic performance after the initial shock had worn off, chose not to say anything about his son's 'secret'. *Perhaps*, Elias thought to himself, *there is something to this boy's love of art and performance*. Thus, when Walter requested to take some classes at the Fine Arts Institute of Kansas City at a nearby Y.W.C.A., learning technique in sculpting, sketching, and drawing animals and the human figure from local professionals, Elias relented due to his belief that it was important for one to hone skills in a specific hobby. However, he intended for his son to pursue the mastery of these skills as a hobby only: art, he believed, could never become a successful profession, as he'd learned due to his failure as a fiddler in Denver.

As Kansas City progressed into the twentieth century, it began to upgrade its technology and infrastructure. In 1915, Elias decided that the home on Bellefontaine needed to be expanded to accommodate the family's needs. Enlisting Walter to help, Elias applied the skills he hadn't used since he had built houses semi-professionally with Flora in Chicago. Together, father and son added an addition to the rear of the home, building an interior bathroom and space that could be used as a bedroom. Their success in building the extension together inspired Elias to construct a garage in 1916 to provide automobile access to the alley that ran behind the house, once again with Walter's assistance. However, Elias's temper often flared when he became frustrated, either with his work or with his son, sometimes resulting in the boy dodging tools thrown at him by his angry father.

This form of discipline wasn't an isolated incident for the boy, even as a young teenager. Whenever Walter made a mistake along the paper route or got into his usual mischief, Elias would send his son into the basement to wait for a whipping. As he got older, Walter began to resent these beatings, which had become more regular in the days following Roy's departure. Remembering his brother's words to him on the night he left, Walter resolved to finally stand up to his father. One afternoon, when

Elias raised his hand to beat his son, Walter caught the man's wrists and held them above their heads, preventing the discipline from occurring.

Elias exerted a brief, half-hearted struggle with his youngest son, before allowing the strength to fade from his arms. Realising he had escaped corporal punishment, Walter slowly let go of his father's wrists and stepped backward, still on guard in case Elias's anger returned. Instead, the man's face fell and without saying a word, he turned and walked silently back up the stairs, closing the door behind him. It was in that instant that the man realised he no longer had power over his youngest son, and from that day forward, Walter never received another beating as discipline from his strict father.

Elias quickly realised that with Walter standing up to him, the boy was more likely to follow his brothers and depart in the middle of the night, leaving him with only the few boys he'd hired to deliver the papers and none of his children to help. As a result, he decided to invest in his son and take it a little easier on the boy to encourage him to continue working the route and to stay with the family. When Walter begged his father to allow him to use his savings from his side jobs to purchase leather boots (considered both a fashion *and* occupational necessity), Elias surprised the boy with a pair for Christmas.

Walter was proud of his new boots: not only did they help keep his feet warm and dry during the winter deliveries, but they also gave him some credibility with the other boys in the neighbourhood, many of whom had a tendency to bully the country boy from Marceline.

One cold evening, while walking home after finishing his paper route, Walter kicked a chunk of ice as he walked down the side of the road. Unbeknownst to him, the chunk of ice contained a large nail, which pierced the toe of his new boot and was driven into his foot. Bending over, Walter grabbed the chunk of ice and pulled on it, attempting to dislodge it from his boot. When it wouldn't pull away, he attempted to remove the shoe, but this only dug the nail deeper into his foot, causing terrible pain. Sitting down on a curb, he began to call for help to those walking past or riding the trams, but everyone thought he was a teen just causing trouble, so they ignored him. Finally, when people nearby saw that he continued to yell after several minutes, they came to help. The driver of a buggy went for a doctor, who explained that he had nothing Walter could take for the pain. Instead, he enlisted the help of a few men who held the boy's legs down while he pulled the nail out of Walter's foot. By this time, his foot had become so swollen that the only way to get it out of the boot to inspect the injury was to cut his precious new boot off.

Over the next two weeks, Walter lay in bed recuperating from his wound. During this time, Elias relied on additional help from his other delivery boys: the only time Walter got off delivering papers for his father in the duration of the paper route. Instead, the aspiring artist practised drawing from his bed, showing off his sketches to his mother and sister who gave compliments on his work. To hone his art skills, Walter once again began to copy from political cartoons that were featured in the *Star* and *Times*, much like he did from Elias's copies of *Appeal to Reason* in Marceline. The long hours spent in bed, his drawing paper at his side and a newspaper spread out across his lap allowed the boy to study the cartoons. He was particularly interested in the depiction of people and animals, symbolism, and the wit of the cartoonists. It was at this juncture that Walter's hobby for art and drawing transitioned to a desire to turn his interest into a career. He had made up his mind: he would become a newspaper cartoonist.

As the second decade of the 1900s progressed, Walter soon found himself in a transitionary period from childhood to young adulthood, becoming increasingly aware of the larger world around him and his place in it. In late summer 1914, the world erupted as the First World War set Europe aflame. While young men in nations like France and Germany quickly enlisted and marched off to war, the United States maintained its policy of isolation: the German Kaiser and his army didn't impact America. Tension in cities throughout North America began to rise as thousands of European immigrants started to choose sides. This resulted in the general public doing the same, joining with Britain and its allies while still maintaining the general policy of isolation and refusing to deploy troops or supplies across the Atlantic. To encourage its citizens to support its allies, the U.S. government started producing wartime propaganda, and political cartoonists for major newspapers began to draw content commenting on the war, the enemy, and events transpiring overseas. It was this environment into which Walter Disney, who had decided to become a political cartoonist himself, was thrust, forcing the young man to become even more aware of the world outside Missouri and its goings-on.

The influence of his increasing global perspective led Walter to begin to see himself as a member of the collective, rather than an isolated individual who wasn't part of the greater community. On 27 January 1917, Walter made his way to the Kansas City Convention Hall where he had been invited, along with every newsboy employed by *The Kansas City Star*, to a screening of the silent film, *Snow White*. As he sat in his chair, he was one in a sea of thousands of boys and young men who braved the elements to bring the news and commentary to the front doors of Kansas City's citizens.

But the screening of *Snow White* had a larger impact on Walter than simply rewarding the paperboy for all his hard work. The boy sat transfixed in the dark of the room, barely noticing the mass of kids around him shouting, throwing things, and climbing over the chairs: his attention was fixed instead on the action taking place on the screen in front of him. He watched in awe as the film's star, Marguerite Clark, held woodland creatures in her dainty hands and spoke to them. He laughed as he watched the seven dwarfs hard at work in their mine and cried with them as they mourned the girl asleep in her bier, cheering for joy as a kiss from the prince woke her from her slumber. It was one of the most ambitious presentations of entertainment Walter Disney had ever experienced and the elaborate sets, colourful characters, rich detail, and engaging plot would influence how he would create entertainment for the duration of his career.

Everything changed for Walter in June 1917 when another new opportunity for investment arose for Elias. As early as 1912, Elias had been investing in a jelly and soda factory in Chicago called O-Zell, believing that he could turn a profit and become wealthier than relying solely on the paper route. Much to Walter's chagrin and disgust, Elias was even forcing his son to invest the money he'd made from tips collected while selling the *Star* on the street corners, attempting to teach him how to be wise with his money instead of merely hoarding it or spending it. Elias was particularly interested in the moral benefits of O-Zell, as its owner, Ernest A. Scrogin, decided to produce fruit soda as an alternative to alcoholic beverages that had become prevalent in Chicago. Thus, Elias purchased 2,100 shares of O-Zell stock from Scrogin at $1 per share, not only investing in the company, but investing in a moral and dry America.

Over the next few years, Scrogin continued to write to Elias, asking for more money, trusting that one of his most prevalent investors would support the company even more as it continued to perfect the formula for its Oriental Fruit Beverage. Between 1912 and 1918, the Disneys purchased more than 7,000 additional shares, but oddly, O-Zell failed to put anything on the market for public consumption.

With the public market not very interested in the sodas available, O-Zell began instead to develop a line of jellies, jams and preserves, which seemed to be more marketable to the average consumer. With this new development, Scrogin realised he was in over his head and needed all hands on deck. On 6 March 1917, Elias received a letter from O-Zell's CEO explaining that the investor needed to decide whether he was all-in when it came to the success of the company. If he was, Scrogin explained, it would be in both Elias's and O-Zell's best interest if he moved to Chicago to help operate the business. Sending $16,000 to Scrogin, Elias purchased a partnership in the company and was awarded the position of head of factory construction as a result of the company's expansion into production of jams and jellies.

Maintaining the same attitude towards her children that she'd had in Marceline, Flora decided that she would remain in Kansas City so Walter and Ruth could complete the school year while Elias went on ahead to secure a home for the family in Chicago. When the children's studies concluded in June 1917, Flora and Ruth packed up their remaining belongings and took the train from Kansas City to Chicago to join Elias, who had acquired a house located at 1523 Ogden Avenue in west Chicago. It was decided that Walter would remain in Kansas City to help provide a smooth transition for the paper route's new owner, who had inherited a much larger route than Elias had originally purchased in 1912 due to the Disneys' success in gaining new subscriptions. Walter wasn't left alone in Kansas City, however: the boy kept his room in the Bellefontaine house, staying with his brother Herbert, his wife Louise, and their child Dorothy. Herbert had pled for Elias's forgiveness and had recently moved back in with his parents.

With the school year done and the paper route having undergone a successful changing-of-hands, 15-year-old Walter was looking for summer work before joining his parents and sister in Chicago for the autumn semester at his new school. Roy, who had worked as a news butcher, selling papers and refreshments to passengers on train rides and on platforms during stops, suggested that his brother do the same. Walter, who had developed a deep love of trains during his time in Marceline, jumped at the opportunity, and Roy loaned him $30 to purchase his first stock of supplies to sell.

Walter was hired to work for the Van Noyes Interstate News Company and was assigned to work along the Missouri Pacific route between Kansas City, Missouri and Denver, Colorado, a distance of approximately 1,000 kilometres. During his trips, Walter would walk up and down the aisles of the passenger cars, offering snacks, beverages, sweets, and cigars to the travellers. On the boy's first day, he decided to keep his store of supplies, as well as empty bottles he could return for a refund on his deposit, in a freight car at the end of the train. While business was steady, the news butcher was dismayed to see soldiers on his line throwing their empty bottles out of the window of the speeding train: it was like throwing his money out the window. Sometime around midday, the train made a stop to restock its supplies of water, sand and coal, so Walter went out onto the platform to attempt to sell to those mingling outside. When the whistle blew, Walter joined the passengers back onto the train, making his way to the rear of the train to put his empty bottles away and restock his supplies before going back up the aisle. However, he found that the freight car holding his supplies and his stock of empty bottles was no longer attached to the train: it had been detached and left behind at the last station, and with it, his investment and income. Walter also found on subsequent trips that he didn't sell fresh fruit fast enough; the majority of the fruit quickly spoiled and attracted flies, forfeiting much of the money he and Roy had invested in the product.

Having had the characteristics of hard work and a refusal to give up imparted to him by his father, Walter, though dismayed at his bad luck, took this as a learning opportunity and devoted himself to his job to provide the best service possible to his customers. The young salesman was so successful and personable that Van Noyes expanded his routes, adding the Kansas City Southern and Missouri, Kansas & Texas Railroad lines to his repertoire. Walter also recognised that he was able to make sales to those who worked for the railroad, not just the passengers. During lean journeys, when the passenger cars weren't as full, Walter would make his way up to the locomotive, where he would sell chewing tobacco and cigars to the engineers and firemen, who would allow the young man to ride in the engine until the next stop. Fondly remembering his time on Uncle Mike's lap in Marceline, Walter was in heaven, getting a chance to see the work of driving a train first-hand.

Working for the Van Noyes Interstate, Walter was able to experience the world outside his hometown, something that was very special for the boy whose family hadn't been wealthy enough to sample life outside Marceline and Kansas City. Unfortunately, his naivety often led to him getting into trouble or being put into uncomfortable situations. One evening, the train stopped overnight during a run between Kansas City and Downs, Kansas. Walter, who wasn't yet tired, checked into a hotel and changed out of his Van Noyes uniform before wandering into town to explore. A local policeman spotted the unknown youth, who was looking into the windows of various shops, and accused him of casing the town for future burglaries. When Walter explained he was staying in town overnight as an employee of the Van Noyes Interstate News Company, the police officer refused to believe him, hauling him back to the train yards before the staff there vouched for him.

On a separate occasion, Walter disembarked a train for the evening in Pueblo, Colorado for an evening off before the route continued on to its destination the next day. As the young man was unfamiliar with the town, he asked around for accommodations and was directed to a 'boarding house' inside a large Victorian-era storefront. Walter felt decidedly upper-class as he stood on the pavement looking up at the building, a large staircase leading up to a heavy wooden door, while the windows were framed by red velvet curtains edged in gold fringe.

When no one answered his knock at the door, the tired young man pushed it open to find a foyer complete with cushioned couches, gilded furniture, and a sparkling crystal chandelier. Beautiful young women, a few years older than he, sat in pairs or small groups, talking quietly, sometimes casting coy glances Walter's way. A full-figured woman came into the foyer, her eyes brightening when she saw the timid young man standing in the doorway. A large smile spread across her painted face, which was topped by a flurry of wild, red hair. Drawing the collar of her bathrobe tighter around her neck, she offered the young man a cold beer while he 'made his decision.'

Walter thanked the woman for her kind offer, his mind confusedly trying to piece together what kind of boarding house would offer patrons an alcoholic beverage. Movement in his peripheral vision caught his attention, and he glanced up to see a young woman, the skin of her neck and upper chest flushed, escorting a cowboy down the stairs. Walter moved to the side for the couple, watching as the young woman opened the door for the man, who smiled back at her over his shoulder as he stepped into the night and she closed the door behind him. Suddenly he understood: this was no boarding house, but rather a bordello, and the 'decision' the matron had referenced was in regards to which girl would be escorting him upstairs! Nodding at a couple of the girls seated nearby, he quietly opened the door and made his way down the front steps before he could be be propositioned again.

At the end of the summer, Walter tallied up the cash he had made from his sales working for the Van Noye Interstate News Company and realised that he had hardly made any money, instead forfeiting the $30 bond for supplies Roy had loaned him to get started. However, his time riding the railways did earn him a number of experiences and reinforced many of the ethics and morals taught by Elias, including hard work, the importance of treating people well, and the refusal to give up. It also proved that the young man didn't want to settle for odd jobs or the 'next best thing' like his father, but rather wanted to find a career that would stand the test of time.

Part V

A lifetime of experience

Chicago, Illinois and France, 1917–1919

Chapter Ten

Odd Jobs

As the summer of 1917 came to a close, Walter's time as a news butcher on the Missouri Pacific came to an end. Packing up his things and leaving Herbert and his family at the Bellefontaine house, he returned to Chicago where Elias, Flora and Ruth were living on Ogden Avenue.

With the autumn term soon beginning, Walter was enrolled as a student at McKinley High School. The 16-year-old quickly found a niche in the life of the school, becoming a regular contributor as an artist for the school newspaper, *The McKinley Voice*. Many of his cartoons featured commentary on current events, including those with propaganda messages relating to the war raging across the Atlantic. One cartoon reportedly challenged young men in the school by asking them if they would spend their summer holiday working or fighting as a part of the United States armed forces. The cartoons that he drew also had a personal purpose: shortly before Walter moved back to Chicago, his brother Roy and Edna Francis's younger brother Mitch felt a surge of patriotism and decided to enlist in the United States Navy. Roy and Mitch were sworn in together on 22 June 1917 and immediately sent to the Great Lakes Naval Station, approximately 60 kilometres from the Disney home in Chicago. Raymond Disney, another of Walter's older brothers, had enlisted as well, but in the Army instead of the Navy. Creating propagandistic political cartoons for *The McKinley Voice* was Walter's way of supporting his brothers who were fighting overseas, as well as doing his part supporting the war effort because he was too young to enlist.

In addition to attending McKinley High as a student, Walter filled his time with hobbies and work. At this point, he wasn't planning to become an illustrator, but he knew he loved art. In order to pursue illustration at night school, the young creative persuaded his strict father that it was merely a hobby and not a possible career. Elias allowed Walter to enrol in night classes at the Chicago Academy of Fine Arts where he studied under

Chicago Tribune cartoonist Carey Orr. The budding artist idolised Orr, who satirised daily news stories and current events in his strip, *The Tiny Trib*. Orr's enthusiastic student would later create a similar segment in his school newspaper which he called *The Tiny Voice*. Unfortunately, Walter found that the classes and styles taught at the Academy didn't necessarily align with his talents: while many of the courses taught the intricacies of producing still lifes and realistic drawings of people, the aspiring cartoonist realised that his real passion was for humorous caricature. By early 1918, Walter stopped attending the night classes at the art school, and instead poured himself into his work on *The McKinley Voice*.

Art and drawing quickly became all-consuming for the young Walter Disney. His education began to suffer as he spent precious class time drawing instead of attending to his studies. Instead of socialising like a 'normal' teenager, Walter would attend school social events for artistic inspiration: perched on a chair along the wall, he would watch the other children mingle and sketch their actions or even occasionally draw trick images to impress his friends and acquaintances.

Despairing that he was too young to enlist like his brothers, the young patriot decided to help his city and country by contributing to the workforce. Shortly after moving back to Chicago, he begrudgingly took work at O-Zell performing odd jobs. Specifically working in the jelly production facilities, he spent time washing out jelly jars, mashing up apples to produce the gelatinous pectin that made jellies thick, capping the jars once they were full, and nailing up boxes for shipment. On one occasion, he was even asked to perform as nightwatchman when the regular security guard called in sick. Recognising that the factory was located in an area of town where crime was abundant and not far from the railroad tracks from which immoral or dangerous vagabonds could wander, Walter was extra vigilant. It certainly didn't help his paranoia when, upon arriving for duty, the manager of the factory handed him a .38 calibre handgun to serve as protection and enforcement. That evening, while on his rounds, Walter kept all the lights on in the factory; he convinced himself it was so that anyone who might potentially try to steal from the factory would think twice when they saw the pistol the skinny, young nightwatchman was carrying.

Walter was lucky enough to live in a city with what seemed to be an overabundance of trains, further feeding his passion. Luckily for him, he was able to secure additional employment working at the elevated train line station located at Wilson Avenue for days when work was lacking at O-Zell. After getting out of school for the day, he would head to the station, don a cap and badge identifying him as a railway employee, and help to load and unload passengers from the elevated train. Manually opening and closing the doors of the train, Walter worked in a team with his fellow gatemen. Starting at the rear of the train, the first gateman would ring his bell, signalling that all passengers were on the train and that his doors were closed. This would prompt the succeeding gatemen to ring their bells, carriage by carriage, until the sound of the bells reached the front of the train, letting the conductor and engineer know that the train was ready to pull out from the station. On one occasion, Walter, situated in the middle of the train platform, gave the signal too early; luckily, his mistake didn't mess up the rest of the process and cause the train to take off before all passengers were secure.

None of these jobs, nor school, seemed to satisfy Walter, however. The war hysteria that swept the United States during the summer of 1917 pulled on his conscience. America officially became an aggressor in the First World War on 6 April 1917, after numerous offences perpetuated by Germany; the biggest was the resumption of Germany's unrestricted submarine warfare on 'neutral' American merchant vessels, which was a reversal of a German promise not to fire on those not considered belligerents. The United States and its citizens activated the domestic war machine, churning out propaganda: even Walter Disney drew propaganda cartoons for his *Tiny Voice* column in McKinley's school newspaper.

As one of America's largest cities, Chicago became a major hub of American patriotism and war fervour. During the summer and early autumn of 1917, the streets of the city seemed to be perpetually filled with war parades consisting of great columns of soldiers from the Great Lakes Naval Station, brass bands, contingents of American Red Cross workers, and floats covered in beautiful girls catcalling the young men watching them drift by.

One afternoon, while Walter stared up at the beauties perched on a patriotic float, one of them called out to the crowd, "Why don't you join up? What's the matter with you? Are you a slacker or something? Enlist! I dare you!" The young man shuddered as he felt goose bumps break out all over his body. The girls were talking to *him*. Why *didn't* he join?

Both Roy and older brother Raymond had enlisted and were fighting for freedom. Wasn't it his duty to serve democracy as well?

The problem was that he was only 16, too young to join any branch of the United States military.

One afternoon in the early autumn, the Disneys received word that Roy was transferring to Chicago's Great Lakes Naval Station and would be passing through the city on his way north. It was rare to hear from Walter's older brother: Elias had been so bitter at his son's betrayal in Kansas City, as well as his choice to enlist in the armed forces, that he had immediately thrown every unopened letter from Roy into the stove.

When it was time to meet up with Roy, Walter went to the train station alone to greet his brother. One of the first things he noticed was how swell and grown up his brother looked in his Navy uniform. It was only a few minutes that the two had to chat, sitting together on a bench along the train platform. Other soldiers milled around, either mingling with each other or talking to their own friends and family. When it was time for the troops to move out, an officer barked out to the troops, "Fall in!" The two brothers stood up and embraced, offering each other well wishes. Roy picked up his things and began to move towards the column of troops. Noticing Walter standing near the bench, watching his brother walk away, the officer marched over to him, believing him to be one of the enlisted men. "Come on! Didn't you hear me? Fall in!" Walter apologised, explaining that he wasn't a soldier and was just there visiting his brother. The officer acknowledged Walter, spun on his heel, and walked back to his waiting troops.

As Walter Disney walked out of the train station that afternoon, back into the sun of an early autumn day in Chicago, he realised something: while he had been busy working numerous jobs and was preparing for an autumn term at McKinley High, none of these were fulfilling. If he truly believed in what America stood for, he should enlist and be a part of this great war happening in Europe, no matter what.

Chapter Eleven

The Postman

As the war bug in America in support of the conflict raging in Europe continued to spread across the country, young Walter Disney quickly caught the fever. Propaganda explained that in order to stop the German Kaiser and the *kultur* he was trying to spread across the Atlantic, young men needed to enlist and it was their patriotic duty to do so. Unfortunately, the minimum enlistment age was 17, and the enthusiastic Walter was one year short.

The school year began at McKinley High, but the young man's attentions were elsewhere. Walter's dreams of serving his country grew, but quickly becoming frustrated due to the age requirement, he attempted to find other ways to help out. It was during this time that he poured himself into *The McKinley Voice*, creating his own propaganda cartoons for his column, *The Tiny Voice*. As inspiration, the budding artist kept a list of visual jokes called a 'gag file' from which to pull to insert into his cartoons; many of these visual gags had been inspired by the scores of vaudeville shows and silent films he had seen during his free afternoons in downtown Chicago. In order to test whether his gags would get laughs in his column, Walter realised that he needed to try them out on someone whose sense of humour was lacking: his father. Careful with how he approached these gag tests with Elias due to his distaste over his son's love of art, Walter would casually bring up a hypothetical situation or tell his father a joke in passing. True to his character, the ever-serious Elias wouldn't flag any facial emotions, just nod at his son, and offer a nondescript compliment: "That's nice, Walter." On rare instances, a few days later, the strict and serious patriarch would approach his youngest son while still maintaining a serious demeanour. "I've been thinking about that joke you told me the other day," he would explain. "It's funny, Walter. Very funny." This reaction told him that, while unable to break the stoic façade of his father, the gag would likely cause his classmates to cackle in response. But even taking a humorous spin on the war overseas didn't satisfy the convictions he had to join up.

As the uneventful school year came to a close, Walter once again continued his occasional jobs at O-Zell and acquired a job as a postal carrier, following in his father's footsteps once more. While working at the Chicago Post Office, Walter had a number of different tasks to accomplish on any given day. Officially holding the position as 'sub carrier', he filled in by picking up and delivering mail if the regular postmen were out sick. On any given day, he and his fellow postmen would walk three or four different routes through downtown Chicago. On some occasions, Walter was able to use a horse and buggy, which allowed him an easier time of collecting large amounts of envelopes and packages. One particular horse had been trained by senior postmen to walk the route and stop at predetermined locations. Walter was instructed not to touch the reins, but rather let the horse carry him along the route. It took a while for him to learn the horse's ways: on numerous instances, after loading several letters and packages into the back of the buggy, the horse would begin its walk to the next stop, leaving the exasperated Walter standing on the curb. Because it had been trained not to respond to verbal commands, Walter often had to try to launch himself into the moving cart or follow until the next pickup location when he knew the horse would stop. Unfortunately, after loading more mail into the back of the buggy, the whole charade would begin again. It didn't take long for him to realise that the sound of the slamming buggy door was the horse's cue to begin towards the next stop; from then on, he quietly closed the door before hopping into the cart.

On one particularly frustrating day, while collecting mail from the hotels along Chicago's Grand Avenue, Walter emerged from the lobby of a building, his arms full of envelopes, to find that the horse and buggy were no longer parked on the curb where he had left them. Running into the middle of the street, he looked up and down the road, but the scores of horses, buggies, trams, and motorcars made it difficult to find the postal vehicle. Remembering that the horse had the route memorised, the panicked postal carrier began to run down the pavement, careful not to drop any of the letters he was carrying. He turned down a side street and then another that ran parallel to Grand Avenue, where he found the horse waiting for him on the opposite side of the hotel building; evidently it had been trained to go around the block and wait for the postal carrier on the other side of the lobby, cutting precious time along the postal route.

Walter's route also took him to the Grand Avenue Pier (today's Navy Pier), the terminal from which tourists could embark on a steamship across Lake Michigan, as well as a port for cargo being imported and exported from the lakeside city to other parts of the country. The 1,000-metre pier was a new addition to the city; originally opened a couple of years before in 1916, the Grand Avenue Pier also served as an outdoor recreation space, as well as the location for a jail for those who had dodged the American draft when the United States entered the First World War.

On one particular day, after collecting postcards from the mailboxes along the pier, Walter boarded a tram back to the post office, his mailbag hanging on his back. It was a beautiful day and he enjoyed admiring the people scurrying down the pavements, the variety of busy traffic on the streets, and the new towers being constructed, billed as some of the tallest in the world. The weather was beautiful and he decided that, with nothing else to do on this Sunday afternoon, he would pick up an additional route collecting letters around the city. Upon arriving back at the post office, he hung his bag of postcards on a peg in the horse barn and took out the buggy that was already hooked up to his favourite horse to fulfil the route.

A few weeks later, Walter was sitting in the mailroom sorting mail for delivery, he and his buddies cracking jokes with each other. Suddenly, he noticed it had become strangely quiet and his cohorts were no longer laughing. He looked up from his pile of envelopes and realised everyone's faces had become solemn, almost a mix between surprise and fear – and they were all looking at him.

"Disney!" came a voice from behind him. Walter started. He turned around to find two tough-looking postal inspectors standing behind him.

"That's me," the young man squeaked meekly.

"Come on with us," they ordered. Walter stood up from his chair and threw a sidelong glance at his friends as he was whisked away. As he walked toward a nearby office, his mind raced, trying to determine what he had done wrong. Had something happened to the delivery horse? Had he accidentally delivered mail at the wrong address? Whatever it was, it must have been bad: these guys looked pretty serious.

After entering an office, one of the inspectors closed the door; both seated themselves on the opposite side of a table in the room from the young man who was now trying to hold his composure while being secretly terrified.

"A few weeks ago, you collected a bag of mail from the Grand Avenue Pier, correct?" one inspector asked.

"Yes, that's correct," answered the young postman.

"What did you do with it?"

"I put it in the mail chute," Walter explained.

"No, you didn't," interjected the second officer, slapping his hand on the table. "What did you do with it? Come clean now, kid!"

Walter jumped. His rising panic made it more difficult to hide his fear. A whirlwind of thoughts sped through his mind. He remembered turning in the mail. What would his father think? Maybe he didn't put the mail in the chute. And Roy? What would he think? He didn't need to worry about his kid brother in jail for mail fraud. As he looked down at his feet, they began to move in a circular motion, but it wasn't because he was moving them – the room had begun spinning.

"Well, we'll tell you what you did with the bag of postcards, Disney," came the voice of the first postal inspector seemingly from a distance. "You hung it on a peg in the horse stable and it's been hanging there for two weeks." The room became silent and stopped spinning. The cold feeling in the young man's chest dissipated as his stomach returned to its normal place. He slowly looked up at the two officers sitting across from him. Both had smirks on their faces.

"That's right," replied Walter in a small voice. "That's exactly what happened." The memory of the beautiful Sunday afternoon and the tram ride back from the Grand Avenue Pier came flooding back to him.

"Be more careful with the mail from now on, kid," said one of the inspectors, standing up and opening the door. "Get out of here."

It took everything for Walter to not stand up and bolt out of the small office. Holding his composure, he slowly left the room and walked back down the hallway to his work station, resisting the urge to find a waste basket to vomit into; he could feel the eyes of the postal inspectors on the back of his head as he walked back into the sorting room. Finding his place at his workstation, he slowly sat down; his co-workers silently continued sorting the mail as though they hadn't noticed his return. When he glanced up at them a few seconds later, he met their sideways looks and locked gazes with them, meeting their wide, questioning eyes

Looking eastward towards the grounds of the World's Columbian Exposition in Jackson Park. Elias Disney often walked through the Midway Plaisance on the way to work while living on Vernon Avenue. (*Library of Congress*)

Pastor Walter Parr personally officiated the ground-breaking of St. Paul's Congregational Church on 19 May 1900. (The Chicago Tribune, *Public Domain*)

PASTOR PARR AND CONGREGATION PLOW THE SITE FOR NEW CHURCH.

The ground-breaking of St. Paul's Congregational Church was significant to both the congregation and the citizens of the neighbourhood. Elias and Flora Disney personally participated in the ground-breaking ceremonies on 19 May 1900. (The Chicago Tribune, *Public Domain*)

1249 Tripp Avenue in Chicago, built and designed by Elias and Flora Disney. The upstairs bedroom over the porch is the room where Roy, Walter, and Ruth were born. (*Andrew Kiste*)

When Elias and Flora Disney realised they had a knack for building houses after constructing their own, they decided to purchase additional lots in the neighbourhood and construct homes to sell, such as this one located at 1209 Tripp Avenue. The house numbers have changed over time. (*Andrew Kiste*)

Marceline, Missouri was instrumental in the life of young Walter Disney: "More things of importance happened to me in Marceline than have happened since," Walt once explained. (*Map by Andrew Kiste*)

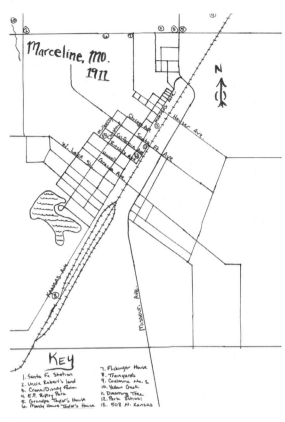

KEY

1. Santa Fe Station
2. Uncle Robert's land
3. Crane/Disney Farm
4. E.P. Ripley Park
5. Grandpa Taylor's House
6. Manly House "Taylor's House"

7. Flickinger House
8. Trainyards
9. Coalmine No. 1
10. Yellow Creek
11. Dreaming Tree
12. Park School
13. 508 N. Kansas

The rural, agricultural environment of Marceline taught Walter the importance of hard work, community and the simple life. (*Andrew Kiste*)

Walter's penchant for performance, creativity and mischief blossomed at a number of locations throughout Marceline, not least of which at the barn that stood on the Disney property. While the barn no longer stands, this reproduction still draws visitors from far and wide to pay homage to the boy who would become Walt Disney. (*Andrew Kiste*)

The close proximity in which Walter and his older brother Roy grew up, as exemplified by the small room and brass bed they shared on the Marceline farm, led them to become incredibly close as both family and business partners for the remainder of their lives. (*Andrew Kiste*)

American Civil War veteran William Crane owned the Marceline farm that would eventually be owned by the Disneys after his death. (*Courtesy of Chris Ankeney*)

'Grandpa' Erastus Taylor lived across the street from the Disney farm and often entertained his young neighbours with tales of his exploits in the Civil War. While Walter later realised that the old man likely never experienced half of what he claimed, the rich detail and engaging storytelling would inspire Walter throughout his career. (*Courtesy of Chris Ankeney*)

'Grandpa' Taylor's house was one of the first built in Marceline and was located across the street from the Disney farm. Often serving as a gathering place for the Crane-Phillips-Taylor clan, Elias and his family were quickly welcomed at the Taylor homestead. Unfortunately, the house burned down in 1909 shortly after Taylor's death, erasing all remnants of the old man from Walter's life, except for memories. (*Courtesy of Chris Ankeney*)

Clem Flickinger, Walter Disney's childhood friend from Marceline. (*Courtesy of Chris Ankeney*)

Young Walter and his friends spent many days swimming, fishing, and ice skating at nearby Yellow Creek, just outside Marceline. (*Andrew Kiste*)

When Flora decided it was finally time to enrol Walter at Park School, the boy spent more time doodling and daydreaming than he did learning. In fact, he spent a few lessons carving his initials into his desk. (*Andrew Kiste*)

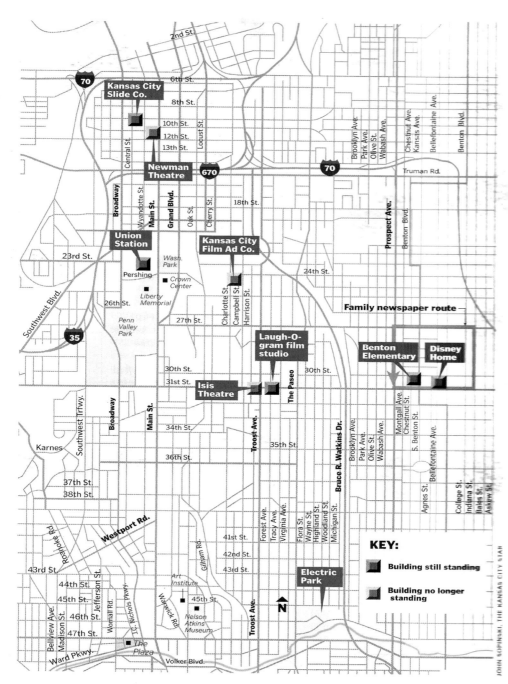

While Marceline helped to define Walter Disney's character, Kansas City's numerous pursuits and businesses, including schools, theatres, advertising agencies, and Walter's affiliation with *The Kansas City Star*, all paved the way to foster his true passion: drawing. (*Map from* Walt Disney's Missouri, *Burnes et. al, reprinted by permission of* The Kansas City Star)

203. Union Depot, Kansas City, Mo.

The original Union Depot served as the main hub by which rail traffic entered Kansas City, as well as the location for the start of Walter Disney's adventure in Kansas City. (*Courtesy of Union Station Kansas City Inc./Kansas City Museum*)

Shortly after arriving in Kansas City, Elias and Roy went to the headquarters of *The Kansas City Star* to apply for a paper route. Over the next few years, Roy and Walter would work the route, located between Prospect Avenue and Indiana Street and 27th and 31st Streets, east of downtown, for their father to help support the family during its time in Kansas City. ('*Kansas City Star Building', Missouri Valley Special Collections, Kansas City Public Library, Kansas City, Missouri*)

Walter and Ruth were soon enrolled in Benton Grammar School, where the young boy continued his trend of causing mischief. However, some of the staff members, including Principal Cottingham and Ms Daisy Beck, had a lifelong impact on the young man. (*'Benton School', Mrs Sam (Mildred) Ray, 1922, Missouri Valley Special Collections, Kansas City Public Library, Kansas City, Missouri*)

A number of ambulance drivers employed by the American Red Cross are inspected at Hospital No. 5 in Auteuil, France prior to rendering a day's service. While Walter Disney never experienced combat situations, he often undertook military-style drills and training during his employment with the American Red Cross, both in the United States and Europe in the days following the First World War. (*Hine, L.W., photographer (1918). Inspection of Staff at Hospital #5. American Red Cross Ambulance Drivers Drilling at American Military Hospital No. 5 at Auteuil, which is supported by the American Red Cross. Auteuil, France, 1918. https://www.loc.gov/item2017682332/*)

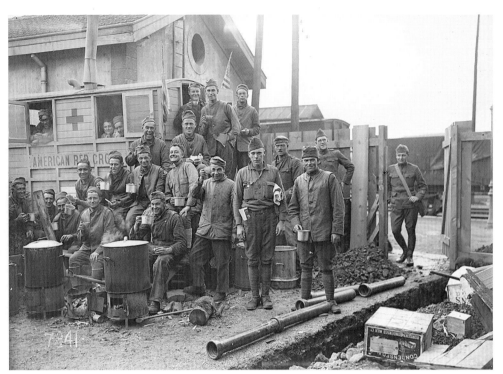

American Red Cross canteens rendered a number of services to European and American soldiers, including providing hot meals and drinks, rest stations, and stationery for writing letters home. The American Red Cross canteen in Neufchâteau, France, pictured here, was famous for providing delicious hot chocolate and fresh doughnuts, made by the matron, Alice Howell, who can be seen in the window of the trailer. (*In the backyard of the American Red Cross Canteen at Neufchâteau, showing tank men enjoying a cup of hot chocolate. Neufchâteau, France, September 1918. Photograph. https://www.loc.gov/item/2017682556/*)

After the flooding of Union Depot, the new Union Station quickly became not only the hub for rail traffic into Kansas City, but also the third largest and busiest train depot in America. Walter spent many hours wandering through the Grand Hall, pictured here, as he bid farewell to his family, as well as visiting weekly to bathe in the station's bathrooms. (*Courtesy of Union Station Kansas City Inc./Kansas City Museum*)

Prior to boarding the train that would carry them to their destinations, travellers would pass below the large suspended clock and seat themselves upon the wooden benches in Union Station's North Waiting Room. (*Courtesy of Union Station Kansas City Inc./Kansas City Museum*)

Upon returning to Kansas City after his time in Europe, Walter secured a job at Pesmen-Rubin where he produced advertisements for local businesses at this desk. It was here that he made a lasting friendship and partnership with fellow artist, Ubbe Iwwerks, and shortened his name to Walt. (*Andrew Kiste*)

When Walt's boss at the Kansas City Film Ad Company wasn't interested in producing animated advertisements, it was recommended that Walt partner with Frank Newman to sell his animated ads. Newman was interested in what Walt created and was soon creating weekly advertisements shown in Newman Theater, pictured here. (*Creative Commons (Attribution) License*)

In 1919, Walt Disney joined the Order of the DeMolay as one of Frank 'Dad' Land's boys. It was here, at Kansas City's Scottish Rite Temple, that Walt learned how to have reverence for courtesy, comradeship, and patriotism, all under the tutelage of Land. (*'Scottish Rite Temple', Mrs Sam (Mildred) Ray, 1922, Missouri Valley Special Collections, Kansas City Public Library, Kansas City, Missouri*)

On 1 November 1921, a ground-breaking ceremony for the new Liberty Memorial took place in front of Union Station. The ceremony drew thousands from around the nation, including dignitaries such as the Allied generals and US president Calvin Coolidge. With not enough standing room, dozens of people perched atop the roof of Union Station to witness the festivities. Walt Disney, in an effort to make some money, attempted (and failed) to capture the event from the cockpit of an airplane soaring overhead. (*Courtesy of Union Station Kansas City Inc./Kansas City Museum*)

During his weekly trip for bathing, Walt often stood on the platforms, watching the trains pull in and out of Union Station, longing to once again be with Elias, Flora and Ruth. However, in 1923, these same platforms would bring a fresh start for him as he left Kansas City behind and travelled to Los Angeles with nothing but a borrowed suit, a cardboard suitcase, and $40. (*Courtesy of Union Station Kansas City Inc./Kansas City Museum*)

When Laugh-O-Gram defaulted on its payments to the owners of the McConahay Building, they were kicked out and moved production to the nearby Wirthman Building, where the Isis Theater was also located. It was here that Walt spent time watching animated films for inspiration for his own shorts, as well as where he met theatre organist Carl Stalling, with whom he would collaborate on future projects. (*Creative Commons (Attribution) License*)

Upon receiving word from Margaret J. Winkler that she was interested in distributing Walt's Alice Comedies, the aspiring film-maker sneaked into the grounds of the Sawtelle VA Hospital located just outside Los Angeles. It was here that he woke Roy, who was recovering from tuberculosis, to tell him the news of Winkler's message. (*Library of Congress, Prints & Photographs Division, HABS*)

After the demise of the Alice Comedies, Charles Mintz asked Walt to develop a new animated character to be distributed by Universal. Together, Walt and Ub Iwerks created Oswald the Lucky Rabbit. This advertisement features an early concept for Oswald that would later be changed to make him slimmer and younger-looking. (*Alamy*)

with a smirk that was characteristic of Walter Disney's sense of humour. This smirk broke the tension and their day of work and jokes continued as it had before the interrogation had begun.

Unfortunately for the young postman, working for the Chicago Post Office was filled with even more drama, some of which became fatal. On the afternoon of Wednesday, 4 September 1918, Walter had just returned from his route to the post office, which was located in downtown Chicago's Federal Building. After dropping off his mail bag shortly after 3 pm, he exited the post office located just off the rotunda of the Federal Building. As he walked across the polished marble floor of the lobby, an explosion shook the building accompanied by a loud *FOOOOOM*. Dust shot out, filling the room, from the direction of the West Adams Street entrance. A few seconds later, a dazed Walter found himself standing up after being knocked to the ground by the blast. Looking around, he noticed others who had been crossing the rotunda doing the same. Walter was confused in noting that a woman who had been walking nearby who had been wearing a white dress was now wearing black; later he realised that her dress had been coloured by the dust and smoke from the explosion.

Screams seemed to echo from all around, magnified by the curve of the eight-floor dome that capped the lobby. Another young man was helping an elderly woman off the floor, her spectacles glassless as they hung crooked from her ears. Across the lobby, a heavyset woman was screaming that she had 'lost all her money'. Scattered across the now dust-covered floor were tattered pieces of cloth including sections of skirts and blouses.

Hundreds of people began running towards the doors, as well as the now-gaping hole where the West Adams Street entrance had been. The mass of humanity quickly came to a halt, as on- and off-duty police officers blockaded the exits and locked the doors in an effort to find those responsible for the explosion. Inserting himself in line, Walter, trying to keep his composure, waited his turn to exit the building. After a brief exchange with the officers standing outside the building, he stumbled over the piles of bricks and shattered wood into the street. Walking away from the building, he barely noticed the sound of crunching glass beneath his feet as he made his way to the pavement across from the Federal Building. As his nerves began to calm, he noticed how the shards of glass seemed almost to cover the street and pavements, as the strong explosion had broken windows as high as five stories on either side of West Adams

Street. The propaganda posters encouraging Americans to purchase war bonds and enlist in the military hung from the sides of the building in shreds, flapping in the breeze created by people running from the scene.

Things outside the Federal Building were more chaotic than inside. Screams from both men and women filled the air. Stunned people sat on the ground or were stretched out in the street. A priest, clad in black, was moving amongst the bodies, tending to the injured and administering last rites to the dead and dying. The body of a young woman lay near the Federal Building, with half of her head blown off. Those nearby were horrified to see that she was still breathing and even more horrified to experience the next few minutes as her breathing became shallower and eventually stopped. The sound of heavy cloth being dragged across the pavement underscored the wailing that filled the streets, as a number of eyes turned to the destroyed entrance of the building. A man was dragging a body clad in a shredded postal worker's uniform down the steps; the unnatural movement of the body led many to believe that every bone had been shattered. Walter was devastated to learn later that this slaughtered individual was William Wheeler, a 45-year-old colleague who delivered mail like him. The sound of brisk horses' hooves clopped down the road as eyes turned to the noise. A lone mail horse was stumbling down the middle of West Adams Street towards a policeman who was surveying the carnage. In an effort to stop the horse from running away, he grabbed the horse by the bit. Blood ran down the side of the horse's face, its eyes wide in terror. Upon stopping the crazed animal, the policeman and others nearby watched as it sank to the ground and died.

The clanging of ambulance bells could be heard in the distance as medical help approached. Hope rose for those standing in the destruction surrounding the Federal Building, but this hope ceased as the sound of a crash ended the ambulance bells. It was later learned that the ambulance, which was rushing to the scene of the explosion, had crashed into the rear of a tram that had stopped for the ambulance to pass, injuring the two physicians and two patrolmen on board.

Finally able to gather himself together to make his way home, Walter glanced at the clock that was mounted to the corner of the Federal Building. The explosion had stopped it to the exact minute of the blast: 3.12 pm. Upon arriving home, his mother and father expressed relief that he had escaped largely unscathed.

Over the course of the next few days, details about the explosion began to emerge. According to an article on page one of *The Chicago Tribune*, at around 3.00 pm on 4 September, an unnamed woman had just finished purchasing war stamps from the post office on the first floor of the Federal Building, located just inside the West Adams Street entrance. She noticed a man standing in the entrance with a cigar box under his arm, a piece of string hanging out from beneath the box's cover. She claimed that he took the cigar he had been smoking and touched the burning end of it to the string, then dropped the box to the ground, kicking it beneath a nearby radiator, before exiting the building. Finding this odd but not disconcerting, she walked away from the entrance and across the lobby towards the Dearborn Street entrance of the building, when the explosion occurred. While her story was not corroborated by other witnesses, a number of other individuals reported seeing a rather short man, weighing approximately 65kg and wearing a fedora or Panama hat made of brown felt, sprinting out of the West Adams Street entrance and getting into a waiting car which sped away just before the explosion.

Eight floors above the scene of chaos, William D. 'Big Bill' Haywood was in a meeting with prosecutors, United States marshals, and officials of the U.S. Court of Appeals. Haywood was a founder and leader of the Industrial Workers of the World (also known as the I.W.W. or 'Wobblies'), a radical socialist-leaning labour union which advocated class warfare through strikes, boycotts, and industrial sabotage. Many of the tactics used by the I.W.W. were often violent and illegal, which led to numerous arrests. In 1917, Haywood and other leaders of the organisation were arrested when they dodged the American draft and encouraged a number of industrial workers in Chicago to refuse to work, which harmed the wartime industry supporting American troops overseas. Law enforcement agents of both the city of Chicago and the United States cited the American Espionage Act, which made it a crime for those inside the United States to hamper the war effort or aid any enemies of the United States, both internal and external.

On the day of the explosion in Chicago's Federal Building, Haywood was upstairs meeting with representatives of the U.S. Court of Appeals asking for a release on bond from their 20-year sentence for those members of the I.W.W. arrested due to the Espionage Act. When the blast shook the building, all the individuals in the room were lifted out of their chairs or found themselves thrown to the ground. Thomas Dolan, a deputy marshal, was stunned to find Haywood still in his chair, tapping a pencil against the table and staring off into space, unperturbed.

"They've bombed the building!" shouted Dolan. Haywood's private secretary, Ms Mary Service, ran to a nearby window and looked down at the road below. Dolan and another deputy marshal, Fred Klika, quickly stepped into the hall, summoning one of the guards that had accompanied Haywood that morning from the county jail, who was also picking himself up off the floor.

After instructing the guard to keep an eye on the I.W.W. leader, the two marshals gathered their colleagues and set into motion a plan to round up other members of the organisation's leadership, convinced that the attack had come as a result of Haywood's appeal plea. While Dolan and Klika were making their plan, Haywood brought his anxiety under control, explaining to the guard and Mary Service that the explosion wasn't tied to the International Workers of the World.

"It might have been a German outrage," he explained, suggesting that the explosion was an attack of America's enemies in the great war happening overseas. "It's a terrible thing. No I.W.W. follower would be as foolish as to do such a thing. I am convinced in my own mind that no man of the organisation had any connection with this outrage."

Over the next few hours, top members of the I.W.W. leadership were captured. Raids were conducted on two headquarters for the organisation, arresting approximately 100 Wobblies. Numerous individuals were taken into custody based on circumstantial evidence of things in their possession. For instance, one suspect, James Connelly, was arrested and accused of being associated with the attacks because he was carrying a small lamp and some receipts from an explosives company in his pockets. Another young man, Kent Rudin, was arrested because he had been seen reading I.W.W. literature. As he was being searched at arrest, he was found to be carrying a rusted revolver, making him out to be seen as a 'dangerous man'. However, out of all the people arrested 'in connection' with the attack on the Federal Building, none matched the description given by witnesses of the short man wearing the brown felt hat.

As the dust finally cleared away and clean-up commenced, it was announced that the explosion killed four: in addition to Walter's colleague, William Wheeler, another postman named Edwin Kolkow, a young serviceman named Joseph Ladd, and the young woman with the head injury, Ella Miehlke, were all killed in the blast. The explosion injured seventy-five others in varying degrees, either from the shock of the blast, flying debris, or falling glass.

In an effort to protect 'Big Bill', he was spirited away down a service elevator to the ground floor, where, handcuffed and under heavy guard, he was loaded into a police wagon and driven to the county prison. In 1919, a woman in Milwaukee, Wisconsin accused her husband, Dominick Costerella, of carrying out the bombing on Chicago's Federal Building, as well as an attack on the Milwaukee Police Station in 1917 that killed ten people. When police finally found Costerella, he was arrested in Pennsylvania on his wife's charges. After learning of his arrest, his wife went to the police and admitted she had made up the story in an effort to locate her husband, who had left her and disappeared. Unfortunately, with the revelation that Mrs Costerella's story was false, the investigation of the United States marshals and the Chicago Police came to a halt and, after some interrogations, most of those arrested in the raids on the I.W.W. headquarters were released. In 1921, after being released on bail during the appeal process, William Haywood fled the country to Russia, where he later died in 1928.

While working part-time at the post office, Walter became friends with a young man his age, Russell Maas. Like many other young men their age, Maas felt strongly about enlisting in the armed forces but was also frustrated by the minimum age requirement of 17. While American young men were able to join the Armed Forces at the age of 16 with parental consent, Walter knew that he would never get this from Elias and Flora: his father was especially bitter and frustrated with his older brothers Ray and Roy for participating in the war. Together, Maas and Walter began looking for a way around this obstacle.

Their first attempt was the United States Navy; Walter admired Roy so much that he was inspired to join the same branch that his older brother served in. Together, he and Maas went down to the recruiting station with the plan to fool the recruiters and doctors: Maas was tall and more mature-looking for a 16-year-old, and they reasoned that if they could convince the recruiters that he was old enough, maybe they would accept Walter too. Unfortunately, after conducting a physical examination of the boys,

Maas was rejected because he wore glasses and it was determined that they were too young, and they were encouraged to return in a few months when they turned 17. The two boys were unable to follow through on the recommendation, however: shortly after their attempt, it was announced that the U.S. Navy had a sufficient number of men for the war and the recruiting office closed.

Recognising that they probably wouldn't be able to fool the American armed forces into believing they were old enough, the two boys decided to investigate other organisations that would take younger boys who wanted to serve. Word soon came that the Canadian Army was accepting young men from the United States. They soon hatched a plan to head north to join up, plotting their escape for the near future. The two didn't have enough foresight, though: in anticipation of their trip, Maas packed his suitcase early with essentials, leading his mother to question her son about the packed bag. When Mrs Maas found out about the boys' plan to abandon their families, jobs, and education, she quickly called Flora Disney and filled her in, bringing the young patriots' desire to join up to another halt.

With their plans to participate in the war seemingly at an end, Walter and Russell decided to pour their summer into their work at the post office. Soon, the school year began, and Walter once again began his work making commentary for *The McKinley Voice* and his column, filling in at the post office when he was available.

One afternoon, while he was sorting mail, he heard the sound of pounding feet as though a flurry of activity was heading towards him in the mail room. Looking up, he saw Maas running up the hallway, dodging carts of envelopes, with other mail carriers jumping out of the way of the sprinting 16-year-old. When he arrived at Walter's desk, the young man was out of breath, but it didn't stop him from getting out the news:

"Walter. There is something forming here in Chicago that will allow us to enlist!" Russell gasped.

Walter set down the stack of envelopes and leaned forward in anticipation. "Aren't we too young?" he asked.

"That's the great part," Maas explained breathlessly. "They don't care if we're too young: they need volunteers. We can drive ambulances to help wounded doughboys. We won't be fighting, so it doesn't matter if we are 17 or not!"

That afternoon, over a pile of unsorted mail, Walter Disney and Russell Maas began to conceive a plan to join this organisation, the American Red Cross, in serving the injured and sick European victims of war and American soldiers. The conversation continued over the next few days; the two wanted to account for everything to ensure that they wouldn't be turned down for the same reasons they had been rejected by the Navy or stopped like they were by their parents when they tried to run away to the Canadian Army.

In late August, Walter and Russell took the tram to the Oakland neighbourhood of south Chicago to the American Red Cross Automotive and Mechanical Bureau Department of Personnel, where they would apply to work for the relief organisation. Upon entering the building located on Cottage Grove Avenue, they found a number of men in American Red Cross uniforms conducting business, as the building also served as the main headquarters for the nearby Camp Scott, a base where the American Red Cross, or A.R.C., trained ambulance drivers that would be sent across the Atlantic. Interestingly, the barracks for Camp Scott was located on the eastern side of Washington Park where it met the Midway Plaisance, less than half a mile from where Flora and Elias first lived at Vernon Avenue upon their arrival in Chicago in 1889.

The Camp Scott training station was not the only way that Chicago was involved with the American Red Cross during the First World War. In fact, the great city and its many citizens were some of the organisation's biggest supporters. Shortly after America entered the war, the American Red Cross organised a membership campaign in the city, encouraging Chicagoans to contribute a few dollars to the relief organisation's fundraising efforts. In one month, from May to June 1917, more than 300,000 new members joined the American Red Cross in Chicago alone, earning it the title of one of the world's first 'Red Cross cities'.

War fever had struck the city, heightened only by its success in the membership campaign. City leaders and Chicago's numerous organisations sought more opportunities to support the American Red Cross. Newspapers took out full-page advertisements, including one describing a wounded soldier who was only saved due to financial contributions such as those given during the membership drive. Publicity stunts that were used to bring attention to American Red Cross efforts were staged around the city, including one where all public transportation in the metropolis was stopped for 60 seconds. Performances were given in the city's theatres telling the stories of American Red Cross medics. Perhaps most importantly were the parades, which streamed through the business district on a daily basis at noon. Attractive girls dressed in American Red Cross outfits called to the men gaping along the pavements, encouraging them either to enlist or to support the American Red Cross, while others walked through the crowds collecting donations. At the end of the parade, seated on a flatbed trailer, was Uncle Sam, a wartime personification of the United States. Wearing his characteristic red striped trousers and white-and-blue top hat, the character sat at a desk, 'calculating' donations on an adding machine and occasionally scratching his white beard. At times, he would look up at the crowds on the pavements, waving to them and calling down that they needed to donate their time and money for the boys overseas. It was probably a parade like this one that Walter experienced when he was patriotically inspired to enlist.

Perhaps the group that did most for the American Red Cross in Chicago and its support of the American effort during the days following the nation's entry into the war was the women. Social organisations, such as the Women's Fortnightly, became active participants in supporting the American government and military in the war effort, as well as relief organisations including the American Red Cross. During the years of active American participation, the Women's Fortnightly created propaganda for the War Information Committee of the Women's Council of National Defence, sold War Bonds, held patriotic rallies, and sewed more than 1,300 garments and bandages to be used by the American Red Cross. The social club also hosted a speakers' series on war matters, including being visited by His Grace, the Archbishop of York, the Most Reverend Cosmo Gordon Lang, D.D, D.C.L., LL.D., Primate of England and Metropolitan.

All of this war fever, both fear and hawkishness, wasn't lost on young Walter Disney. After some investigation, he and Russell Maas realised that they did, in fact, have to be 17 to join the American Red Cross. However, they were so determined to serve that they concocted a plan to ensure that their youth wasn't discovered. The applications that the two submitted on that late summer day weren't for Walter Disney and Russell Maas, but rather for Walter and Russell St. John, twin brothers who were determined to help the sick and injured.

After answering a few questions about themselves to one of the enlistment officers, the American Red Cross employee handed Walter and Russell a piece of paper and told them that it needed to be filled out and submitted to the government in order for them to travel overseas. Walter looked down at the United States Passport Application in his hand. As he skimmed over the questions it asked, his stomach dropped: he was required not only to put down his birthday on the application, but also to obtain a parent's signature because he was younger than 18. Not only would it be difficult to convince Elias and Flora to let him serve in Europe, there was no way he would be able to convince them to allow him to forge his birth date so he was 'old enough' to serve.

Handing the two boys their American Red Cross training uniforms, the officer explained that they would receive notification of when they should report to Camp Scott. Trying to hide their excitement, Walter and Russell grinned at each other as they turned and walked out of the office back into the city that had so inspired their patriotism for the American war effort.

Chapter Twelve

Camp Scott

While Elias and Flora Disney weren't thrilled that their son had joined the American Red Cross, they assumed that he was assisting the charity organisation on the home front, serving as a driver who would transport returning troops either to rehabilitation hospitals or their homes upon arrival back to the States. However, Walter wasn't quick to correct his parents: if they allowed him to serve out of ignorance for what he was really doing, he was willing to take advantage of this. Elias and Flora's misunderstanding was further perpetuated by Walter's training at Camp Scott, which could begin before receiving his parents' official permission.

On 25 September, Walter and Russell arrived at Camp Scott, on the southeast edge of Washington Park where it met the Midway Plaisance, near the intersections of 62nd Street and Cottage Grove Avenue. An American Red Cross officer met them at the headquarters where they'd originally applied and explained to the two eager young men that they could carry their bags with them as he gave them a brief tour of the small camp on the way to their barracks. The three men walked through the beautiful Midway Gardens, which was dotted with makeshift white tent structures, the canvas edges flapping in the wind. The trio approached the Washington Park Refectory, which was being used as the Mess Hall where participants in Camp Scott's training programme took their meals. The building, which had been designed by World's Columbian Exposition Head of Works and Head of Construction, architect and designer Daniel Burnham, served as a community dining location that could be rented out, surrounded by the natural beauty of Washington Park and the nearby Midway Plaisance. Sticking their heads in, the two young men marvelled at the remarkable cafeteria. With his keen artist's eye, Walter especially noticed the beautiful statuary on either side of the hall, as well as the way the sunlight shone through the lightly pigmented glass windows, illuminating the entire room in a kaleidoscope of colour. Stepping back into the bright sunlight, the officer then guided the boys past various recreation areas, framed by tall pillars and covered seating areas from which the enlisted men could enjoy the sights of Washington Park to the west and the Midway Plaisance to the east.

After a brief overview of the grounds, the three approached a large brick structure that housed the barracks. As they entered the lobby, the officer explained to Walter and Russell that they would be making this building their home for the next six weeks, along with approximately 500 other men during their training programme. All the features and amenities of the building thrilled Walter: the barracks include large showers, an expansive library with books covering topics from military subjects to automotive engineering to pieces of fiction, as well as smoking and recreation rooms. The final room the two young men were shown was the sleeping quarters, a large area where dozens of the American Red Cross drivers and mechanics would sleep. The officer led them to their cots; as he set his small bag on his new bed, Walter was thrilled to see that each enlisted man was provided with woollen blankets, a pillow, and a comfortable sleeping arrangement.

Throughout the remainder of the day, Walter and Russell sat with the officer back in the headquarters building, as he explained to the boys what their course of training would be. Those training as American Red Cross mechanics typically went through the programme over the course of a month, but due to the large number of trainees and the limited availability of places in each class, the trend of completing the programme was closer to six weeks. The training itself consisted of learning the different structures and functions of various vehicles used on the war front. Classes were taught by experienced mechanics from area automotive garages and those employed by Chicago's Yellow Cab Company. Guest lecturers from various American and Chicago automotive corporations also regularly visited the camp to give talks on important car parts and repair processes, including bearings, lubricants, carburettors, and tyre repair.

After the initial training, the men visited the workshop attached to the barracks, as well as area automotive garages, where they had experience taking apart and rebuilding various vehicles over the course of a sixteen-lesson class. It was here that Walter would learn the way an engine functioned, how to correctly time motor valves, how to adjust a carburettor, how to wire an ignition system, and how to change a car's oil and refill its cooling system. Once they were given a cursory overview of the process of automotive repair in the barrack's workshop, the newly-trained mechanics would be sent to area automotive garages, where they would be trained by, and work alongside, professionals repairing customers' vehicles from around the city.

Following mastery of automotive repair, the American Red Cross men would be trained in driving vehicles that they would use during their service in Europe. While this training began on regular roads around Camp Scott to ensure that the recruits had a handle on how to properly manoeuvre the vehicles, they were soon brought to a driving course approximately 4 miles away from the camp, which had been set up like a mini 'No Man's Land'. This special course, which was meant to mimic the battlefields of Europe, was complete with trenches, shell holes, craters, and piles of debris in order to ensure the ambulance drivers really could drive their vehicles through war-torn areas. The final test, which would determine whether or not an American Red Cross man was ready to be deployed to the European Front, was mastery of driving through Chicago's 'No Man's Land' at night. For those who became arrogant in their final driving test, they were introduced to Maude, a Ford truck that had been damaged, taken apart, and repaired dozens of times during the A.R.C.'s testing of potential ambulance drivers in the fake 'No Man's Land'. This ancient vehicle provided numerous challenges for the self-confident youths, breaking down as many as three times per run, leading to the expectation that those being tested not only drive flawlessly, but also repair the truck, all in the darkness of the Illinois night.

Throughout the entire training on driving and automotive repair, Walter and Russell would also be going through extensive training and drilling in military discipline. While not officially part of the American armed forces, each man who passed through Camp Scott was well-versed in how a military man should act, as well as different troop formations and manoeuvres. In the American Red Cross, there was also a similar hierarchy to that of the Army or Navy, as well as a rank equivalent to the branches of the military. Each man who completed the American Red Cross training at Camp Scott held the status of private in the Army upon arrival in Europe, and those who took over individual ambulances achieved the rank of lieutenant. This meant that while serving as a part of the medical service, they weren't seen as outsiders by the American military establishment, but rather as equals, and in some cases, superiors.

"We should probably discuss compensation," the officer explained with a smirk on his face. "While there are 70,000 Red Cross drivers working on the fronts in Europe, only those who successfully complete training here at Camp Scott will receive pay for their work. During your time here, you will be provided $20 a month, as well as necessities like food and board. Once you embark, your pay will increase to $40 a month including necessities. You will also receive a paid-up insurance policy of $1,000."

"Looks like we picked the right place to train then," Russell stated, eliciting a nod from Walter.

Several weeks later, as his training at Camp Scott began to come to a close, he realised he still needed to submit his passport application, giving him permission to be deployed overseas for relief work with the American Red Cross. Walter began by filling out the application himself, using one of the typewriters available to trainees at the American Red Cross camp. On the first page, Walter listed details about his origin, including when and where he was born, as well as information about his parents' citizenship, and his current home address and place of employment. At the bottom of the application, he read the short paragraph to which he was to agree as his Oath of Allegiance to the United States and signed his name.

In order for his application to be processed, he was required to supply two letters of recommendation: one from someone who could attest to his character and another from a parent giving permission for him to serve as a minor. Walter convinced one of the engineers he had recently met on his job at Chicago's elevated railway, George H. Peirce, to vouch for him, and on 26 October, the two men went together to the clerk of the U.S. District Court's office in downtown Chicago for Peirce to sign his statement, and swear an oath that his statement was truthful and accurate. However, Walter still needed to formulate a plan to win his parents' favour in allowing him to have an American passport as a serviceman. Even though he was living at Camp Scott during his training, he was still able to move about the city, including paying the occasional visit to his family at the house on Ogden Avenue.

Emboldened by his accomplishment in securing one reference and motivated by his desire to join his countrymen in this great war,

Walter decided to make his move in convincing his parents to sign off on his passport application the same evening he had received Peirce's endorsement. Upon arriving home, Walter found Flora working in the kitchen. This distraction was the perfect opportunity to bring up the passport application.

"Mother, I applied today to serve overseas for the American Red Cross. I was wondering if you could write out a permission thing for me since I'm under 17."

Without looking up from her work, Flora responded: "We will discuss this with your father later this evening."

As the evening progressed and the Disney family was spending time together, Flora could tell that Walter was apprehensive about bringing the topic up with his father. Deciding to help him, she broached the subject herself.

"Elias, Walter has something he would like to talk to us about." Elias looked at his son. As Walter began to explain his desire to enlist as an ambulance driver in Europe for the American Red Cross, he could tell that his father was becoming frustrated.

"I don't want my grandchildren asking me someday, 'Why weren't you in the war? Were you a slacker?'" he explained, hoping that this last summary would convince his father of his desire.

"I won't give you permission," Elias stated, standing up to walk out of the room.

"Elias," Flora tried to reason, "the boy is determined." The family patriarch spun around.

"I won't consent. It would be signing a death warrant for my son." Through his father's frustration, Walter detected pain and betrayal in his voice.

"Three of my sons have left our family in the dark of the night. I would rather sign off on this and know where he is than to have him run off somewhere like Herbert, Raymond, and Roy," Flora retorted, herself becoming indignant about her husband's stubbornness.

Elias's eyes widened in pain and a look of shock registered on his face as he processed his wife's stinging comment. Quickly gaining control, this emotion was replaced with deadpan emoting. "Well, you can sign it," he grumbled, turning around and stalking out of the room. "And you can sign it for me too, because I won't."

The room was silent for a moment. Walter looked over at his younger sister Ruth, who was sitting nearby listening to the conversation, and the two locked eyes. The young man could see empathy in her eyes, as she too was familiar with their father's lack of reasoning. The sounds of Elias moving around in a room elsewhere in the house could be heard, probably as he was attempting to distract himself and hold himself together in the light of this news. A few seconds later, their mother gave an almost inaudible sigh and looked at her son.

"Well, that's that." Flora reached for a small notebook nearby and a pen, and leaning over a small side table, she began to scribble out a note. A few seconds later, she ripped it out of the notebook and handed it to her son. "This should do," she explained. Replacing the notebook and pen in its place, she stood up and walked into the next room to calm down her fuming and pained husband.

Ruth stood up and came to sit by her older brother. Together, they read through the note. At the top, Flora had written in her scrolling cursive script the family address, proving that Walter did, in fact, reside where he had noted on his passport application. The body of the note was simple, stating that Walter E. Disney had been born on 5 December 1901 at the Tripp house in Chicago. At the bottom of the note, Flora had listed both her name and her husband's.

There was one more thing to do to complete the process of securing his employment as an American Red Cross worker. Feeling a touch of betrayal towards the mother who had lovingly stood up for him against his worried and strict father, Walter rose from his seat and crossed the room to the side table where his mother had written the note. While the permission was exactly what he needed to complete his application, his mother had identified him as only being 16, a year too young to participate in the war. Ruth watched from where the two had been sitting, but when she saw him pick up his mother's pen, she joined him at the side table, curious about what he was going to do. Very carefully, so as to make the writing appear natural, Walter changed the second one of his birth year to a zero to show that he had been born in 1900 instead of 1901. The work made the correction almost indiscernible. Replacing the pen exactly where his mother had left it so that she didn't suspect anything, Walter took the note to his room and placed it with the other papers that made up the passport application, intending to submit it to the District Clerk's office of Chicago. A few days later, the clerk notarised his application after Walter gave an oath as to the validity of the information and accepted it for processing.

After Maas submitted his passport application, the two began to craft the last piece of their plan: to remedy the fact that while their passports named them as Walter Disney and Russell Maas, their applications for employment with the American Red Cross identified them as Walter and Russell St. John. Acquiring new copies of the American Red Cross application, they filled them out identically to their first submissions, altering only their names. Having made an acquaintance with one of the office staff working at the American Red Cross headquarters in the Oakland neighbourhood, they submitted the new applications; the ones for the St. John brothers were replaced by the applications for Walter Disney and Russell Maas instead, officially granting them legitimate entry to participate in the First World War by way of the American Red Cross.

As Walter and Russell's training came to a close in mid-October 1918, Walter almost became a casualty of the war. Raging across every continent, stealing silently into civilian homes and military barracks at home and abroad, and storming into the trenches at the front, was an invisible enemy: the Spanish flu.

The Spanish Influenza, which was a strain of swine H1N1 virus, was easily transmitted between individuals by direct contact or by inhaling infected droplets that had been thrown into the air either by the sneeze or cough of an infected individual. The lay name for the virus was seemingly misleading: the ailment didn't originate in Spain, as the name suggested, but rather got its name because Spanish news coverage of the illness was most accurate during a world war when propaganda and news censorship abounded. Rather, the first cases of the flu emerged in Haskell County, Kansas in spring 1918 before it quickly began to spread across the United States. It was here that the Army burned more than 9,000 tons of pig manure monthly in an effort to dispose of it. However, a violent dust storm in March 1918 ripped through the Kansas prairie, blowing the dust and ashes from the manure through nearby Fort Riley. A few days later, the first reports of flu-like symptoms began to emerge. Those infected by the virus experienced a number of symptoms such as high fevers accompanied by delirium and hallucinations, coughing and sneezing, body aches, and headaches. Over the course of the week after the dust storm, more than 500 troops at Fort Riley reported flu-like symptoms, resulting in forty-six fatalities.

As the illness progressed throughout the human body, it quickly led to pneumonia, filling the infected person's lungs with fluid and, in severe cases, blood. While this new strain of the influenza had a mortality rate of 2.5 per cent, this was significantly higher than the 0.1 per cent of previous strains of the flu. By the time the global epidemic ended, the Spanish flu had infected around 500 million people, or one third of the world's population in 1918, killing approximately 50 million people, with 675,000 in the United States alone.

As America continued to mobilise for war, the American military establishment served as the primary vehicle through which migration occurred throughout 1918 and 1919, transferring recruits between military bases and camps, accepting draftees into training programmes, and deploying troops to the front lines in Europe. The movement of these men led to an increased transmission of the Spanish flu across the United States, and across the Atlantic into Europe. A couple of months after the virus emerged in Kansas, troops from Fort Riley were deployed to France, and the sickness quickly spread through the lines of the Western Front.

Over the course of a calendar year, the virus went through three waves. The first wave, which began with a few undocumented cases of flu-like symptoms in January, became a recognised viral problem in March and lasted until May 1918, taking the form of localised outbreaks, especially in the American Midwest and in and around military training camps. After a couple of months of dormancy, the virus emerged again in July until November, bringing the largest effects of the illness and leading to the most fatalities from complications. The final wave emerged in February 1919 and lasted only a few months, tapering off in April, concentrated primarily in northern European nations where American troops had been deployed to fight the Central Powers.

During the last few months of the First World War, thousands of deaths occurred as a result of the Spanish flu and its complications from pneumonia, continuing into the thousands even after the signing of the Armistice in mid-November. In 1918 alone, more than 2.4 million enlisted men and officers required hospital treatment as a result of the influenza epidemic with a mortality rate of 1.9 per cent, or approximately

47,300 men. Close contact between the American troops and natives of European nations and the enlisted Allies quickly led to a spread of the disease to other groups. Interestingly, African American troops had a lower incidence rate of catching the Spanish flu, which can likely be tied to the segregation of military barracks and units; however, those who did catch the illness had a higher mortality rate from complications from pneumonia than their white counterparts.

While easily communicable diseases were nothing new in the first decades of the twentieth century (doctors had been combating illnesses such as smallpox and the mumps), it was the groups impacted most by the Spanish flu that frightened Americans the greatest. Described by doctors and epidemiologists in recent research, the mortality rates of Americans as a result of the 1918 influenza epidemic can be described as a 'W-shaped curve': those most at risk of dying from the disease were very young children, young adults between the ages of 20 and 40, and those over the age of 65. However, there was a disproportionate number of low incidences of death for those between the ages of 5 and 20 and those from 40 to 65 years old. One theory for this is that these two groups had achieved partial immunity as a result of similar, yet less fatal, illnesses to which they had been exposed in the 1840s and in 1889. This didn't diminish the extreme danger that the Spanish influenza epidemic posed, however: in Philadelphia, on 10 October 1918 alone, the virus killed more than 750 people, while two weeks later, on 23 October, more than 850 people succumbed to the virus in New York City. The domestic death rate in America replicated high mortality rates from the Spanish flu around the world. Throughout the last week of October 1918, war-related injuries killed 2,700 Americans, but the Spanish flu caused the deaths of more than 21,000 Americans domestically. The virus was very quickly becoming a major threat to people worldwide.

To combat exposure to the flu virus, Americans took a number of precautions. Because it soon became obvious that the disease was initially spreading as a result of troops moving from camp to camp, not only exposing other enlisted men and civilians working alongside the military but also the surrounding urban areas, a halt was placed on transfers of individuals to or from infected camps, including Camp Devens in Massachusetts and Camp Dix in New Jersey. Mess halls throughout all military training bases began to implement strict cleaning measures of dishes and silverware, going as far as publishing literature instructing staff how to disinfect equipment and dishes. Once it became obvious to military medical personnel and leadership that the illness was spread by airborne droplet infection, overcrowded barracks and troop-ships were addressed, cutting occupancy down by approximately one-half. Overseas, one in three American troops caught influenza, while troop transport ships across the Atlantic became floating infirmaries as the hundreds of troops onboard either came down with the flu or were exposed to the virus. According to studies, in one Army unit, the mortality rate for soldiers with influenza was as high as 80 per cent.

Civilian groups also implemented measures to attempt to control the spread of the virus. While the masses lacked a true understanding of what caused the illness and how it was spread, it quickly became obvious, especially with the high incidence of mortality in usually strong young adults, that an attempt needed to be made to curb the spread. Social distancing measures were encouraged, with some communities going as far as advocating self-isolation and quarantine. City-wide bans on public gatherings forced thousands of businesses, stores, schools, and churches to shut down, leading to many of them going out of business. The government published literature to teach citizens safe coughing and sneezing techniques and handwashing protocols were enacted, while many were encouraged to wear masks, especially if they were experiencing flu-like symptoms or were particularly susceptible to the disease. It was at this time that using a handkerchief became popularised, as one was using it to protect oneself, rather than exposing others to potential airborne germs. Even kindergarten classes taught children the importance of using a handkerchief, conducting occasional drills in an effort to teach them proper sneezing and coughing etiquette. Local and state governments began to create emergency hospitals and sanitoriums to accommodate patients struck by the epidemic. A number of patent medicines, many of which were scams, were introduced to the market, touting that they would prevent one from catching the disease or heal those who had been infected. A few medicines were created which claimed to address symptoms of the Spanish flu; one in particular, Vicks VapoRub, which had been invented in Greensboro, North Carolina and had gone on the market in 1905, gained particular popularity for its ability to calm bronchial irritation that could cause virus-spreading coughs. While the United States Army attempted to create a vaccine to address the Spanish flu, it was ultimately unsuccessful in curbing the disease.

The Spanish influenza very quickly spread to the urban areas surrounding military training camps as troops and military personnel moved about the local cities and interacted with civilians. Lower income areas, especially those in large cities, were hit particularly hard by the virus, probably due to a number of factors including higher population density, limited access to healthcare facilities, and illiteracy, which made it difficult for the affected populations to be educated on methods of treating the illness and prevention of catching the virus from infected individuals. In fact, during one of the worst periods of the Spanish flu, from 29 September to 16 November 1918, there were 7,971 deaths from influenza and complications from pneumonia in central and south Chicago, which is where the majority of the city's population was living.

Chicago was lucky in that the primary training camp for wartime American Red Cross workers was located in the heart of the city. As the virus overcame the city's population, Camp Scott's trainees were dispatched to provide relief to those stricken by the illness. The health organisation quickly jumped into action, setting up emergency hospitals, transporting both the sick and the dead, providing meals to the convalescent, and even creating pamphlets and literature for the U.S. Public Health Service to educate Americans on how to care for themselves in the face of the epidemic. After the Armistice was signed in November 1918, the American Red Cross and its citizen supporters quickly converted their relief supplies; instead of their wartime military uniforms and surgical dressings for those injured at the Front, they created hospital gowns and gauze masks for the infected. However, while providing great relief services to their neighbours, their work was also exposing the American Red Cross volunteers to the virus due to its high likelihood of contagion.

As enlisted men from Chicago's various military bases moved about the city and interacted with its citizens, they brought the illness back to their camps, where it quickly spread amongst the troops and volunteers. The Great Lakes Naval Station, Camp Scott, and the University of Chicago's Student Army Training Corps were all heavily impacted by the Spanish flu, primarily due to the fact that trainees lived in close quarters and the camps were often overpopulated. In October, influenza broke out at the University of Chicago, hitting the Student Army Training Corps particularly hard. The Corps served as a programme at the university to train young men how to be effective officers in the Army, allowing them to be concurrently enrolled in their college classes, as well as on an officer training programme. Rather than living in dormitories, however, these young men were accommodated in military-style barracks, often in close quarters with each other, making them more susceptible to spreading and catching the virus. Section B of the Corps was particularly hard hit, mainly because of a lack of isolation efforts for the infected: out of 234 men living in Section B, ninety-two were infected by the disease within a single week.

The University of Chicago and its Student Army Training Corps was located on the north side of the Midway Plaisance, only a few minutes' walk from Camp Scott, where young Walter Disney was stationed. The American Red Cross work assisting the city's sick, as well as official interactions between the personnel of Camp Scott and the university's training corps, spread the disease between them, while the close quarters shared by the American Red Cross workers at Camp Scott quickly caused influenza to spread through the camp. As a camp used primarily to train members of the American Red Cross Ambulance and Motor Corps, Camp Scott didn't have extensive medical supplies or facilities. Consequently, as volunteers and workers began to fall ill, they were removed from common barracks and placed in white canvas tents, where they stayed with others who had contracted the virus. If one of the infected got too sick, they were driven by their colleagues in an American Red Cross ambulance to a nearby hospital for care, many of which were already overwhelmed with patients suffering from the Spanish flu or the subsequent pneumonia.

At first, Walter's symptoms were minor: a low-grade fever and a sore throat. Over the next couple of days, his symptoms worsened as his fever increased, leading to body aches, chills, low appetite, and delirium. A few times each day, American Red Cross workers carrying stretchers visited their sick colleagues, going from tent to tent to check on them. On one particular afternoon, after stopping by Walter's tent, it became obvious that he was too ill to remain at Camp Scott and was in need of medical attention.

"Kid," one of the camp medics asked as he ducked into Walter's tent. "Do you live in Chicago?" Walter could only answer an affirmative with a croak.

"We're gonna take you home," the medic explained. "You've got a better chance there than you do at the hospitals. If we take you there, you might not come out alive." The medic waved over his shoulder, and another medic entered the tent. Squatting down, the two men helped Walter onto the canvas stretcher and slid him out of the tent into the back of an ambulance waiting nearby.

The next few days spent at the Disney home on Ogden Avenue were marred by a series of fever-induced hallucinations and long periods of sleep. Flora Disney cared for her youngest son, accompanied by Ruth, who worried about her brother. Flora even called a local doctor to the house, who administered quinine to Walter, a medicine typically given to patients fighting malaria. Finally, his fever broke; it would still be a few weeks, however, before his strength returned sufficiently and he could return to Camp Scott. Caring for her son came at a cost: Flora soon caught the Spanish flu, followed shortly by Ruth. However, she soldiered through the illness to continue providing care for her two youngest children, nursing them back to health in the midst of her own illness. Walter was one of the lucky ones: he soon learned that two of his friends from Camp Scott had been taken to the hospital the same day he was sent home with symptoms of the Spanish flu; true to the medic's word, neither of them left the hospital alive.

Word of his friends' deaths wasn't the only disappointment Walter Disney experienced as he lay in his convalescent bed at his parents' home. On 3 November, Walter's company from Camp Scott, including Russell Maas, left Chicago for the battlefields of Europe, where they would aid the American Expeditionary Forces (A.E.F.) and the Allies on the front lines in France.

Adamant not to miss out on his chance to serve his country, Walter, still weakened from the effects of Spanish influenza, left the Disney home and returned to Camp Scott the next day, 4 November. However, because his unit had shipped out, he was assigned to Company C of the Personnel, Automotive, and Mechanical section of the American Red Cross Motor Corps. This required a transfer from Camp Scott to Camp King, located at South Beach in Greenwich, Connecticut.

Walter and the other American Red Cross servicemen transferred from Camp Scott were billeted in Ye Olde Greenwich Inn, a 100-year-old beach resort that was left vacant during the winter months and had been commandeered for use by the American Red Cross after the U.S. became involved in the war.

The young Walter Disney wasn't happy that he had been left behind by his unit and had instead been sent to a new camp on America's East Coast: he spent his time waiting for deployment, moping about and sketching rather than interacting with his new colleagues. When other young men assigned to Company C went into nearby towns to flirt with local girls, Walter was standoffish, deciding to stay back and draw instead. On the rare occasions that he let himself have fun, he would receive demerits and be assigned to guard duty at the camp entrance as punishment.

Unfortunately, Walter's attitude soured even more when, on 11 November 1918, the Allies and Central Powers signed the armistice, which ceased the fighting on the battlefields of Europe. The end of aggression meant that the United States would begin to demilitarise, as well as bring home the troops and auxiliary organisations, such as couriers and medical services, that provided battlefield support. The evening of 11 November was especially sombre in the mess hall: the usual chatting and laughing was absent, replaced instead by a low murmur of whispers as none of the American Red Cross workers wanted to disturb the others who were obviously disappointed in missing out on deployment. With nothing else to do after dinner, many of the servicemen slowly trudged to bed, expecting to hear when they would be discharged the next day.

At 3 am the next morning, however, pounding came at the doors of the resort rooms as an officer yelled from the hallway.

"Up, everybody! Up!" came the call.

One of Walter's room-mates dragged himself out of bed to the door, cracking it open. Doors up and down the hallway were opening as dozens of young men were pulling on shirts and rubbing their eyes. One of the other drivers came to the door and spoke through the crack.

"Fifty guys going to France!" he called into the room.

Walter's room-mate left the door and rushed to his bedside, shaking him awake. "Come on, Diz. Fifty guys going to France!"

"*I* won't be going," Walter grunted, rolling over in bed and pulling the blanket over his head.

Down in the mess hall, most of the American Red Cross workers gathered, sitting at the tables. The silence that reigned the evening before at dinner was replaced with a new buzz of energy, excited chatter from young men who hoped to travel overseas in the days following the end of the First World War. Over the course of the next hour, fifty names were called out. After each name, a chorus of disappointed groans was overshadowed by a single cheer of excitement by the young man whose name had been chosen.

At the end of the meeting, the American Red Cross workers whose names weren't called went back to their rooms, hoping to get a few more hours of sleep before they needed to get up and pack before heading home. Walter Disney's door slammed open, however, as his room-mate sprinted into the room, practically jumping onto his bed.

"Get up, Diz!" he yelled. A few other young men joined the room-mate, pulling Walter out of his bed.

"You lucky son of a bitch!" one yelled. "They called fifty names and yours was the last one called!"

"I'm going to France?" Walter asked, a smile breaking across his half-asleep face.

"You're going to France!"

Over the course of the next hour, an exhausted Walter Disney gathered his things and put on his American Red Cross uniform. The excited young man and forty-nine of his colleagues arrived at a train station a few minutes after leaving Camp King, boarding a train for Hoboken, New Jersey. The sound of the wheels on the rails lulled the young man to sleep; those around him could have sworn that a small smile played across his face who, after sixteen years, finally felt like he was going off to do something that would make a difference.

Chapter Thirteen

The American Red Cross

While it initially remained neutral in the conflict that raged across Europe, the United States supported the Allied nations by providing medical relief and mobility services through various volunteer organisations. One such group, the American Field Service, arrived in Europe as early as 1915, operating sixty ambulances to transport the wounded and dying to field hospitals behind the front. Over the course of the next few years, more volunteer relief organisations would arrive in Europe to support the American Field Service in caring for Allied wounded, such as the American Red Cross, the Knights of Columbus and the Young Men's Christian Association.

As soon as the aggressors declared war against each other in late summer 1914, the American Red Cross began ramping up to provide essential support to all wartime belligerents, including the Germans and the Austro-Hungarians. American Red Cross director Henry P. Davidson believed that only through providing medical relief would the world become at peace once again: "[O]ur job in the American Red Cross," he explained, "is to bind up the wounds of a bleeding world…[and] succour wounded nations." As a result of this belief, on 12 September 1914, a ship called *The Red Cross*, nicknamed 'The Mercy Ship', left New York City for the war-ravaged and bloodied battlefields of Europe, carrying 170 surgeons and nurses organised into eleven units that would provide relief to each of the aggressor nations fighting in the war.

Over the course of the next thirteen months, the American Red Cross provided medical relief to Europe, spanning from Britain to Serbia. In October 1915, however, medical teams were withdrawn from European battlefields: British leadership was fearful that the medical supplies used by the American Red Cross could fall into the hands of the Central Powers and be hoarded as an alternative tactic of attack against its enemies. Instead, the relief organisation began to provide support to the 130 other groups that provided relief services to the aggressors across the Continent.

In 1917, the United States formally entered the war on the side of the Allied Powers, allowing it to provide additional services through the U.S. Army Ambulance Service, a branch of the United States Army Medical Department. This was much better equipped than the volunteer organisations due to funding from the U.S. Army and the American federal government. Employing more than 350,000, the Ambulance Service included more than 21,000 nurses and 31,000 physicians, equivalent to 24 per cent of all doctors in the United States.

The medical branch of the U.S. Army utilised forty-six ambulances manufactured by American automotive companies including Ford and General Motors, and were modified to handle the difficult wartime conditions of the European battlefields. A favourite vehicle used by the Ambulance Service was Ford's Model T, which, according to a report filed by the U.S. Army Medical Department in 1925, was easily able to navigate the high-grade roads of Western Europe and was light enough to be lifted by three or four troops should the vehicle get stuck in a shell hole on the battlefield.

The United States Army Medical Department also established 152 base hospitals and more than 100 camp hospitals intended to treat both American and Allied soldiers wounded on the Western Front. In order to address the high number of patients arriving at the hospitals, as well as providing care for those stricken by illnesses such as the Spanish flu, the medical service began to triage patients upon arrival, designating them as either requiring immediate care, providing comfort to those expected not to survive their injuries, or requiring services that could be delayed a few days if necessary. In fact, it quickly became the official policy of the U.S. Army Medical Department to perform as few surgeries as necessary on those needing delayed care at the field hospitals in order to save as many beds and resources as possible for those requiring immediate or end-of-life care. Instead, those with battlefield injuries or illnesses not requiring urgent treatment were loaded onto medical trains and transported to evacuation hospitals near Paris or other areas away from the front.

The U.S. Army Medical Department and its various branches, such as the Army Ambulance Service and the Sanitation Service, quickly became overwhelmed in providing relief not only to American troops but to Allied troops as well. Within the first month of American involvement, President Woodrow Wilson requested that the American Red Cross begin mobilising and fundraising for its war efforts. By August, the American Red Cross had put together an official policy regarding its involvement on the battlefields across the Atlantic: in regard to providing medical assistance to the wounded, the neutrality of the American Red Cross ended at the same time as official American neutrality in February 1917. However, they did explain that when they came across a wounded soldier lying on the battlefield, they "would not recognize the ethnicity of the wounded," providing a loophole for the American Red Cross to provide healthcare to all, ally and enemy alike. The relief organisation not only promised to provide aid and assistance to civilian populations, but also agreed to partner with other groups providing aid to the war-torn nations, including the Y.M.C.A, Jewish Welfare Board, the Society of Friends, and the Salvation Army. In total, during the time that the American Red Cross supported the Allies during the First World War, more than 91,000 were treated in the makeshift hospitals in France alone.

Members of the American Red Cross, the U.S. Army Medical Department, and other volunteer organisations that participated in providing relief during the war weren't immune from danger. Ambulance drivers and medical personnel, who provided support to troops on the front lines, were constantly at risk and were so close to the fighting that they were required to wear earplugs to protect their eardrums and goggles to prevent gunpowder and dust from getting into their eyes. Some injuries of those in the trenches were so severe that surgery and procedures were conducted in the back of the vehicles only metres from the battle, shells exploding all around. In other cases, as ambulances carried the wounded, fleeing from the danger of warfare, they dodged explosions, bounced through shell holes, and were riddled with bullet holes. As a result of this violence, approximately 300 American Red Cross nurses and more than 120 ambulance drivers were killed, while hundreds more were injured. Some volunteers were recognised for their bravery, continuing to provide essential care to their wounded after being injured themselves: author Ernest Hemingway, whose leg was filled with shrapnel after an explosion, dragged an injured soldier out of harm's way while providing aid in Italy. The foreign governments of Western and Central Europe recognised the value of American medical staff and ambulance drivers; while the French government awarded the Croix de Guerre to the most heroic members of the American medical service, the Italian government decorated *all*

American ambulance drivers for their role in providing aid and relief to civilians and soldiers alike.

The United States government and the U.S. War Department also recognised the importance of troop and civilian morale during the war. General John J. Pershing, commander of the American Expeditionary Forces on the Western Front, understood the importance of locals' morale when he ordered Major Grayson M.P. Murphy, European Commissioner of the American Red Cross, that it was necessary for the relief organisation to "buck up the French…[as] the value of the service [to Americans and foreign governments] is beyond computation…[I]f they are not taken care of nobody can tell what will happen to us." The American Red Cross helped local populations by rebuilding homes destroyed by the war, providing seed to restore farmers' destroyed crops, building and operating orphanages for children whose parents were killed in the conflict, and creating convalescent homes for those recuperating from war-related injuries or illnesses like the Spanish influenza epidemic. French general Marshal Philippe Pétain later explained that "nothing has contributed more to the morale of my soldiers…[than] the American Red Cross in France."

In addition to providing medical care, relief, and aid to the sick and wounded, and relief and work to local civilians, the American Red Cross, partnering with the various relief organisations, was expected to 'provide recreational, educational, and religious activities for servicemen'. This would primarily be carried out by the American Red Cross Canteen Service, which operated 130 canteens inside military camps and American Red Cross hospitals and at train stations along important lines throughout France. These canteens featured a number of services that were critical to the care and morale of American troops serving overseas, including dormitories, restaurants serving free or reduced-price meals, lounging and recreation rooms, baths, barber shops, and even theatres showing films.

The American Red Cross also provided services for Americans at home during the time of war. Thousands were recruited as emergency American Red Cross nurses, aids, and helpers to provide care to the unprecedented number of victims struck by the Spanish influenza epidemic. The American Red Cross Motor Service was established in February 1918, using 12,000 volunteers to transport the sick, as well as wounded servicemen that had arrived home in the United States, to evacuation hospitals situated on American Red Cross and military bases. New organisations were sponsored by the American Red Cross to provide services for the disadvantaged, such as occupational training programmes for the blind, an institute for those who were crippled and disabled during the war, and a Sanitation Service, which ensured clean and sanitary conditions in large cities, as well as areas plagued by the Spanish flu. The American Red Cross also provided help to families of American servicemen overseas, such as mortgage assistance, writing letters to families on behalf of injured and sick soldiers, and even investigating the fates of servicemen who were missing or killed in action. On some occasions, the American Red Cross even took photographs of grave markers for soldiers who had been killed and buried overseas so that families had closure.

The relationship between American civilians and the American Red Cross didn't just favour those at home; instead, it was mutually beneficial. While fundraising drives helped to provide much-needed capital for the organisation, civilians also provided physical resources to support the hospitals and wounded. For example, American women sewed and knitted more than 23 million items of clothes, 300 million bandages, and 14 million pieces of hospital supplies such as hospital gowns and garments. They even supported the American Red Cross by sewing 1.4 million masks to help alleviate the Spanish influenza epidemic. In some cities, like Chicago, where war hysteria was strongest, hundreds of sewing circles each produced thousands of garments.

After the Armistice, as American servicemen were sent home and relief organisations were decommissioned, the American Red Cross found itself continuing to be of importance in the process of rebuilding a war-torn continent. Divisions were dispatched to dozens of countries to assist the victims of war, such as providing milk and meals to orphaned children in Czechoslovakia; caring for those stricken by the typhus epidemic in Poland and the Baltics where hospitals had been destroyed; operating relief stations and dispensaries in southeastern Europe; and even helping to reunify refugee families in Russia. Throughout France, the organisation assisted more than 1.7 million refugees, providing food and clothing, rebuilding homes, and offering jobs and medical care. These services were continued until the various governments were able to re-establish their own medical infrastructures, at which point workers and resources would be reallocated to other nations, or volunteers were sent back to

America. After the Russian Revolution and the rise of the Bolsheviks, leadership of the American Red Cross, with the support of the United States government, decided to withdraw their services from Russia, afraid the ideas of the communists would be spread to the capitalist nations of western Europe and America. By 1922, services of the American Red Cross had begun to be withdrawn, with the last volunteers arriving back in the United States a year later.

As a whole, providing assistance to the victims of war, warriors and civilians alike, was an essential and honourable contribution in the years during and after the First World War. Henry Pomeroy Davison, Chairman of the War Council of the American Red Cross and the founder of the League of Red Cross Societies, was absolutely right in his assertion that "A contribution to the Red Cross [was] a contribution toward victory." Without the support of the American Red Cross, or the American people who in turn supported the voluntary relief organisation itself, Allied victory in Europe wouldn't likely have been guaranteed.

Chapter Fourteen

France

After a quick train ride from Camp King, Walter Disney and his forty-nine Red Cross colleagues arrived in Hoboken, New Jersey, where the SS *Vauban* sat in the city's port of embarkation. The steam-powered ship was propelled by three screws, which sat below the water and originally launched in 1913 as a passenger, cargo and mail vessel that travelled across the Atlantic. The ship likely amazed the young man from the American Midwest as it was rather large; at peak capacity, the *Vauban* carried 610 passengers and 250 crew. During the war, the steamship had been used by the U.S. Army, as well as to transport passengers from South America; it had recently arrived in Hoboken after travelling from Buenos Aires on a passenger trip.

The American Red Cross men walked up the gangplank onto the deck of the ship, the sound of water sloshing below as the small waves gently rocked the boat. The young men, carrying their rucksacks, were shown to their bunkroom, deep in the belly of the ship. The *Vauban* would not only be carrying the relief workers across the Atlantic; the ship would also be transporting paying passengers to Europe, as well as tons of beef that had been loaded in Argentina prior to its arrival in New Jersey. As a result, the crew of the ship had to be creative when finding somewhere for the American Red Cross workers to sleep. Consequently, a series of bunks had been erected inside one of the cargo holds. Walter was assigned to a bunk that sat above a hatch. When his innate curiosity caused him to ask what was below, he was told that the small door led into the ship's magazine, and while the war was officially over, the ship continued to carry explosives and powder as a precautionary measure. The chance of being at the epicentre of a potential ground zero should the explosives detonate only added to the excitement that Walter likely felt at this new adventure.

Over the course of the next twelve days, the ship made its way across the choppy Atlantic. Near the end of November, the coast of France came into view. As the SS *Vauban* approached the continent, Walter stood at the railing on the ship's deck and watched as the cities beyond the rocky beaches seemed to float by. Upon entering the English Channel, the ship slowed down as it began to navigate waters made treacherous by the war. A loud voice called from behind him; looking over his shoulder, he found that a crewman had climbed into one of the ship's temporary guns and was helping the ship's pilot to navigate amongst the wreckages of ships sunk by the aggressors. The sound of smaller boat engines rose over the din of the waves against the large ship's hull, as two small fishing trawlers came alongside and then passed the *Vauban*. The crews of the small boats let down their netting from long boom arms that hung from the sides of the boats. Walter soon realised that these craft were makeshift minesweepers, ensuring that no explosive mines were in the way of the transport ship sailing through the English Channel.

With its nose pointed toward the Cotentin Peninsula, the *Vauban* slowed even more. Large buoys floated in a line across the mouth of Cherbourg Harbour. The boat plied through a narrow gap in the buoys, and as one was swept against the hull of the ship, the young American noticed that netting was strung between them, which he later learned was used to prevent German U-boats from sneaking into Cherbourg Harbour and attacking the ships stationed there.

After twelve days at sea, Walter and his compatriots were ready to disembark onto dry land and get to work supporting the sick and wounded. However, Cherbourg wasn't their port of disembarkation. Instead, the ship anchored in the harbour for the next three days as the British government determined where best to deliver the meat being transported from Argentina. On 2 December, it was decided that the meat was destined for Le Havre, a few hours east. Walter's disappointment in being unable to get off the boat at Cherbourg was quickly forgotten as he began to observe the shells and skeletons of more sunken battleships, whose hulls stuck out of the water or were wrecked against the large rocks that littered the approach to the French beaches.

Finally, on 3 December, the SS *Vauban* docked at Le Havre, where the young men practically sprinted down the gangway to reach dry land. A representative from the French Army was waiting for the fifty American Red Cross men. Once everyone was settled on the dock, the Frenchman led the group into the city where they checked into the Hôtel Continental, a luxurious experience for the young man from the American Midwest. Walter was especially impressed by the view: the hotel was located on a boardwalk along the harbour, allowing for magnificent vistas of military ships, passenger and cargo steamers, and the ocean in the distance.

The young American Red Cross relief workers spent that afternoon and early evening exploring Le Havre, experiencing the culture and marvelling at the multitude of differences from America. Self-organised into small groups, they flitted from building to building, taking in the sights, sounds, smells, and tastes that the French city had to offer. While some enjoyed coffee and a pastry at a bistro, others found themselves dwarfed by the city's sixteenth-century churches. The young men were especially interested in the numerous French girls that lived in the area, attempting to strike up conversation, but mostly failing due to the language barrier.

There was one thing that the naïve young men found lacking at first glance, however: public restrooms. As the afternoon wore on, the urge to relieve themselves became unbearable. Some of them asked local civilians for directions, even going as far as asking the men behind the counters of the bistros and delis for directions. When the inability to communicate in French made the message impossible to convey, the young men embarrassingly resorted to charades to explain their request. The Americans were pointed toward a small stone kiosk sitting at the curb alongside the road where a row of men was standing, their backs to the public. Horrified, they quickly realised that this was the *'pissoir'* the civilians had been talking about when they asked for a restroom: an outdoor urinal where French men could relieve themselves as they went about their business in the city.

The young men quietly talked together, complaining that there was no screen to provide privacy and that the lack of modesty would make it difficult to relieve themselves. They were fascinated, and slightly jealous, by the men, young and old, who casually stepped up to the *pissoir*, went to the bathroom, and then walked away as though it was a normal daily experience.

"If someone else goes, I'll go," one of the American Red Cross workers said aloud to the group.

Puffing out his chest, one member of the group stepped forward. "Aw, hell. I've gotta go! I don't care who sees me." As his colleagues watched, he quickly stepped up to the *pissoir* and fumbled with his trousers. His shoulders visibly relaxed as he was finally able to relieve himself. After he finished, he turned around and walked back to the group, a smug smile plastered on his face. One by one, the others made their way to the *pissoir* until the entire group of young men was lined in a row, using this foreign restroom, the relief it provided outweighing their embarrassment.

The next day, after their first truly restful sleep in almost a month at the Hôtel Continental, the workers of the American Red Cross boarded a train for a ten-hour journey to Paris. Upon arrival, they were once again put up in one of the city's beautiful hotels for the evening. It was during this leg of the journey that evidence of the First World War became more obvious. Sandbags littered the city in an attempt to protect buildings, while many had glassless windows. Soldiers marched through the streets, moving between military bases or conducting patrols.

The next morning, the group loaded onto the back of flatbed trucks and were carried to the nearby small village of Saint-Cyr, located approximately 6 kilometres from Versailles, where a French military academy and Algerian soldier labour camp were located. The American Red Cross had rented two châteaux for the workers to sleep in. However, compared to the previous two nights staying in luxury hotels, the young men were less than thrilled with their new accommodation: the buildings were old and, with no heat, it made sleeping difficult in the French December weather. While the American Red Cross had supplied the men with cots and blankets, these weren't sufficient in the near-freezing temperatures. They resorted to creative solutions, wrapping themselves in newspapers to trap the heat.

On the morning of Walter's first full day in Saint-Cyr, he woke up shivering. As his eyes registered the vision of a cloud of steam emerging from his mouth and nostrils due to the cold air in the château, he remembered it was his birthday: he was finally of legal age to be serving in the American Red Cross. After spending the morning and afternoon getting settled and learning how they would be serving in Saint-Cyr, it was time for some relaxation. One of his American Red Cross colleagues, after learning it was his birthday, invited Walter to a nearby bistro to celebrate with a drink.

As they entered the bistro, Walter's eyes took a moment to adjust due to the darkened, deserted room. Suddenly, dozens of young men jumped out from behind the walls and from beneath the bar and tables.

"Happy birthday, Diz!" they yelled, followed by a rousing chorus of 'Happy Birthday'. As soon as the song was finished, a number of his friends came over to him, clapping him on the back or shoulder, and giving him warm wishes. Others went to the bar and began to order drinks. Someone brought Walter a grenadine, while others filled their glasses with cognac. Together, the American Red Cross boys enjoyed a few hours at the bistro, wandering out on occasion to return to camp, until only Walter and a few others were left.

"Happy birthday," they smiled at their friend as they walked out into the cold, leaving Walter alone in the bar. He turned back and smiled at the barkeeper, heading toward the door himself. The man behind the bar grunted at him, holding up a piece of paper and waving him back to the counter. Closing the door, Walter returned to the bar. Through a series of signs, charades, and pointed fingers, he eventually realised that the barkeeper expected Walter to pay for all the drinks he and his friends had ordered. He couldn't believe it – it was *his* birthday and he got caught with the bill! Pulling his money out of his pocket, he soon learned with discouragement that the tab cost every cent that he had brought with him to Europe. As he turned to walk out of the bar, the barkeeper grunted again and waved him back. Holding up the paper the tab was recorded on, he was even more discouraged to learn that he still owed money. He was able to communicate to the man that he didn't have any more money and would have to go back to the camp to get more.

Upon arriving back at the American Red Cross billets, Walter complained to his colleagues that he couldn't believe they had stuck him with the bill. He also explained that he was short of cash to pay the remainder of the money.

"Well, they gave you two pairs of shoes when you got your uniform, right?" one of the guys asked.

"Yeah," Walter responded, not quite sure how this question related to his problem.

"Just sell one of the pairs and use the money from that to pay off the bartender," the other guy explained. "You can probably get thirty francs for them." After asking around, Walter soon found someone in Saint-Cyr who was interested in purchasing his shoes, giving him enough money to pay off the bar tab.

A week later, Walter accompanied his fellow American Red Cross workers back to Paris for a special event: President Woodrow Wilson had arrived to attend the Peace Conference and was participating in a state parade on his way to Prince Murat's residence, where he would be staying for the next few months as the Treaty of Versailles was worked out between the Allies. As the motorcade carrying Wilson made its way down the Champs-Elysées, Walter and his friends realised they had arrived too late to the parade: thousands of American and French soldiers, relief workers, and French civilians had turned out to see the American president. One of the boys found a ladder and a number of the young men, including Walter, climbed into a tree overlooking the street in time to see their president roll by. The spectacle stirred pride in Walter's heart, reinforcing his choice to participate in the war effort: cheers of "Vive l'Amérique! Vive Wilson!" echoed through the city, creating a cacophonous din of excitement.

This day trip wasn't the last time Walter would spend time in Paris. A few days later, he received a transfer, leaving behind Saint-Cyr and arriving at Evacuation Hospital No. 5, located on the western outskirts of Paris. The American Red Cross established a total of thirty-seven evacuation hospitals in France, each of which had a capacity of 1,000 beds, but often cared for more patients than could be accommodated. These hospitals typically didn't provide essential medical services for the sick and wounded, but rather acted as middlemen, transporting those with non-critical injuries to hospitals in England and the United States for care. While sometimes located near the front, evacuation hospitals were more often found along major rail lines, making it easier to transport patients by medical train to other large cities or embarkation ports.

Working at an evacuation hospital certainly made the war real for the young Walter Disney. The base featured five Bessonneau tents in a line, standing side by side, each housing different departments of the hospital: admission, dressing, X-ray examination, pre-operative, and operation. Smaller tents were scattered around the area to provide accommodation for patients, administration offices, a canteen, and barracks for the American Red Cross workers. A nearby field served as parking for ambulances, cargo trucks, and a fleet of touring cars, which were used to run errands and transport workers, leadership, and visiting dignitaries. On the edge of the parking area, in a grassy field, was a large white canvas cross, fastened to the ground, with each arm measuring approximately 3 metres by 2 metres. This symbol was large enough for enemy planes flying overhead to see; a mutual agreement between the Allies and the Central Powers created the understanding that by marking hospitals, neither would attack the places where the sick and wounded were being treated.

Walter was not employed in helping those who had been wounded in battle at Evacuation Hospital No. 5, however. As a result of the Armistice, the U.S. Army and American Red Cross had begun to withdraw some forces, allowing for Europe to take charge of rebuilding its nations. Walter was therefore employed in helping to close the evacuation hospital. He took part in a number of odd jobs around the camp, including packing up medical supplies and helping to carry litters holding patients from the recovery tents to waiting medical trains for transport to nearby hospitals and other hospital camps. In fact, things were so busy over the couple of weeks Walter spent working at Evacuation Hospital No. 5 that he and the other 700 American Red Cross and medical workers worked right through Christmas, not having a break to celebrate the holiday until a week later on New Year's Day.

Once his services were no longer needed at the hospital, Walter was given a transfer to serve as a chauffeur for the American Red Cross Motor Pool in Paris. Featuring approximately 1,400 cars, the motor service was used to transport supplies for the United States armed forces; to provide food aid to the nearby civilian population living in areas destroyed and impoverished by war; to move wounded or sick soldiers from hospitals to trains, ships, or convalescent homes; and to provide transportation for American Red Cross workers, military officers, and the occasional VIP.

On one occasion in February 1919, Walter and another American Red Cross employee were assigned to transport beans and sugar to Soissons, located approximately 110 kilometres from Paris. After boarding the 5-ton truck, the two young men made their journey northeast past landscapes devastated by war. As the afternoon wore on, large wet snowflakes began to fall. As the truck began to wind its way into the higher elevation just southwest of Soissons, a bearing on the vehicle failed. At this point, the snow had become heavy and the wind began to blow, making it difficult to see outside. Walter, who was behind the wheel, decided to push on, hoping to make it to the delivery destination, where they could spend the night somewhere warm and dry, and hoping to employ his training from

Camp Scott in fixing the truck before heading back to Paris the next day. However, the condition of the truck continued to worsen, as a loud knocking began to drown out the sound of the whistling wind blowing past the truck's cab.

Approximately 10 minutes from Soissons, the connecting rod of the truck came loose, causing it to smash through the engine block, grinding the motor to a halt. Walter cursed loudly and coasted the truck a dozen metres before pulling it off to the side of the road. A short distance away was the railroad, a small watchman's shack alongside the line slightly identifiable through the snow by the yellow glow of light emitting from its windows.

The two relief workers bundled up their coats, pulling on their hats and woollen mittens, being sure to bring their small bag of emergency supplies with them, as they trudged through the shin-deep snow towards the watchman's shack. After taking a moment to warm up inside the 4-foot-square building, it was decided that the other American Red Cross worker would go for help; as the driver of the supply truck, it was Walter's responsibility should anything happen to it or the supplies in the back.

Walter's colleague, leaning into the wind and blowing snow, walked to the nearby train station, from where he would take a train back to Paris to inform the American Red Cross of the broken engine and get assistance in bringing the truck back to the motor pool's headquarters. In the meantime, Walter took off his coat and sat on a crate next to the watchman, who occasionally went into the cold to pull down the gates to prevent traffic from crossing the tracks when a train was coming. As the evening wore on, the young American Red Cross worker opened the emergency supplies, sharing a loaf of bread and some beef and cheese with the watchman in return for the railroad employee's gracious sharing of his space and heat, which emitted from a small stove in one corner.

After 48 hours of sitting with the guard, awaiting his colleague's return, Walter was beginning to lose patience; keeping watch over the truck was his responsibility so he hadn't slept in two days. While the blizzard had stopped, the snow remained, but he was determined to brave the frigid weather to go off for help himself. Over the course of the next hour, Walter pushed through snowdrifts on the way to Soissons. After enjoying a warm meal of French peas, bread, and a lamb chop at a local restaurant, he rented a room where he could get some rest before going back to check on his truck.

When he returned to the watchman's shack the next day, he was horrified to find that the truck was missing. The watchman was unable to provide Walter with any information other than explaining in his very broken English that someone had come to take the truck and driven south. Unable to blame anyone for this misfortune but himself due to the fact that the truck had been his responsibility, Walter went down to the train station from where his co-worker had departed and purchased a ticket back to Paris. As he sat in the waiting room, a wave of discouragement and worry swept over him. What would happen? Would he be charged for the value of the truck and cargo? Court-martialled? *Arrested?*

Upon arriving back at the American Red Cross headquarters in Paris, Walter soon learned that he was indeed up for a court martial for abandoning the truck as a result of 'dereliction of duty'. When the day of his case arrived, Walter stood before the American Red Cross leadership, admitting his guilt. One of the sergeants he had worked with at Evacuation Hospital No. 5 stood up and began to tell the story about what really happened.

When the other young man who had been in the truck with Walter left the watchman's shack the evening of the breakdown, he arrived in Paris too late to report the incident to the American Red Cross headquarters. Instead, he decided to fight the cold weather by visiting a local bar for a drink. He got so drunk that he slept off his intoxication and corresponding hangover over the course of the next two days. Finally, on the third day, he was feeling well enough to report the incident to the American Red Cross, who immediately sent a second truck to Soissons to retrieve the broken one, which was repaired and driven back to Paris before Walter arrived back at the watchman's shack later that morning.

"Don't forget," the sergeant finished, gesturing towards Walter, "that this boy sat in that shack, awake, for two days and two nights, keeping watch over his truck. Why punish him if you have not punished the other fellow?"

After a few moments of silent contemplation, it was decided that while Walter had abandoned his truck, it was really his colleague who was at fault. Walter was forgiven for the incident, while the other young man was court-martialled and sent home to the United States.

As a member of the Paris motor pool, Walter also performed the duty of taxi driver for various American Red Cross workers and leadership, as well as commanding officers of the American and French armed forces. While waiting for a job in the lobby of the Hôtel Régina, the motor pool's headquarters, Walter enjoyed chatting and playing poker with fellow American Red Cross drivers. During his time as a chauffeur, he was able to explore the city, noting a number of features of cultural interest including the old city walls, churches and cathedrals, gardens, and cultural icons such as the Eiffel Tower and Arc De Triomphe.

On 11 February 1919, Walter was transferred to the village of Neufchâteau, located approximately 300 kilometres east of Paris. Neufchâteau was the location of one of the American Red Cross headquarters in France, and it was there he was employed as a driver for the canteen and rest station that serviced the train station through which thousands of troops passed as the country was demilitarised.

The American Red Cross Bureau of Canteen Service was first established in France in September 1917, when the first American-operated canteen opened in a converted barracks at the Châlons-sur-Marne railroad depot. Serving the thousands of French and American troops that passed through the station on the way to the front, the canteen provided services such as haircuts and first aid care, sleeping accommodation and showers, and even supplied meals and hot beverages to soldiers stopping by for a break. The American Red Cross recognised how important the canteens were to the American and Allied war effort: in 1918 alone, expenditure on the canteen service totalled almost $900,000, almost as much as the hospitals operated by the American Red Cross, which had cost the organisation just over $1 million in the same year.

The success of this canteen led to the creation of hundreds more across France, situated not only along major rail lines, but also in evacuation hospitals, outside major cities, and at ports of embarkation. These rest stations were significant as they provided services such as recreation and entertainment lounges, technical libraries, and psychological care for troops and civilians alike. They were also locations for storing and providing resources to military leadership, as well as the auxiliary services that accompanied military divisions, such as materials for army chaplains and first aid supplies for divisional medics.

While all of these services helped to boost military and civilian morale alike, the most important thing offered by the American Red Cross canteens was the preparation and serving of meals. Through cooperation with local organisations, the American Red Cross was able to provide full meals, beverages included, for 75 centimes or less. On occasions that troops were lucky, their military divisions provided them with vouchers that could be used at the canteens, so they could have a meal free of cost. American Red Cross canteens didn't just provide cheaply-made meals, but prepared three-course meals for those who took advantage: visitors to the canteens' kitchens noticed that they were 'full of cauldrons and chopping blocks and meat and things,' and at busy times 'could possibly feed five hundred at a clip'. In the first year alone, the American Red Cross canteens provided between 2,000 and 4,000 meals each day, totalling almost 700,000 by January 1918, less than three months after the first canteen opened at Châlons-sur-Marne.

The canteen that Walter was transferred to at Neufchâteau was well known throughout France. However, it wasn't famous for the services it rendered or the food it provided. Rather, it was beloved due to its head cook and surrogate matron, Harriett Alice Howell. Howell had first arrived in France in June 1918, fulfilling a similar desire to Walter in serving her country in a way that would benefit it and its allies during the war. She volunteered with the American Red Cross as the United States armed forces had few opportunities available for women. Howell made sure that every soldier who visited her canteen was comfortable, relaxed, and had a full belly before he went on his way. In addition to the meals she prepared for the troops, Howell was well known for her fresh-baked doughnuts, producing 800 each day and personally delivering them to the troops at the front and to the wounded at area hospitals.

Walter quickly settled into life at the Neufchâteau canteen and the nearby Evacuation Hospital No. 102. His daily assignments as a driver for the canteen included transporting supplies for Howell or the hospital staff, taxiing American Red Cross employees to and from work, and even providing tours for visiting dignitaries, American Red Cross leadership, and military officers.

During his downtime, Walter would sit in the kitchen of the canteen, awaiting his next assignment. He became close friends with Howell and also took this time to hone his art skills, even applying for some artistic work back in the United States. He sent gag drawings making fun of the life of a soldier to a number of American newspapers and magazines, including *Life* and *Judge*, but received rejection letters from them all.

Instead, he decided to draw cartoons for friends back home, including his old school newspaper, *The McKinley Voice*, as well as a bound scrapbook full of illustrations that he sent to a lady friend in Chicago.

Desperate to make some money from his craft, he began doing some commissioned work for other workers around Evacuation Hospital No. 102. After he drew a *Croix de Guerre* on his American Red Cross jacket, other young men noticed it and were astounded at how realistic Disney's work was. They began to request that the budding artist draw the French medal on their jackets as well. Recognising Walter's talent, Howell commissioned him to create a few advertisement posters for the canteen, encouraging passing soldiers to try the hot chocolate and other delectable treats.

On a few occasions, when he practiced his craft for the sake of self-improvement, it created new opportunities. When out in the field or on an assignment, Walter often found himself without paper. It was during this time that he resorted to drawing on the canvas top of his ambulance truck, illustrating the side with an image of his American doughboy character. Liking how the side of the truck looked with the drawing, Walter decided to paint his footlocker, attempting to try his hand at a camouflage pattern. While he wasn't particularly pleased with how the camouflage turned out, another young man who stayed in Walter's barracks, who went by the nickname 'The Cracker', noticed his colleague's talents and saw the opportunity to make some money. While on a number of assignments through the French countryside, the enterprising young man began to collect German helmets that he found abandoned in fields and in trenches. After bringing them back to camp, he enlisted Walter in painting them to make them look old and worn from battle, even going as far as shooting bullet holes through them, painting fake blood and attaching hair to the holes to make them look like they had been worn by slain German soldiers. The Cracker then took his helmets to the nearby train station and showed them to the French and American troops passing through, who couldn't resist purchasing the 'rare souvenir' from the con artist. Walter always got a cut from The Cracker's sales for his part in decorating the helmets.

After a few weeks at the canteen, however, Walter had less time to engage in his artistic pursuits, as it was discovered that he had quite the potential as a tour guide for visiting dignitaries throughout Paris due to his explorations while stationed at Evacuation Hospital No. 5. As a result, his assignments at Evacuation Hospital No. 102 and the Neufchâteau canteen became more focused on chauffeur and tour guide work, rather than running errands. When Howell learned that her friend, General Pershing, would be sending his young son to visit her at the canteen, she decided to use Walter's skills in giving the boy a tour of the French countryside.

On 20 April 1919, Walter stood outside the canteen as a large car pulled up, driven by an Army sergeant. Opening the rear door so Warren Pershing could get out, Walter immediately noticed the boy's outfit: he was wearing a miniature uniform identical to his father's, complete with medals and stripes. When Walter offered to tour the boy in the fancy Army car he arrived in, Warren insisted that they take a canteen car, wanting the full experience of life and likely feeling the desire and fascination that all young boys have of riding in different types of vehicles. After loading the young Pershing, the sergeant accompanying him, and a couple of American Red Cross girls into the canteen car, Walter drove to Domrémy-la-Pucelle, the birthplace of Joan of Arc, approximately 11 kilometres north. After their brief sightseeing, the group found a field nearby and enjoyed a picnic of fried chicken, which was a special treat for the American Red Cross employees who were used to the canteen food at the evacuation hospital. After their meal, the group headed back to Neufchâteau, and Walter allowed young Warren to drive the car back, letting the boy steer while he pressed the pedals.

A few days later, Howell received a personal note from General Pershing who raved about the treatment his son was given by the driver of the canteen car, who was a fantastic tour guide. The hospital canteen leadership heard of this, giving Disney more assignments touring visiting dignitaries around the area. He often took visitors on rides east to Alsace and the Rhine River, which had become occupied by the British and French on 1 December 1918 after the conclusion of the war.

On one occasion, while touring a visiting lieutenant in the Alsace region, the young man was showing off the city of Strasbourg which had played a significant role in both the Franco-Prussian War of the nineteenth century and the First World War half a century later. He was surprised to find the buildings decorated with ribbons and red, white and blue bunting and cockades, while colourful banners and French flags flapped in the breeze, hanging from windows, flagpoles, and balconies.

The entire city, it seemed, had turned out and was standing along the curbs as a grand parade marched down the city's main thoroughfares. It took but a moment for Walter to realise that it was 14 July and the city was celebrating Bastille Day – the first time in fifty years.

Walter, like many other workers at the American Red Cross canteen, also utilised the help of German prisoners of war who were stationed at Evacuation Hospital No. 102. One of them, a mischievous prisoner named Rupert, had become the de facto leader of the group, and had a tendency for taking advantage of Walter's naivety. On one occasion, Rupert brought an empty wine bottle to Walter, explaining that Harriett Howell wanted him to go into town to get another bottle. While the young driver found it odd that the canteen's cook hadn't asked him to run the errand herself, he took the empty bottle and some money from Rupert to get new wine. When he returned to camp, Rupert was waiting to meet him and took the bottle from the young man, explaining he would take it to Howell himself. Later, when no one could find Rupert or any of the other German POWs, Walter discovered them in the shower room, heavily intoxicated from the bottle of wine. It was then that he realised that Howell hadn't wanted him to refill the wine – Rupert was tricking him all along.

The German's naughty streak wasn't always aimed at Walter, however. One afternoon, after Mrs Howell had asked Walter and Rupert to retrieve some wood for a fire, they ran across some French children, who recognised the man accompanying the American as an ex-German soldier. The children began to throw rocks at the two, hurling insults including the derogatory slang for a German, 'Boche'. Walter instructed Rupert to fill his own pockets with rocks, and on command, the two men began charging the schoolchildren, engaging in their own battle against the French locals.

Unfortunately, Walter's grand time at the Neufchâteau came to an end when, on 9 August 1919, the canteen was shut down and Harriett Alice Howell was sent home to America. With no more work at Evacuation Hospital No. 102, Walter was sent to Paris. Finding himself becoming very lonely and homesick, he applied for a discharge from the American Red Cross, which was finally granted in mid-August. While waiting to be sent back home to the United States, Walter witnessed the end of General John J. Pershing's service in Europe, when a ceremonial parade was held for him as he left the city before being sent home on 1 September.

During his time in Paris, Walter reconnected with Russell Maas. The two young men had much to catch up on and made a pact to travel down the Mississippi River like American literary character, Huckleberry Finn, when they returned to the United States. The two also decided to each purchase German Shepherd puppies, which would join them on their trip rafting down the river. When Maas received his discharge first, he packed up his supplies and left, taking Walter's puppy with him, promising to care for it until Walter could return and the two could make their trip.

After a month of waiting for his discharge, drama during a dock strike in Marseilles, a transfer to the coastal town of Nice, and some time enjoying the sights and experiences of Monte Carlo, the young Walter Disney finally boarded the SS *Canada*, embarking from Europe on 4 September 1919, finally arriving back in New York on 9 October, before heading home to Chicago two days later.

Walter's arrival home brought an abundance of disappointment. He soon learned that in his absence, Russell Maas had got married and was no longer interested in rafting down the Mississippi River with his friend.

"At least," Walter thought to himself, "I still have my puppy to keep me company." Unfortunately, he soon learned that his puppy had died on the journey home across the Atlantic while in Maas's care.

Walter was also disappointed by his parents' reaction to him arriving home. One of the first conversations he had with Elias was the elder Disney asking him what his plans were now that he was no longer employed with the American Red Cross.

"My boss at O-Zell, Mr Scrogin, has a job for you," Elias explained.

"Dad, I don't want to work at O-Zell," Walter explained.

"It's a good job, Walter. You'll make $25 a week."

"I don't want to work in a factory, Father. I want to be an artist."

Elias harrumphed, and recognising his own stubbornness in his youngest son, let the conversation drop. He had done everything that he could to instil morals in his children, so if they decided to engage in immoral and shiftless behaviour like creating art for a living, he decided he couldn't take responsibility.

Walter took some of the artwork he had drawn in France to *The Chicago Tribune* to apply for a position. After meeting once again with Carey Orr, he was disappointed to learn that there were no positions available.

He soon realised that he was unlikely to find the type of work he wanted in Chicago and that his father wasn't going to support his dream, so Walter decided to move back to Kansas City. After being discharged from the Navy in February 1919, Roy had returned to Missouri to his job at the First National Bank, and to Edna Francis, who had waited for him during his deployment. Walter's parents tried unsuccessfully to convince their youngest son not to move away to pursue his interest in an art career, and they helplessly watched him prepare to leave. After requesting the money that he had sent home to Flora for safekeeping while overseas, Walter kissed his mother and shook his father's hand before boarding a train and heading back to Kansas City.

Part VI

I want to be an artist

Kansas City, Missouri, 1919–1923

Chapter Fifteen

Advertising

As Walter stepped off the train and onto the platform at Kansas City's Union Station, he was met by Roy. Walter put his suitcase down to shake his brother's hand, finally looking forward to being with a member of the family who wanted him around and believed in his dreams. Picking up his luggage, Walter followed his older brother across the platform which stretched below the metal awnings and into Union Station.

While Walter had travelled from Union Station before when he joined the family in Chicago, he had been more focused on finding the appropriate platform for the train headed to Illinois rather than the beautiful storeyed building that would become so important to him over the next few years.

Kansas City's original Union Depot opened in 1878, serving the city's numerous railroads from the West Bottoms district, located just east of the Mississippi River. In 1903, a flood devastated the area, with waters rising as high as almost 2 metres, causing thousands of dollars of damage to the depot, which was one of the most important buildings contributing to the economic life of the city. When the waters finally receded, it was discovered that sediments carried by the flooding of the river had been deposited around the building's foundations and inside the building to be piled against the walls. It was quickly determined that as the city's importance continued through the expanding railroads, a new and larger depot needed to be built on a higher elevation away from the river to prevent such occurrences from happening again.

Representatives from the twelve railroads that passed through Kansas City met together and settled on a site a few miles away, south of downtown, and set to work searching for an architect to design the new structure. The new depot would take the name Union Station, signifying the united efforts of the dozen railroad companies in constructing and operating what would become the largest railroad station west of the Mississippi River. This new organisation became incorporated and was called the Kansas City Terminal Railway, specifically for the purpose of overseeing the construction of the new Union Station.

Over the next few years, a number of architects presented their ideas to the Kansas City Terminal Railway, but the contract was awarded to Jarvis Hunt, nephew of Richard Morris Hunt, who had designed many of the buildings at the 1893 World's Columbian Exposition of Chicago and New York's Metropolitan Museum of Art. While Hunt had experience in designing railway stations in the past – he had designed the 16th Street Station in Oakland, California and Joliet, Illinois' Union Station – his plans for the Kansas City station were unique enough to pique the interest of the railroad executives. Access to the station was gained through one of two grand entrances, which were set beneath three 12-metre tall arched windows. Tall marble columns stretched to the roofline, supporting the heavy roof that covered the structure. The entire building faced south, which at first glance seemed odd, as the central business district of Kansas City was actually north of the station. However, Hunt had two reasons for this. First, electric lighting, especially in large interior spaces, was in its infancy during the first few decades of the twentieth century. As a result, the large south-facing windows provided abundant natural light to those waiting in the station. Secondly, while downtown Kansas City was located to the north, Hunt recognised that the city was going through exponential growth, especially with the expansion of the railroads and the rumour of Kansas City being America's next site for a Federal Reserve bank. Thus, Hunt believed, and rightly so, that as the city expanded, his new Union Station would sit at the future centre of the city as its boundaries continued to expand southward.

As Hunt designed the building, he drew extensively on the City Beautiful movement advocated by *Kansas City Star* owner William Rockhill Nelson and employed by designers of the World's Columbian Exposition. Like his uncle and Nelson, Jarvis Hunt believed that by designing a grand beaux-arts style structure, Union Station would inspire the citizens of Kansas City to live a noble life, one which would instil civic order and pride in their city.

Construction of Union Station began in the autumn of 1910, utilising the day's newest methods and technology, including the rerouting and enclosing of OK Creek, the dynamiting of rocky hillsides to flatten the land for the building's footprint, and the use of concrete, steel and limestone to construct the station. More than 500 men worked on the station at any given time to construct the building, which covered more than 5 acres and had approximately 900 separate rooms.

When Union Station officially opened on 30 October 1914, nearly 100,000 people arranged themselves in front of the structure to welcome its first train before making their way into the Grand Hall. Kansas Citians stood within the cavernous room, marvelling at the 27-metre high ceilings, which were coffered and intricately painted, lit by three enormous crystal chandeliers. A semi-circular mahogany ticket desk protruded towards the centre of the Grand Hall, while small shops, shoe-shines, and restaurants lined the hall's outer wall. In fact, Fred Harvey, the nation's largest operator of restaurants along the railroad, was headquartered in Union Station, ensuring that all Fred Harvey restaurants throughout the United States provided consistent and quality meals at each of its locations, including its new restaurant sitting next door to the Santa Fe station in Marceline.

Passing beneath the 2-metre diameter, back-lit clock hanging from the ceiling, visitors to Union Station entered the North Waiting Room, a 100-metre-long hall which ran perpendicular to the Grand Hall. This room was filled with wooden benches, upon which travellers perched awaiting their train. Black signs hung next to a series of doors along the east and west walls of the room, listing the departure times of the scheduled trains, as well as the various cities each train would service. When the time came, passengers would walk through the doors and down a narrow staircase to one of eight train platforms collectively servicing sixteen individual tracks, which ran below the North Waiting Room.

As the United States slowly began to mobilise its resources and personnel with the outbreak of the First World War and ultimately entered the fray in 1917, Union Station quickly became a hub of action in Kansas City. The depot soon began offering services to travellers and railroad workers alike, including bookstores, grocers, a pharmacy, a barber shop, restaurants, and lounges servicing both men and women. The station was soon hailed as the third largest and busiest train depot in the United States, second only to Grand Central Station and Pennsylvania Station, both located in New York City. As troops began deploying across the North American continent as America became committed to the conflict, Union Station quickly became one of the busiest in the country; it serviced more than 79,000 trains in 1917 alone, including a record-breaking 271 trains in one day.

Thus, when Walter Disney arrived in Union Station in the autumn of 1919, he and Roy found themselves within a bustling depot where immigrants, soldiers returning from war, businessmen, and young families arrived and departed the city, took meals at Fred Harvey's, or attended meetings in one of the station's many rooms. Stepping out of the front doors and into the bright sunlight, Walter's eyes quickly adjusted, observing a smattering of buildings of the expanding city surrounding a tall, green hill directly across from Union Station. Together, the two brothers made their way to a nearby tram station, boarding a conveyance that took them to the neighbourhood in which they had lived before the war.

Walter had made arrangements to stay with the family of his brother Herbert, who had moved into the house owned by Elias and Flora on Bellefontaine. While he had a place to live, Walter needed work to support his expenses, and started looking for art jobs to pursue his dream of becoming a cartoonist.

Walter began by visiting *The Kansas City Star*, for whom he had delivered newspapers during his childhood. He figured that his experience with the paper would give him an edge over potential competition in becoming a part of the organisation's art department. He took a portfolio of the work he had done for *The McKinley Voice* and some of the pieces he had created while stationed in France. Unfortunately, he was told that there were no openings as an artist for the *Star*. Shortly after, however, he saw an advertisement in the paper that they were looking for a candidate as an office boy and his heart leapt: any position for the newspaper, however lowly, could eventually lead to a position in his dream job as a cartoonist.

The fact that Walter was still a minor and should probably still have been in high school could pose a problem in securing a job with the paper. Would they even be interested in someone with so little perceived experience? The memory of he and Russell Maas fooling the American Red Cross into believing they were older than they were came flooding back, so he began to hatch a plan to once again convince a hiring agent that he wasn't too young for a position. He remembered the comments his mother and sister had made when they saw him in uniform after returning from France, and donned his American Red Cross uniform, feeling that it made him look more grown up, mature, and experienced. Marching through the door and into the foyer of *The Kansas City Star*, the young man removed his uniform cap and walked up to the reception desk.

"I am here to apply for the position of office boy," he explained, lowering his voice a half-octave.

The man sitting behind the desk in the hiring office glanced up from the papers scattered across his desk and looked Walter over. His eyes lingered on the uniform with its American Red Cross patch and realistically drawn-on Croix de Guerre. The newspaper man looked back down at his papers.

"Too old," he muttered in a dismissive way without looking at Walter.

"But I'm only 17," Walter insisted.

"You wouldn't want this job anyway. It wouldn't pay enough to support your family." Walter was frustrated as he realised that the man still thought he was older than 17.

"Sir, I would like to work for the *Star*," he insisted.

Frustratedly, the man sat back from his desk and looked up from his papers. "What have you done for work?"

"I drove ambulances for the American Red Cross in France after the war." The man's face changed upon learning this information.

"Well, then you need to visit the transportation department. Give them your name, and when they have an opening for a position as a delivery driver, they'll contact you."

Walter was discouraged: he didn't want to deliver newspapers like he had for his father and it obviously hadn't done him any favours now. He was a creative and his passion was art – he didn't want to spend his life working with his hands in a blue-collar job like his father.

With the *Star* as a dead end, Walter decided to apply for a job in the art department of its competitor, *The Kansas City Journal*, this time in civilian clothes, not wanting to be mistaken for being older than he was due to his American Red Cross uniform. Once again, the answer was the same: no openings.

Walter was very disheartened. He was starting to wonder if his father had been right – that cartooning wouldn't be a feasible way for him to make a career. He found himself wandering the streets of Kansas City until he arrived at the front door of the First National Bank. If anyone could encourage him at this time from being in such low spirits, it would be Roy. Pausing outside the door, Walter was captivated by the soaring architecture of the building. Tall marble columns supported a grand flat roof stretching above a frieze and decorative guttae, all of which symbolised that the financial institution would stand the test of time, much like the Greek and Roman architecture the building's façade was modelled after. Would Roy *really* encourage him? Walter wondered. Roy was so successful, serving as a bookkeeper for one of Kansas City's leading financial institutions. He was so good at what he did that the bank had held his job when he went off to war.

Taking a deep breath, Walter decided to take a chance and heaved open the heavy wooden door of the bank. The grand design of the interior didn't make him feel any better about his situation. His shoes clicked on the tile floor, drawing the gazes of the tellers sitting behind the waist-high counter stretching around the lobby's perimeter, as well as the other patrons doing business. Tall columns stretched up to support the elegantly designed coffered ceiling, from which hung chandeliers, sunlight pouring in from the floor-to-ceiling windows causing the crystal fixtures to sparkle. A clock perched along the back wall ticked as the second hand circled its face, reminding Walter of the short time he had to make his career choice before it was too late and he was relegated to a life of manual labour like Elias.

A bank employee asked Walter how he could be served, and Walter asked if his brother was available. Moments later, Roy came to the teller's counter and waved him behind the counter, leading him to his desk. It turned out that Walter's worries were unfounded; Roy was completely supportive, assuring him that something would come along sooner than later.

One of Roy's colleagues, sitting at a nearby desk, overheard the brothers' conversation.

"You're into art and drawing?" the bank employee asked. "I have a couple of friends by the names Pesmen and Rubin. They own an advertising agency, and the other night they'd mentioned they were looking for an apprentice to join them." Walter got the address of the agency and thanked Roy's colleague, rushing to Pesmen-Rubin from the bank.

After Louis Pesmen met Walter in the lobby of his business, the young man realised he didn't have any pieces of artwork with him to prove he was qualified for a job. Walter's enthusiasm impressed Pesmen and he encouraged the boy to return the next day with some samples.

The following day, during another brief meeting with Pesmen, Walter showed off some of the work he had done overseas of his doughboy character, caricatures, and political cartoons that he had sent to *The McKinley Voice* and American humour magazines. Pesmen was impressed and asked Walter if he could start the following week, explaining that he wasn't sure what they could afford to pay him. Walter was excited about the opportunity, realising that a pay check wasn't essential, as he was living with Herbert for practically nothing and a job at Pesmen-Rubin would give him the experience necessary to make him attractive to the *Star*.

A few days later, when Walter sat down at his drawing board in his new position working for Pesmen and Rubin, he was given the assignment of designing an advertisement for farm equipment in a local Christmas catalogue. Towards the end of the week, as Bill Rubin was making his rounds, he stopped by Walter's station to survey his work. Walter looked up at his new boss, dismayed to see him with a slight frown and shaking his head. Walter's stomach dropped: he had worked so hard, finally securing an art job for himself, and management was already displeased with his work!

"I don't know," Rubin said to Walter, keeping his voice low so the other artists couldn't hear. "How about fifty a month?"

"Dollars?" Walter gasped. Rubin nodded. "That would be perfectly okay," Walter stuttered. In fact, it was better than okay: he had not expected to get paid so much. As Rubin walked away, he offered encouragement, patting Walter on the shoulder as he moved on to the next artist's station.

Walter could hardly focus on his work for the rest of the day. He couldn't wait to tell everyone important to him the great news of finally finding success in his new job. At last, when it was time to leave for the day, he quickly pulled on his jacket and practically ran to a nearby hotel where Uncle Robert and Aunt Margaret lived. Bursting into their room, Walter went to the bed, where he found Margaret propped up.

"Auntie! I got a job and they are paying me money to draw pictures!" he exclaimed.

"That's nice, Walter," his aunt mumbled between hacking coughs. An older woman now, her body was beset by pneumonia and she was unable to muster the strength to be excited for the nephew she had purchased art supplies for when he was a small boy in Marceline. Walter spent a few minutes talking to his favourite aunt but left disappointed that she hadn't shared in his excitement. She succumbed to her illness shortly afterwards, adding to Walter's disappointment that she, who had fostered his passion, hadn't lived to enjoy the fruits of her investment.

Over the next couple of months, Walter was assigned a number of advertising and layout jobs at Pesmen-Rubin including designing letterheads and illustrations for advertisements for area businesses. Because of the technical nature of the job and the deadlines expected, the budding artist had to learn a number of time-saving techniques, which he picked up from other artists working for the agency. One of these artists, a Dutch-American young man named Ubbe Iwwerks, was something of an expert at lettering and commercial art. The time that Walter and Ubbe spent together at work quickly evolved into a close friendship. As the two young artists became especially close, Ubbe began referring to his friend as Walt. It was a nickname that stuck.

Completing successful work in the advertising world could often lead to the opening of an account with the agency, providing regular work for the agency and guaranteed jobs for the artist. In late autumn 1919, Walt was assigned to design the weekly programme for the Newman Theater, a nearby movie palace owned by Frank Newman, a Kansas City businessman who owned a small theatre chain throughout the city. Newman was trying to drum up interest in the film industry in Kansas City with his theatre programmes. He had opened the Newman Theater the previous June, deemed at the time to be the most expensive and ambitious movie palace built in Kansas City. While Walt only designed the programme for a few weeks, more importantly, he established a relationship with Newman that would serve him in the years to come.

As November 1919 came to a close, the work at Pesmen-Rubin began to slow down: most of the advertising work for the Christmas catalogues had been completed and there were more artists than jobs. Because he had only been hired six weeks earlier, Walt was among the first to be laid off. While he was very likely disappointed about losing the job that paid him for 'drawing pictures', he recognised that more importantly, he had gained not only experience but also a reputation for his work throughout the city.

Ubbe was soon laid off as well, and the two began to discuss ways they could pool their talents to go into business on their own. Inspired by the lettering, layout and advertising work they'd done at Pesmen-Rubin, Walt and Ubbe began canvassing area businesses to design and provide illustrations for a number of newsletters. Upon entering a local business, they introduced themselves as the owners of Iwwerks-Disney Commercial

Artists (rather than Disney-Iwwerks, which sounded too much like the name of an optometrist's office) and showed off some of the best work they'd done for their previous employer.

While many of the businesses they approached turned them down, the boys did establish a few accounts. Walt remembered his old friend Walt Pfeiffer, whose father had set up a newsletter for the local chapter of the United Leatherworkers' International Union. Remembering the talent Walt had exhibited as a boy, Mr Pfeiffer quickly hired the two artists to design the letterhead for the newsletter, featuring small illustrations of a number of leather goods.

But simply working out of their homes didn't make the pair feel or look very professional. Walt soon learned that office space existed at the Mutual Building, where the headquarters for *The Restaurant News* was located. *The Restaurant News* was a weekly publication provided to local restaurants full of advertisements for customers to read while they had their meal. The owner of the paper, Alvin Carder, was a few years older than Walt and had grown up as his next-door neighbour when the two lived on Bellefontaine.

At first the meeting was congenial, as the two young men shook hands and reminisced about growing up as neighbours. After asking about each other's parents, Walt pulled out the portfolio of work he and Ubbe had compiled and explained that Iwwerks-Disney wanted to serve as the art department for *The Restaurant News*.

"Gee, I'm sorry, Walt," said Carder. "I don't have enough work to keep you busy here. I don't really need an art department."

"That's okay," Walt explained. "We are really looking for a place to work. We will do work for you when you need it for free. Besides, then you can brag that you have an art department."

The newspaper owner thought for a moment. "Okay," he agreed. "I typically pay the guys that do the printing ten dollars a week for their work. I'll not only give you space in the office for two desks, I'll even give you the ten dollars I would normally pay the printers. I'll also encourage the businesses that advertise with me to employ your services for their ads."

Iwwerks-Disney was in business.

Needing the capital to invest in the supplies to fit out his business, Walt sent a letter home to Flora, who was safeguarding money he'd sent home while working for the American Red Cross in France. Elias was furious and tore up the letter: not only did Walt dare to write home after abandoning the family in Chicago, he had the gall to ask for money when he knew his parents were struggling. O-Zell had hit some financial trouble and Scrogin had asked for additional funds from investors to help keep the factory afloat.

Flora, ever the mother trying to keep the peace between her husband and their sons, quickly wrote to Walt, asking what he planned on doing with the money. Insisting that the cash belonged to him and he had only entrusted his parents to watch over it until he had need of it, Walt explained that he and a friend planned to go into business and needed the money to support the purchasing of supplies. Disgust was added to Elias's fury at his son, and he reiterated that art was no way to make a career. But not wanting a fight, Elias and Flora relented. However, feeling that they had better foresight than their naïve son, they only sent him half of the money he requested; they were afraid that this newest pursuit might be a squandering of his hard-earned money and they didn't want him to go bankrupt.

A few days later, Walt and Ubbe carried their few boxes of art supplies into the headquarters of *The Restaurant News*. They soon learned that Carder had indeed found space for them to work – in the bathroom. The space was tight, allowing for only two desks and the few pieces of equipment they had managed to purchase with Walt's wartime pay, including an airbrush and tank of compressed air for Ubbe to work his magic on the drawing board.

Carder was true to his word: over the next month, Iwwerks-Disney was able to secure work illustrating for *The Restaurant News*, as well as a number of the businesses that advertised in the paper. Soon, the pair had enough money saved up to move their office to the nearby Railway Exchange Building, where there was more space.

One morning in late January, Walt walked into the Iwwerks-Disney office to find Ubbe sitting at his desk looking over the morning edition of *The Kansas City Star*.

"Walt, there's an ad in the paper," Ubbe explained without looking up. Taking his hat and coat off and placing them on his desk, Walt turned to his friend. "They're looking for a cartoonist."

Intrigued, Walt walked over and stood over Ubbe's shoulder to read the ad. The inquiry was for the Kansas City Slide Company, requesting someone who could draw cartoons and wash slides. After discussing the opportunity, it was decided that Walt should answer the advertisement for the pair, as he was more enthusiastic and eloquent than the introverted Ubbe.

Choosing some of the best samples the pair had created at Pesmen-Rubin and *The Restaurant News*, Walt went to the Kansas City Slide Company where he met with the owner, A.V. Cauger.

"I'm going to be honest with you, sir," Walt explained. "I'm looking for part-time work; I have my own art business with a friend that I would like to keep on the side."

"Well, I'm really looking to hire someone full-time. I am willing to pay 40 dollars a week."

The aspiring artist felt a grin tugging at the corners of his mouth. Earning a consistent 40 dollars each week was more money than he'd ever earned. Keeping his voice steady, he thanked Cauger for his time and explained he would contemplate the offer. It took everything in him not to run out of the building and back to the Iwwerks-Disney office.

Upon his return, Walt explained to Ubbe that Cauger was really only looking for a cartoonist, not someone to create professional art. However, he explained that he was hesitant to take the job because their joint venture had just begun.

"Why don't you take the job?" Ubbe offered. "I'll make sure that our contracts here get fulfilled. You can work at the Slide Company during the day and do some work here on nights and weekends."

It was agreed, and thanks to one of his closest friends, Walt Disney had got his first job creating art for the motion picture industry.

Chapter Sixteen

Early Animation

In early February 1920, Walt began working for Cauger's Kansas City Slide Company, which changed its name to the Kansas City Film Ad Company in 1921. He was fascinated to learn that while the business originally created static advertisements drawn on glass slides which would be projected on the screens of theatres between films, A.V. Cauger's business had begun to dive into the developing world of animated and live-action advertisements to play between shows.

Walt didn't know much about animation; in 1920, the industry was in its infancy. During his informal orientation, the curious young man was shown how artists working for the Kansas City Film Ad Company created figures made of paper, moving the figures' hinged joints slightly before photographing them in different positions to create the illusion of movement when played at a normal speed through a projector.

This new art form opened a new world to Walt. While he loved creating cartoons and caricatures, the chance to give his drawings movement brought him joy. Shortly after he had started working for Cauger, he finally heard back from *The Kansas City Journal*, offering him a job in the cartooning department. However, Walt was pleased with his new role and turned down what he had previously thought of as his dream job.

In March, work for Iwwerks-Disney began to slow down, probably because the company's introverted Ubbe Iwwerks didn't sell his product as well as his enthusiastic partner. The lack of consistent work caused Iwwerks-Disney to go under, leaving Ubbe without a job. A.V. Cauger was pleased with Walt's work, and Walt was soon able to secure a position at the company for his newly-unemployed friend.

Upon joining his friend making the animated advertisements, Ubbe quickly caught on, becoming one of the top artists at the Kansas City Film Ad Company, as well as inventing a better motor for photographing drawings for the films. However, the two young men soon realised they weren't content with the quality and style of art they were producing and began to research more professional animation techniques.

After a visit to the Kansas City Library, the pair discovered a book by British photographer Eadweard Muybridge titled *Animals in Motion*, which featured a series of photographic stills of dozens of animals in various stages of movement. The young artists were especially interested in this book, as it helped them to see how a number of still frames tied together could create accurate and lifelike motion. While Muybridge's book was originally published in 1899, the photographer's study of animal motion had begun decades earlier as a result of another man's work. French scientist Étienne-Jules Marey was interested in proving natural selection by observing animal locomotion. However, because the movement of animals was often uncooperative, it was difficult to study a creature's gait. Using photographs he had taken of people in motion, Marey used his working knowledge of animal locomotion to write *Animal Mechanism* in 1873.

Across the globe, around the same time Marey published his book, former California governor and horse breeder Leland Stanford hosted a dinner party. Marey's book was mentioned, and Stanford got into an argument with one of his guests over whether or not a horse in full gallop has all four hooves lifted off the ground at the same time. Money placed as a bet convinced Stanford that he needed to prove his side of the argument, and he reached out to Muybridge, whom he had learned had recently returned from a stint aboard the USLHT *Shubrick*, taking photographs of lighthouses along California's Pacific coast.

After a series of meetings over the next few years, Stanford and Muybridge created a plan to determine how to capture the photographs of a galloping horse, something that Marey had been unable to accomplish. Muybridge installed twelve cameras along a racetrack attached to tripwires, and when crossed by the speeding horse, this caused the cameras to snap multiple photographs. The results fascinated the literary, artistic, and scientific worlds alike, as no series of photographs like this had ever been taken before. Not only did the intellectuals find Muybridge's experiment a success, but so did Stanford: he won his bet, proving to his adversary that all four hooves of a horse are airborne at the same time.

Enjoying his new-found fame, Muybridge created a device, printing each of the photographs around the edge of a disk and using light to project the images in motion onto a screen to showcase his work. Calling his device a zoopraxiscope, Muybridge toured throughout Europe during the first few years of the 1880s to show off his discovery of animal locomotion and bring himself prominence as a photographer.

It was Eadweard Muybridge's invention of the zoopraxiscope that really impressed enterprising individuals. In 1893 at the World's Columbian Exposition, American inventor Thomas Alva Edison debuted his Kinetoscope, a box that allowed individuals to look through an eyepiece to see a series of photographs printed on a celluloid film which, when pulled through the machine at a fast speed, created the illusion of motion. Celluloid film had been invented by George Eastman in 1888 to print photographs more easily. Edison's new device was so popular that he began to distribute the machines to penny arcades and Kinetoscope parlours throughout America's big cities in the years following the World's Columbian Exposition.

Watching film was not just a personal experience in the last years of the nineteenth century. A number of inventors and scientists began to develop technology to make the art form a communal experience. After developing the praxinoscope in 1877, which allowed a viewer to see images on the interior of a spinning drum on a set of central mirrors, Émile Reynaud built a larger version in 1882 allowing the mirrored images to be projected on a screen. Over the next seven years, Reynaud perfected his machine, allowing him to exhibit short animated sequences to audiences throughout France.

Many realised that the projecting praxinoscope was a fairly large piece of equipment and sought to make a smaller machine which would allow longer films to be displayed. Utilising Eastman's celluloid film process, Auguste and Lyon Lumière developed a film projector, allowing for short films to be exhibited to audiences beginning in 1895.

Not to be outdone, Thomas Edison decided to attempt to be the first to exhibit films in America, developing the Vitascope projector, which was used to project films between vaudeville acts. As Edison began to develop his own short films, other early studios emerged, such as W.K.L. Dickson's American Mutoscope and Biograph Company.

As film became increasingly popular, especially for the working classes, storefront theatres began to open in the heart of American cities, charging an entrance fee of between 5 and 10 cents. Due to the low prices collected, these theatres became known as 'Nickelodeons', as admission cost a mere nickel (5 cents) for a day's entertainment.

As the film industry began to develop, new leaders in film production emerged, including Carl Laemmle and Adolph Zukor. Taking inspiration from the work of Reynaud and Muybridge, other film pioneers started making drawings move, beginning the craft of animation. One of the earliest projects, *Humorous Phases of Funny Faces* created by J. Stuart Blackton in 1906, featured a number of photographs of different phases of faces taken while being drawn on chalkboards which, when run quickly on film through a projector, created the illusion of motion. Two years later, Émile Cohl developed *Fantasmagorie*, which featured a stick man who encountered a number of objects that slowly morphed into different objects. While Blackton and Cohl's films were only around a minute in length, they were critical accomplishments that helped the craft of animation develop, demonstrating that simple photographs strung together in a stop-motion fashion could create the illusion of movement.

While Cohl and Blackton's animated sequences garnered attention for their novelty, others used the new medium for the purpose of entertainment. In 1911, American cartoonist Winsor McCay, inspired by children's flipbooks, single-handedly drew and hand-coloured more than 4,000 individual frames for an animated cartoon based on his *Little Nemo* comic strip. This animated short featured no plot, but rather used the characters from McCay's strip to perform gags and experiment with the new medium, such as stretching the characters to see how far animation could go before looking ridiculous.

In February 1914, McCay released *Gertie the Dinosaur*, his first animated short for a public audience, which he once again single-handedly drew, this time featuring more than 10,000 individual frames. However, rather than releasing the film to be shown in a silent theatre, McCay created an act for vaudeville theatre, where he would interact on stage with the projected dinosaur by giving her commands, feeding her a pumpkin, and eventually 'jumping' into the screen before riding her away. The popularity of his act led to studio executive William Fox offering McCay a distribution deal for theatres, which the artist accepted. McCay added a live-action introductory scene and title cards to provide context to the film, and it was released to theatres in December 1914.

Animation during the first two decades of the twentieth century wasn't very popular with the masses. Rather, the art form was merely a novelty, drawing small crowds that chanted "ooh" and "ahh" at the magical lines that performed illogical feats as they danced across the screen. These early cartoons didn't tell a story, but with an approximate run-time of only 1 minute, simply demonstrated visual tricks or small gags that weren't possible in a live-action film.

Because of animation's lack of popularity in the early years, little was done to develop the craft; instead of focusing on creating short films to draw audiences, the medium was used as fillers between features or to advertise products, as in the case of the Kansas City Film Ad Company. As a result, the films that Walt and Ubbe created for Cauger used limited animation techniques for the sake of convincing theatre audiences to purchase products from Cauger's clients.

As Walt began to find his groove at the Kansas City Film Ad Company over the next year, he earned the trust of his boss and was able to convince Cauger to allow him to write his own ads, as well as insert some humorous gags to make them more memorable. Walt particularly used this favour when Cauger requested he create advertisements featuring people, much to the chagrin of Walt's direct supervisor, the art manager, who was upset he wasn't consulted with regard to Walt being hired.

While he struggled to portray humans realistically, the budding artist had become a master at caricature. The art manager, who was jealous of the favour Cauger had shown the new hire, saw an opportunity to get rid of Walt. For example, after receiving an assignment for a local haberdasher, Walt placed drawings of realistic hats for sale atop the heads of humorous caricaturised faces. Watching the art being created, the manager explained that the assignment was to create realistic people wearing the hats.

"I can't draw pretty boys," Walt explained. "I'm a cartoonist."

"We do what is expected of us around here," the manager explained smugly. He couldn't wait until Cauger saw the work the new artist had done for the company's important account.

When the ad was completed, Walt submitted it to his boss for processing: "It's about time we got something new around here!" Cauger chortled. Cauger soon realised that he preferred the kid's unique art style and encouraged Walt to do similar work.

As Walt and Ubbe continued to improve their craft in animation, they proposed to Cauger that the company begin to utilise more advanced animated advertisements, giving them an edge over the competition. In an effort to conserve funds, however, Cauger explained he wasn't interested. However, he was willing to invest time and resources in his top artists, so when Walt and Ubbe asked their boss to loan them an old camera to experiment with animation technique, he was happy to oblige.

Walt convinced his brother Herbert to allow him to create a rough animation studio in the garage behind the family home. On his evenings after work at the Kansas City Film Ad Company, Walt would close himself off in the small garage to experiment with photographing his sketches under different types of incandescent light to create the best illusion of motion.

In early 1920, O-Zell had recently gone bankrupt and its owner, Ernest A. Scrogin, was convicted of embezzlement charges, presumably of money invested by employees and members of the community, including Elias. Unfortunately, not only was Elias out of the money he'd invested, he was also out of a job. He, Flora and Ruth once again packed up their things, sold the Chicago house, and returned to Missouri, moving back into the Bellefontaine house and relieving Herbert of his leadership role over the family members living in Kansas City. While Elias didn't own a car – and never would during his lifetime – he wasn't keen on his youngest son using the family garage in the house's backyard as his animation studio. He allowed him to continue to draw and experiment there in the evenings as long as he made a rent payment of $5 per month.

After establishing the best methods for photographing drawings in the family garage, Walt began to develop ideas for short sequences, animated and live-action. He determined that if Cauger wasn't interested in developing hand-drawn animated advertisements, he would create his own to market to area theatres. Not only would he be making a pay-check creating professional advertisements through the Kansas City Film Ad Company, but he was also using the skills developed creating these advertisements to become a more accomplished artist for the emerging medium of animation.

Taking a cue from Carey Orr's *The Tiny Trib* in the *Chicago Tribune*, Walt decided to create his animated sequences as social commentary on political and economic issues around Kansas City. After searching through the latest editions of newspapers, he came across a headline talking about the terrible quality of Kansas City's roads. After adding a spin of humour that has since become characteristic of Disney entertainment, he took his finished product to Louis Pesmen for criticism. Instead, Pesmen loved it and recommended he immediately show it to Frank Newman, the owner of the Newman Theater Company of Kansas City. Walt added a title card to the beginning of his advertisement, giving the reel the moniker 'Newman Laugh-O-grams' in confident anticipation that Frank Newman would invest in the animated advertisements.

Upon arrival at the office headquarters of the Newman Theater Company, Walt introduced himself to Newman, who was unsure of what to make of this skinny kid, standing in front of him with an uncanned film reel clutched to his chest. Together, Newman and Walt made their way to a small room with a projector, the theatre mogul standing next to the kid as he fumbled at getting the film fed correctly into the projector. Finally, Walt turned on the machine and heat and clattering filled the air as the projector began to pull the film through, shining the image on the opposite wall.

At first the screen was empty, but then the image of a human hand holding a pen – belonging to Walt – filled the screen and began to move across the blank surface, leaving a still image in its wake. As the hand left the screen, the image came alive, showing a road filled with potholes. Cars drove back and forth across this street, the drivers and passengers shuddering with each bump, at times so violently that hats flew off their heads, car parts were ejected from the vehicle, their teeth fell from between their lips like a pair of dentures, and one passenger even fell from the car.

As the short film, only 91 metres (298.5 feet) in length, came to an end, Newman let out a barking laugh. Opening the office door, Newman called down the hall to Milton Feld, the general manager of one of his local theatres, to come and see what Walt had drawn. The manager, like the theatre chain's owner, was impressed.

"I like your work, kid," Feld explained. "I'll take one film per week. How much do they cost?"

Walt did some quick maths in his head: "Thirty cents per foot," the young artist explained. Feld's mouth dropped open at the luck of this great deal and agreed with the young man that they had a new partnership.

As Walt left the offices of his new distributor that day, he was ecstatic and couldn't wait to tell Ubbe and Roy. Suddenly, he stopped in his tracks as his stomach dropped: the deal he'd struck with Feld and Newman would merely pay him for his work at cost, not providing him any profit. While certainly disappointed, Walt was obviously excited about the opportunity to have his work showcased in a local theatre before an audience, especially one who would invest their emotions with the action he'd created on screen. It was slowly becoming clear that Kansas City would have as much impact on his future as Marceline had on his childhood.

While employed by Cauger at the Kansas City Film Ad Company, Walt found another way to become involved in his community, which could ultimately benefit him as he continued in his desire to further himself in the art world. During the nineteenth and early twentieth centuries, many men, including those of influence, belonged to fraternal orders, which played a major part in bettering the local community through service and charity. Feeling a sense of pride as a Kansas Citian, 19-year-old Walt joined the Order of DeMolay, an organisation founded in Kansas City in 1919 for young men between the ages of 12 and 21.

It was in 1919 that Frank S. Land, the social services director for the Scottish Rite organisations throughout Kansas City, first met a young man named Louis Lower. Lower had come to the Scottish Rite, which oversaw numerous fraternal groups throughout the city, looking for work to support his mother after his father died earlier in the year. Land hired Lower, who began to work around the headquarters building, and as the young man became closer to his employer, he confided in Land that he missed his late father and the strength and guidance he had provided.

Recognising the need that Lower and many other young men throughout Kansas City had for paternal influence, Land decided to create a fraternal organisation for young men to be mentored by local businessmen and community leaders, where they could support each other, and learn how to become responsible individuals in America. Lower invited eight friends, and together they became the first members of this new organisation, choosing the name DeMolay after Jacques DeMolay, the final Grand Master of the Knights Templar, who had exhibited bravery and loyalty during his torture by the king of France.

Land soon became known by 'his boys' as 'Dad', serving as a father figure to the original cohort and thousands of members that would join over the next few years. Along with the mentorship that DeMolays received, Land also held lectures to instruct his pupils in the way of the 'seven cardinal virtues': love of one's parents, reverence for sacred things, courtesy, comradeship, fidelity, cleanness, and patriotism.

Upon returning to Kansas City, Walt remembered when Dad Land had visited Benton Grammar School before he had joined Elias and Flora in Chicago. Land had come to the school to advocate for his organisation and offer guidance to any young men interested in living the life of the DeMolay. Walt was inducted as the 107th member of the Order of DeMolay on 29 May 1920 at the Scottish Rite temple located at the intersection of 15th Avenue and Troost Avenue, about 4 kilometres northwest of the family home on Bellefontaine. It is possible that while Roy provided some paternal guidance to his younger brother, Walt still felt as though he lacked a strong father figure with Elias living in Chicago and unsupportive of his youngest son's dreams. Walt was incredibly proud of his membership in the fraternal order, sporting a gold DeMolay ring on his left-hand ring finger and attending meetings on a regular basis.

As a member of the DeMolay, Walt was mentored directly by Dad Land. However, many of his peers within the order were mentored by area businessmen and entrepreneurs, which allowed him to build relationships with the city's professionals. When they found out about Walt's new venture into animated advertisements, they began to commission his work which would be seen by patrons of Newman's theatre. When an auto detailer requested that the artist create an ad for their service painting automobile tops, Walt drew a car driving down the road, the top shooting off sparks like fireworks. A man standing nearby spoke to the driver: "Hi, Old Top. New car?"

"No," the driver replied. "New top, old car."

Another advertisement, especially popular with the male patrons of the theatre, was purchased by the Petticoat Lane shop. The title card explained that the stockings it sold were so long that women had to roll them down from the top. As the title card cut away, the image of Walt's hand appeared, drawing a pair of women's legs, the hose rolled beneath the knees. However, as the ad continued, the hand began to sketch a pair of busts on either side of the legs, revealing that the legs actually belonged to a mannequin, not a real woman, in the front window of a dry goods store.

As Walt began to perfect his craft and become increasingly confident due to the Newman contract, the quality and technical aspects of the Laugh-O-Grams became more complex. Taking a cue from other animators of the time, the early cartoons showed Walt's hand drawing the ads, which included captions, title cards, symbolic labels, and dialogue. However, Walt's hand was unable to fit between the camera and the drawings to be photographed for the film. The proximity between the camera and drawings also made it difficult for the camera to focus on anything that was not two-dimensional. Instead, he photographed his hand and cut it out, taking individual stop-motion photographs of the hand moving as it 'drew' the cartoon, creating the illusion of real-time movement.

As he experimented in the Bellefontaine garage and studied the Muybridge book, as well as another by artist Edwin Lutz titled *Animated Cartoons: How They Are Made, Their Origin and Development*, the Laugh-O-Grams began to transition from stop-motion line drawings to rough animation. In a Laugh-O-Gram titled *Kansas City's [S]pring [C]lean-up*, a line of police officers is seen walking stiffly into the police department. The building begins jumping off its foundation, clouds of smoke bellowing from the barred windows, before a caption of someone yelling "YOUR FIRED" [sic] issues from the doorway, followed by the same police officers tumbling head over heels into the street dressed in plain clothes. Just before the shot irises out at the end of the 40-second film, a well-dressed individual steps into the doorway, hanging a sign with the message "COPS WANTED," making it obvious that the title of the ad alluded to a clean-up of police corruption that Walt was commenting on.

The success and popularity of Walt's Laugh-O-Grams led to Newman and Feld requesting that he do other art jobs for the theatre. For instance, he was asked to illustrate a scene for the theatre's birthday by showing caricatures of celebrities of the day springing out of the centre of a cake. Walt was also requested by his patrons to come up with a creative solution to the problem of audience members reading title cards out loud. Ever one to incorporate humour, Walt created an animated character named Professor Whosis who showed off his new invention of a machine that would remove animated theatregoers not adhering to proper film etiquette from their seats by way of a trap-door beneath each chair.

As Walt began to find success through his contract with Frank Newman and continued to pull income from his job with the Kansas City

Film Ad Company, he soon found he had accumulated enough money to purchase himself a Universal camera for $60 and return the borrowed one to Cauger. When another young man working at the Kansas City Film Ad Company named Hugh Harman heard that Walt was going to invest more time in creating animated advertisements, he asked Walt to assist him in his venture. Together, the two young men created the Harman-Disney Studio, later changing its name to Kaycee Studios.

Walt wanted to do more than just create social commentary or animated advertisements, desiring instead to try his hand at creating animated fairy tales. Recognising that he and Harman were unable to accomplish this alone, he took out an advertisement in the *Star* asking for local boys interested in learning animation. A young man named Rudolf 'Rudy' Ising quickly answered the ad. Together, the trio began to animate their first short film, *Little Red Riding Hood*, starting in October 1921.

As the three young men worked, they became fast friends, spending a lot of their time together. They also began to experiment with film effects that could be incorporated into their animated shorts. It was soon discovered that special effects could be achieved by speeding up or slowing down a film strip in a projector, or even running the film backwards. These experiments were conducted around Kansas City, and Walt often enlisted his friends and family to participate. In one clip, Walt used his young niece, Herbert's daughter Dorothy, who dropped a milk bottle on the ground, which shattered and spilled milk everywhere. When the film was run in reverse, however, it appeared that the shattered bottle became whole and leapt off the ground and into her hand. In another example, Walt had climbed on top of the garage he'd helped Elias build behind the Bellefontaine house, jumping off the roof and into the backyard. When played backwards, it seemed that Walt had leapt onto the top of the building from the grass, a superhuman feat. Even Flora got involved, with the reverse film showing a speeding newspaper flying into her hand, and a small smile on her face.

While Walt was enjoying success as a pioneer in the Midwest American market and discovering the process of filmmaking, he also experienced some personal difficulties that caused him to pour himself more heavily into his work out of loneliness.

In the autumn of 1920, Walt's brother Roy came down with a severe case of the flu. As part of the treatment, it was decided that he needed to have his tonsils removed. While working at the bank provided ample income, Roy decided he would save some money and instead went to a doctor that offered the surgery significantly cheaper than what seemed reasonable.

A few days later, Roy decided to visit this doctor during his lunch break from the bank, have the surgery, and return to work within the hour. However, while returning to the bank after the operation, the sutures in the back of his throat haemorrhaged, causing him to cough up thick blood as he walked up the street. Upon returning to the bank, his friend and Edna's brother, Mitch Francis, recognised something was wrong and rushed Roy to the hospital. After listening to his chest and hearing his cough, the doctor ordered an X-ray of Roy's lungs, which showed a spot of tuberculosis on his lung.

Common medical practice of the time recommended that those with respiratory illnesses, including tuberculosis, would be best served by spending long periods of time in a hot, dry climate. Taking advantage of his benefits as a veteran of the First World War, Roy moved to Santa Fe, New Mexico, where he took up residence at a Veterans Affairs hospital. Not pleased with the level of care he was receiving, he soon transferred to another VA hospital in Tucson, Arizona. After a few months, Roy felt he was feeling better and got himself discharged, against doctors' orders, from the hospital. Hearing about opportunities available further west, he decided to move to Glendale, California, where he could establish himself before sending for Edna. Walt was once again disappointed as his favourite brother and one of his best friends left, but wanting Roy to stay healthy, he understood what was best for his wellbeing.

Around the same time Roy headed west for recovery, Herbert learned he would be transferring to Portland, Oregon for a new position there as a postal carrier. With his failure at O-Zell, Elias was once again feeling the itch for new opportunities, making the decision that he, Flora and Ruth would accompany Herbert and his family to Oregon. Walt, who had begun finding success in his new venture producing the Newman Laugh-O-grams, as well as continuing to hold his steady job at the Kansas City Film Ad Company, decided to stay behind, the only member of the Disney family remaining in Missouri. Arrangements were made to sell the Bellefontaine house, which would necessitate Walt finding a new place to live.

On a crisp day in November 1921, Walt accompanied his family down to Union Station. As the mass of Disneys made their way through the bustling station, Elias and Herbert pushing carts full of luggage, the realisation of what was happening began to sink in for Walt. The anxiety and sadness he felt dulled his senses, hardly noticing the sound of the announcers standing on the balconies of the wings of the Grand Hall or the large clock hanging from the ceiling that had always fascinated him. Time seemed to creep by as he sat between his mother and Ruth in the North Waiting Room, until at last the announcement was made that the train had arrived. The family made their way to the appropriate doorway along the west wall of the room and down the wooden stairs to the platform below. Walt stood stoically while Elias and Herbert helped load their carry-on bags onto the train, as Flora primped her youngest son, devastated at leaving him behind in Kansas City. An announcement was made by the train's conductor that it would be departing soon, and Elias walked over to his wife, telling her it was almost time to board. Wiping a tear from her eye, Walt's mother embraced him tightly, pulling away and getting on the train to avoid the pain. Elias and Herbert both shook Walt's hand, and Ruth hugged her big brother tightly, boarding the train last.

Left alone on the platform as the train went through its final procedures, Walt felt empty. Not wanting to perpetuate the loss he was experiencing, he made his way back up the steps to the main floor of the station and into the west midway, where arriving passengers bypassed the North Waiting Room. As he exited the front doors of Union Station, the blast of a train whistle cut through the air as it pulled away from the platform and headed west. It was then that the 19-year-old Walt Disney realised, for the first time in his life, he would finally need to define himself on his own.

Chapter Seventeen

Laugh-O-gram

As the sole Disney still living in Kansas City and the Bellefontaine house sold, Walt now found himself without anywhere to live and responsible for providing for himself. He had recently moved in with Dr John Cowles and his young family: Dr Cowles had been the family physician for the Disneys for years and had developed a close relationship with them. Shortly after, Walt moved into an apartment on nearby Charlotte Street. In order to stave off the loneliness, the young man decided instead to fill his time with work. Using the Universal camera that he'd purchased with his income from the Kansas City Film Ad Company, Walt was contracted with Pathé Newsreel, Selznick News, and the Universal Film Manufacturing Company to produce newsreels around Kansas City. When he wasn't hard at work, Walt carried his camera around town, looking for newsworthy events to record which could be sent back to Hollywood for incorporation into Universal's newsreels.

One of the more important events that Walt was able to capture was the ground-breaking of Liberty Memorial, located in downtown Kansas City across from Union Station. In anticipation of opening the memorial on 11 November 1926, the eighth anniversary of the signing of the Armistice, the ground-breaking took place on 1 November 1921. In addition to hundreds of thousands of Kansas Citians who turned out to the ceremony, a number of dignitaries were invited to participate in the day's events, including President Calvin Coolidge, as well as Marshal Foch of France, General Pershing of the United States, General Diaz of Italy, Admiral Lord Beatty of Britain, and Lieutenant General Jacques of Belgium, the first time all five Allied commanders had appeared together in public.

Unable to get close enough to record the day's ceremony in detail, Walt decided to take a different approach to capturing the footage. As a military parade wound down Grand Boulevard towards Union Station,

Walt climbed onto the roof of a building overlooking the *Kansas City Star* building, where Coolidge, Foch, and Pershing sat in a reviewing stand. Cranking his camera, Walt was able to capture footage both of the parade marching southbound, as well as the powerful trio enjoying the show.

Walt had also heard that some First World War pilots would be performing air stunts over the city. While most people were accustomed to enjoying air shows from the ground, the young film-maker wanted the viewers of the newsreel to feel like they were participating in the dogfight and had secured a seat on one of the aeroplanes. With very little experience filming things at high speeds due to his work in stop-motion animation, Walt sought advice from another photographer, who explained that he should decrease the size of the lens aperture: this would reduce the amount of light entering the camera, allowing for greater dimension in the film.

When the time came for the show to begin, Walt climbed into the cockpit of the First World War plane, along with the pilot and Hugh Harman's younger brother, Fred. As the plane went airborne, Walt, who was sitting on Harman's lap, stood up and aimed the camera toward the other planes performing stunts. Harman remained seated, steadying the tripod so the camera wouldn't blow over.

As Walt began to yell down to Harman that he was going to start cranking the camera, his voice was lost in the bluster of the wind. Their eyes met as Walt motioned what he was going to do, and Harman nodded to show he understood. The two young film-makers were thrilled by the action they witnessed and filmed, with the planes performing barrel rolls and loop-the-loops.

When the plane ended its stunts, Walt hopped onto the runway, taking the camera from Harman as he handed it down. "Boy!" he yelled, practically jumping. "They're going to buy this one! Maybe they'll even give us a bonus!" A few weeks later, Walt received the developed film. Gathering his animators and Fred Harman at the Kansas City Film Ad Company, he loaded the film on a projector and ran the film. He was devastated to see that it showed nothing but a grey background over which a rotating black shape flickered. He soon realised the film showed nothing but the airplane propeller. Suddenly, a jolt shook across the film and the screen went dark, leading him to realise he had set the aperture too low so that not enough light could get to the lens. His footage was a bust.

Recognising that perhaps he should stick to what he knew best, Walt gave Cauger his notice in early 1922, explaining that he had decided to go into the full-time business of creating Laugh-O-Grams and other short animated films for Newman. While Cauger was obviously disappointed to lose one of his top artists, he understood that this was where Walt's ability and passion truly lay and sent him on his way with warm wishes.

Walt soon set out to acquire capital to finance his new venture. With the Bellefontaine house now sold to a new family, he was no longer using the garage he'd built with Elias as his makeshift studio. Over the next few months, Walt used his charisma to secure investments from a number of people in the community, including Dr Cowles and his wife Minnie. It was particularly helpful when Frank Newman learned of Walt's need for capital and offered to show one of the Laugh-O-gram films in his theatre for the purpose of attracting investors. Soon, several individuals had purchased stock in Laugh-O-gram, with many owning between $250 and $500 worth of stocks. By May 1922, Walt had secured more than $15,000 in investments, enough to officially create a new film-making company. On 23 May 1922, Walt Disney officially incorporated Laugh-O-gram, dropping Newman as the prefix because he was hoping to distribute to a wider audience than just those who patronised the Newman-owned theatres.

Using the newly-acquired capital investments, Walt decided to add to his staff as they poured themselves into the creation of their newest venture: drawing modern-day depictions of fairy tales. Before long, Walt had a staff of eleven, including the recent additions of Carman Maxwell, Lorey Tague, Otto Walliman, Walt Pfeiffer, camera operator Red Lyon, distribution salesman Leslie Mace, stenographer/bookkeeper Nadine Simpson, and Aletha Reynolds, who was responsible for tracing and inking the artists' sketches onto celluloid for photographing.

As *Little Red Riding Hood* was completed in May 1922, Mace was sent to New York, where distributors for animated shorts were headquartered, to find someone interested in distributing Laugh-O-Grams to the nation's theatres. While Mace was unable to find anyone from the big film companies interested in the animated fairy tales, he was referred to William R. Kelley, a representative of the Tennessee branch of Pictorial Clubs Incorporated, a company that distributed films to schools and churches. While this was less than ideal, Walt recognised it was an open door that could lead to bigger things and instructed his salesman to sign a deal, which was done on 16 September. The contract, which called for a total of six animated shorts, would pay a total of $11,100 for the series with the studio receiving a $100 advance upon signing the contract, the remaining $11,000 due by 24 January 1924. Walt saw the contract agreement with Pictorial Clubs as an opportunity to bring Ubbe Iwwerks to Laugh-O-gram, and Ubbe soon quit his job at the Kansas City Film Ad Company, joining the burgeoning organisation in their new venture.

With their investments, incorporation, and the promise of thousands of dollars from Pictorial Clubs, Walt decided the Laugh-O-gram staff needed somewhere more official to work in producing their animated shorts. A new building located at the intersection of 31st Street and Forest Avenue in southeast Kansas City, located only a few kilometres from the Bellefontaine house, piqued Walt's interest. The structure, known as the McConahay Building, was designed by prominent Kansas City architect Nelle E. Peters, who had also designed a number of local hotels and apartment buildings, and was completed in 1922. When Laugh-O-gram moved in, the studio occupied a series of five rooms on the second floor of the building, situated above a shoe store and restaurant, the Forest Inn Café.

The atmosphere at Laugh-O-gram's studio was one of cooperation, fun and companionship, more akin to a fraternity rather than a place of business. The artists would often play tricks on each other or on unsuspecting Kansas Citians. In one example, the boys put a sign on their car identifying them as being from a studio and mounted their camera onto the back of the car, drawing attention from those nearby who wanted to be seen in newsreels that would be shown across America. At other times, they would bring their camera to Union Station and stand in the Grand Hall or North Waiting Room with Walt cranking the empty camera, the artists performing antics to the delight of the surrounding crowd who believed they were seeing a movie being made. The artists also hung out at nearby Swope Park, spending time at a log cabin in a wooded area of the park.

Shortly after moving into their new studio, Walt and his artists began their second animated fairy tale, *The Four Musicians of Bremen*. This was quickly followed by *Jack and the Beanstalk*, *Goldie Locks and the Three Bears*, *Puss in Boots*, and *Cinderella*, rounding out the list of films guaranteed by the contractual obligations agreed to with Pictorial Clubs.

These early animated fairy tales often featured jerky movements and limited detail, especially in the background. They also used time-saving techniques, including cycling and repeat action: for example, the first scene in *The Four Musicians of Bremen* included more than fifteen seconds of people throwing bricks and glass bottles at the main characters of the film as they ran away, repeating the same animations every two seconds. This technique allowed for fewer drawings to be completed, photographing the same stills multiple times to make a cartoon longer. The staff often also recycled stock characters from one film to another, rather than spend time developing new, unique characters: thus, the same minor cat character may be seen as an 'extra' in multiple Laugh-O-gram films. In spite of the rudimentary nature of these early works, they still featured what made the films of Disney popular to millions around the world over the past century: an integration of plot and gags, smart humour, and likeable animal characters.

The studio soon created short joke reels, which were given the name 'Lafflets', allowing for experimentation of the emerging medium of film animation with a focus on humorous gags rather than plot. Disney's artists began to try their hand at stop-motion, claymation, and animation using celluloid sheets (also known as cels), which they had first used when making *Jack and the Beanstalk* for Pictorial Clubs. Composing these experimental films into a single reel, Walt began looking for a large studio distributor who could use the Lafflets as fillers between feature films and newsreels at theatres. Unfortunately, there was very little interest in this new product.

As Laugh-O-gram developed the animated fairy tale shorts for Pictorial Clubs, there wasn't a steady income for their work: the remaining $11,000 wouldn't be paid until after the six contractual films were submitted. As a result, funds were often tight, with Walt resorting to paying his artists in shares of studio stocks rather than in real money. Also, rather than paying for the services provided to the studio every month, debts began to accumulate, which Walt intended on paying off upon receiving the final payment from Pictorial Clubs.

Unfortunately, this didn't come to pass. At the end of 1922, the Tennessee branch of Pictorial Clubs, Inc. folded. This meant that all the work Laugh-O-gram had done on the six animated fairy tales was all for naught. The New York branch of Pictorial Clubs absorbed the Tennessee branch, which meant that while the company acquired the assets of the bankrupted company, they refused to pay any of the liabilities owed. As a result, the New York branch wouldn't pay Laugh-O-gram for the agreed-upon $11,000.

Walt began to scrape together ideas for paying off debts accrued over the previous few months, including those owed to the companies that provided utility services to the studio, as well as stores that sold supplies for the production of their films.

One afternoon, while the artists were hard at work, a gentleman in a suit carrying a briefcase came walking up the stairs and into Laugh-O-gram's lobby.

"Is Mr Dinsey here?" he asked Nadine Simpson, who was sitting at her desk near the stairway. She looked over at Rudy Ising, who was sitting nearby, then at Walt, who was hard at work on the other side of the room.

"No, I don't think so," Walt said, without looking up.

"Well, I'll be back," the man explained. The sound of his footsteps receded as he walked back downstairs, the door to the street opening and closing behind him.

"What?" Walt asked his staff who had all stopped and looked at him. "He's obviously a debt collector who is looking for a Mr *Dinsey*. Nobody by that name works here," he explained with a smirk.

The collector returned several more times, each time continuing to mispronounce Walt's name. Each time, Walt or one of his staff, who had come to see this as a funny game, turned him away.

One afternoon, when the debt collector returned, however, Walt was discussing a scene with Walt Pfeiffer. The discussion began to get heated as they disagreed over a scene, while the collector stood at Simpson's desk, once again exasperated that he'd missed 'Mr Dinsey'.

Suddenly Pfeiffer raised his voice. "Now listen, Walt…"

The debt collector's head snapped around to the pair. "Walt?" he asked. "Walt *Dinsey*?"

"Yeah," Walt responded, frustrated over his disagreement with Pfeiffer and the collector's persistent incompetence. "That's me. But it's pronounced *Disney*, not Dinsey."

The debt collector explained that he needed to discuss the settling of accounts with Walt, and together the two stepped into a corner and sat at an animation desk where they could go over paperwork. An agreement was made as to how the debts would be paid, but it quickly became obvious that the capital needed to continue to create animated shorts was lacking, and the likelihood of getting new contracts was slim. Some of Walt's artists began to leave Laugh-O-gram, seeking out other art positions, including Ubbe, who returned to his job at the Kansas City Film Ad Company.

Most of the investment capital he had received had been exhausted in producing the Laugh-O-Grams, so Walt had to dip into his own savings to pay off some of the debts accumulated by the studio. The decision had to be made: to pay rent for either his apartment on Charlotte Street or the Laugh-O-gram studios. Walt decided to keep the studio on 31st Street and moved out of his apartment, choosing instead to live at the studio. While sleeping in a desk chair was incredibly uncomfortable, Walt never gave up on his dream, choosing to work *and live* film animation.

Because the studio didn't have a full bathing suite, Walt walked several kilometres to Union Station on a weekly basis for a hot bath, where paying a dime would get him a small cake of soap, a clean towel, and an opportunity to bathe in semi-private quarters. As he walked through the front doors of Union Station, Walt was hit with discouragement as he saw well-dressed businessmen meeting beneath the large clock. Checking in with a small desk near Pierpont's, a waiting room for women and children situated just off the Grand Hall, Walt was escorted upstairs to enjoy his weekly bath. Afterwards, he would treat himself to a cigarette in the men's smoking lounge or wander through the doors of the North Waiting Room, where he would stand on the train platforms, a wave of sadness overtaking him as he remembered Elias, Flora and Ruth's departure for Portland.

Meals were usually taken at the studio, where Walt had started eating unheated cans of chilli and beans as it was all he could afford. On special occasions, the homeless and hungry young man would go downstairs to eat at the Forest Inn Café, where he had befriended owners Louis Katsis and Jerry Raggos, who allowed him to rack up a tab when he promised to pay them back. This agreement ended, however, when Walt's debt to the restaurant totalled $60 and Katsis cut him off. One day, when Raggos went upstairs to request money to pay off the tab, he found Walt sitting in the middle of the empty room eating from a tin can. His frustration immediately evaporated.

"Walt, I don't care what Louis says," Raggos said, walking up to him. "Come down to our place and have a bite to eat on us."

While he was able to enjoy the mercy of the restaurant owners downstairs, Walt still felt very alone; not only had his family left for the west, but his animators, including best friends Walt Pfeiffer and Ubbe Iwwerks, had given up on working for the studio. Roy's fiancée, Edna Francis, still lived in Kansas City, and she often welcomed her boyfriend's little brother over for the occasional meal and company, but this only eased the loneliness for a few hours before he returned to the cold darkness of the studio.

Walt was also lucky enough that while his former Laugh-O-gram employees had parted ways with him professionally, some of them remained in touch. When she became aware that Walt was struggling to find money for food, his former stenographer Nadine Simpson came to the rescue. While attending a church social, Simpson learned that the grand prize of the raffle drawing was groceries and a ham. She immediately thought of her former boss and purchased $2-worth of tickets. One of her tickets won the raffle and she brought the food to Walt, who was too gracious to be embarrassed.

Luckily, Walt had also made some friends who lived with him in the studio: a few small mice who had been living off the crumbs of his leftover meals. When the studio had still been a bustling place of creating animation, one of these mice had been moving crumpled papers around inside a wire wastebasket, causing Walt to discover him and fondly give him the name Mortimer. The studio boss quickly made Mortimer and his friends the mascots of the studio, keeping them in a small cage on his desk and putting them in one of his desk drawers at night.

Walt was able to make a little money by fulfilling some local film jobs. In the early autumn of 1922, Dr Thomas B. McCrum, a Kansas City dentist and head of the Deaner Dental Institute, heard about the local film-maker. McCrum reached out to Walt, and the two worked out a deal where Walt would produce an educational film for the dentist about the importance of dental hygiene. Titled *Tommy Tucker's Tooth*, the short film, which featured primarily live-action, provided a commission to Disney for $500, which he used to help pay off some of his debts.

When it was time to write up the contract and pay Walt the advance for *Tommy Tucker's Tooth*, McCrum called Walt at the studio.

"I've got the money for your film. I'd like you to come to my office so we can set the deal," the dentist explained.

"I'm sorry, but I can't come over," Walt stated.

"Why not?" asked McCrum.

A silence hovered over the line. "Well," the young artist began hesitantly. "My only pair of shoes were falling apart. So I brought them to the cobbler downstairs to get repaired. The price for repair was more than I anticipated, and he won't let me have them back until I scrape up a dollar and a half."

"I'll be right over," McCrum said. Before Walt could protest, the dentist had hung up the phone. Within the hour, Walt's new patron was knocking at the door of the studio. Walking down the darkened staircase to the first floor in his stocking feet, Walt opened the door to find Dr McCrum standing on the pavement with Walt's shoes in hand: he had paid the cobbler what he was owed for the repair work on the artist's behalf. After closing things upstairs, Walt climbed into McCrum's car and together they drove to the dentist's office where they signed the deal for the educational film.

Walt scoured the neighbourhoods near the Laugh-O-gram studio for children who could play the parts in his film, ultimately choosing a young man named Jack Records as the lead actor and even filming at Benton Grammar School, where he himself had attended as a youngster. While the footage was filmed, Walt stood nearby, a cardboard megaphone in his hand and a cap on his head, instructing the children what to do and say between takes. It was obvious that Walt's vision for the film was in his head, as none of the children had been given a script to memorise. Instead, Walt would act out what he wanted the performers to do, call for the camera to begin rolling, and shout out cues and actions while the children reproduced Walt's performance.

While funds were hard to come by due to very little work, Walt often paid the 5-cent admission to the local theatres to stay abreast of what the big animation studios in New York were doing. It was at the Isis Theater, a mere 120 metres from the Laugh-O-gram studio on the corner of 31st Street and Troost Avenue, that the young Walt Disney developed a relationship with Carl Stalling, a musician who played the theatre organ to accompany the silent action on screen. Stalling explained to his friend that the Isis Theater wanted to develop a series of films, called 'Song-O-

Reels', which would project the lyrics to a song beneath filmed action, to encourage audiences to sing along, serving as a filler between features and newsreels. Short on funds, Walt accepted the offer and began meeting with representatives of the Isis Theater and the J.W. Jenkins Music Company of Kansas City.

It was decided that the first Song-O-Reel would accompany the newly-published song *Martha: Just a Plain Old-Fashioned Name* by Joe L. Sanders. As film-maker, Walt was given leeway to cast the characters. On the day of shooting, Walt met his cast – some of the old Laugh-O-gram girls and Ubbe as their object of affection – at Swope Park. While they had been equals in the past, with Walt working alongside them on the animated films, in this new medium they submitted to Walt, the director giving direction, calling out cues by megaphone and showing them their movements by miming them himself. However, much like *Tommy Tucker's Tooth* and the Lafflets, *Martha* ended up being the only Song-O-Reel made by Walt.

Unfortunately, none of these projects led to additional work for the aspiring artist. Walt recognised that he had experienced more success with animation than with his local live-action work. For inspiration, he continued to visit theatres throughout Kansas City to see what the big animation studios were doing.

One afternoon early in 1923, after the conclusion of one such cartoon short, a still advertisement for Warneker's Bread flashed onto the screen. The advertisement, which was produced by the Kansas City Film Ad Company, featured the image of a smiling girl holding a piece of bread covered in jam, a speech bubble filled with the words, "Oh, yum, yum!" off to one side.

One of Walt's eyebrows shot up as he sat in the darkened theatre. He hardly noticed when the next film began, the dim grey light flickering across his face. He had an idea, one that no one had ever tried before.

Chapter Eighteen

Bankruptcy

While animation merely served as a novelty during the early years of the twentieth century under pioneers like Émile Cohl, J. Stuart Blackton, and Winsor McCay, some innovations allowed for the films to be produced more quickly and cheaply, and more easily distributed to larger audiences across the nation, ultimately leading to the emergence of dedicated animation studios.

While early animators hand-drew each individual frame photographed, it was quickly realised that this wasn't the most efficient way. On 11 August 1914, John Randolph Bray, who had become successful for launching one of the first animated series, *Colonel Heeza Liar*, received the exclusive patent for using celluloid in animation. Bray had discovered that he could draw backgrounds for the scene on translucent paper, with any new character movement on blank paper, which could be seen through the background.

A few months later, artist Earl Hurd improved upon Bray's process by simply flip-flopping the process: drawing backgrounds on blank paper, with the characters and new animation on the thin, clear piece of celluloid, which was placed over the top of the background. This also allowed for the addition of dimensionality to the scene, as multiple layers of celluloid could be placed on top of each other. Hurd applied for and received the patent for this process on 9 December 1914.

The discoveries made by both Bray and Hurd greatly improved upon the process of animating. Rather than drawing the same background thousands of times on individual pieces of paper like McCay had done, one only needed to draw the background once, simply adding the new animation on the cel which was layered over the background. This made the entire animation process easier, quicker, and cheaper, allowing for more animated shorts to be produced in a shorter amount of time.

This new technical discovery encouraged those interested in animation to open their own studios in New York, where the industry was centred in the 1910s and 1920s. However, when many of the big film studios moved their production west to Hollywood, the animation studios often stayed put: the creation of hand-drawn films wasn't reliant on the weather or landscape like live-action films were, and many of the film distributors were located in New York City due to their close relationship with the business and financial world of America.

During the 1910s, some new animation studios emerged, none of which lasted very long, but each of which made discoveries or technological improvements that helped pave the way for the prominent studios that came after. The first major studio, Raoul Barré, was founded in 1914 and invented the peg system by which blank pieces of paper were held on an animator's desk by a series of pegs situated above the drawing surface. In this way, artists could easily layer their drawings, allowing them to flip between the sketches to determine whether the right amount of movement had been achieved by the character.

As these animation studios began to develop, a fierce system of competition emerged. In an effort to compete with Hearst International, another major studio, Raoul Barré began to offer art classes for their animators, which included Dick Huemer, Bill Tytla, Albert Hurter and Ted Sears, all future Disney artists, to ensure that characters had accurate movements.

Another of the studios, J.R. Bray, took pointers from McCay's *Gertie the Dinosaur* by allowing their cartoons to break the fourth wall. For example, in their series *Bobby Bumps*, which was syndicated by Universal in 1915, the unseen animator interacted with the characters by drawing props to help them get out of problematic situations. To meet the increasing need for animated shorts for Universal, Bray began to employ the assembly line system of animation, which sorted artists into different roles in the studio. For example, while one was quickly sketching the characters on blank paper, another would be tracing the sketch onto a piece of celluloid with ink, while a third would be filling in the inked cel with paint to create different shades and details on screen.

Toward the end of the century's second decade, newly-established studios eclipsed Barré, Hearst and Bray in popularity, technique and quality. In 1919, Pat Sullivan and Otto Messmer released a short titled *Feline Follies*, which was syndicated by Universal and distributed by Margaret Winkler in 1921. The short's protagonist, Felix the Cat, quickly became recognisable throughout America as Winkler worked with Sullivan to develop a marketing campaign utilising merchandise that could be purchased by fans of the mischievous character. Felix was also incredibly popular to audiences due to the fact that Sullivan and Messmer had given him a personality, something that was relatively new compared to the dozens of emotionally flat characters that had preceded him on screen. The humour conveyed in the Felix shorts was unique as well, because Felix often used his body parts, such as his tail, to help him solve problems.

Sullivan and Messmer soon found themselves a suitable competitor in a new animation studio headed by Max Fleischer. However, Fleischer took a different approach to the medium than Sullivan and their forebears. While many in the industry had concentrated on improving the quality of animation through devising new techniques, Fleischer instead focused on discovering ways to implement technology in improving animation. He was particularly interested in the process known as rotoscoping, or projecting live-action film one frame at a time onto a blank piece of paper while an artist traced the figure and added details of his own. This process made the movement of animated characters much more fluid and lifelike, leading to more buy-in from audiences to the believability of an animated sequence.

Fleischer tested out his new technique by developing the character Koko the Clown, portrayed by his brother Dave. After tracing Dave's figure and movements on the sketch paper, Fleischer added a clown outfit and make-up. When projected on film, Koko's movements were incredibly realistic as he spun and leapt across the screen. Recognising that he had discovered something special, Fleischer travelled to Hollywood in 1919 to meet with Adolph Zukor, founder of Paramount Pictures. When he ran into John Bray in Zukor's outer office, Bray was impressed by the artist's test reel of Koko and offered him a deal for Paramount to distribute one of Fleischer's reels every month as part of the Paramount Pictograph screen magazine. This partnership with Paramount lasted until 1921 when Fleischer created his own studio, Out of the Inkwell Films, Inc. and partnered with Samuel Goldwyn.

Not only was Fleischer's animation technique revolutionary, but so were the subjects of the cartoons themselves. True to the name of the series, 'Out of the Inkwell', each short began with a shot of Max Fleischer seated at his artist's desk. After dipping his pen in an inkwell, the artist began sketching Koko, who magically came to life. Over the course of the shorts, Koko would entertain audiences by fighting against live-action flies who landed on the paper, running away from ink blotters, or even leaping off the artist's desk and running around the live-action office or sliding down the leg of a chair. This technique of introducing the animated Koko into the live-action world was completed through the use of another technological process developed by Fleischer known as rotographing, or overlaying the cel of animation over a still frame of a photograph. The novelty of an animated character interacting with real-world objects, people and locales is what drew audiences, but unfortunately, the animated shorts lacked coherent plots, often resorting to gags and two-dimensional personalities.

Thus, the cartoons that fascinated and delighted audiences in the early 1920s featured an animated clown who inserted himself into the real world and a cat chock-full of personality that used body parts to help escape desperate situations. As young Walt Disney sat in that darkened theatre, staring at the hungry girl in the bread ad, he knew that if he wanted to edge into the animation world, he would have to create something new that would be just as appealing to modern audiences.

The little girl in the bread ad was Virginia Davis. At 4 years old, the curly-haired, bright-eyed little girl was already a local face on Kansas City theatre screens through her occasional modelling jobs with the Kansas City Film Ad Company. Her parents wanted more for their young daughter than just being featured in still ads and sent her to the Georgia Brown Dramatic School where her skills in singing, acting, and dancing could be honed.

After learning the girl's name from his contacts at the Kansas City Film Ad Company, Walt sent a letter to Mr and Mrs Davis, inquiring whether they would be interested in their daughter starring in his newest film. When he offered to pay Davis 5 per cent of all income made from the film, they jumped at the opportunity, officially signing a contract with Walt on 13 April 1923.

Walt recognised that this new project, *Alice's Wonderland*, was potentially his last chance at getting into the animation world and began to pour himself into his work. While his artists had left him, he was able to convince a few, including Rudy Ising and Ubbe, to help, with Ising running the camera, Ubbe doing most of the animation, and Walt directing the live-action sequences.

The concept for *Alice's Wonderland* was merely the opposite of Fleischer's popular series. While audiences had been enthralled by Koko the Clown's exploits into the real world, Walt took a bet they would be just as invested in a real little girl finding herself in the cartoon world. Walt Disney, however, didn't have the same technical expertise as Max Fleischer, so he relied on Ubbe's ingenuity to help devise a way to make this vision come to life. The solution, they found, was to photograph Virginia in front of a white backdrop. Once the live-action was complete, the images were printed and animated characters and scenery were drawn on a cel where the white space was. The cels were then photographed and the two prints – the live-action film and the animated film – were combined into a single reel.

As Walt began to realise that he would be able to finish producing *Alice's Wonderland* without running out of funds, he started to look for a distributor. When he brought up his newest venture to Milton Feld, general manager of the Newman Theater, Feld suggested that he write to Margaret Winkler, distributor of Sullivan's *Felix the Cat* cartoons. Walt wasted no time in jotting out a letter on 14 May, heralding something that had never been seen before in the medium of animation. He went on to explain that his film would appeal to all, regardless of class or age, and promised to have a completed print available to send within a few weeks. Winkler wrote back, enthusiastic about the prospect of a new series.

Unfortunately, production soon fell behind schedule. Shortly after sending the letter to Winkler, the McConahay Building was acquired by a new landlord, Clifford Collingsworth, who soon learned that the Laugh-O-gram studios was historically behind on its rent payments. To compensate for the money owed, the new owner placed a lien on the studio's property, including the furniture and art equipment, afterwards putting a padlock on the door to prevent anyone from entering the studio until rent was paid. Eventually, Walt and his staff were allowed back into their offices to remove the studio's equipment and furniture and transported it to the nearby Wirthman Building, which accommodated office space as well as the Isis Theater where the *Martha* Song-O-Reel had premiered.

Walt, who had come to love his mouse companions during his residency at the McConahay Building, decided that the owners of the Wirthman wouldn't appreciate more rodents. Carrying them in a small box to nearby

Swope Park, he found a secluded wooded area, set the box on the ground, and gently tipped it over so the mice could walk out. At first, Mortimer and his friends crawled out of the cage, sniffing the ground around them. A short distance away from the cage, they stopped and looked up at him as if to question what he wanted them to do: in their time with the young man, they had become somewhat domesticated. In fact, a few of the mice ran back to the box, waiting for their friend to pick it up and return them home to the studio. Saddened once again by loss, Walt eventually had to shoo the mice away and snatch the box up to prevent them from returning, turning about and walking away before he changed his mind.

Discouraged at their continued declining prospects, more of Disney's artists left Laugh-O-gram, including Rudy Ising and Carman Maxwell. Later in the summer, business manager Jack Kloepper not only left the company, but sued for back pay; Walt escaped the court summons by being lucky enough to not be at the studio when a police officer came to serve the warrant. Hugh Harman, who had stuck by Walt's side since their time working together at the Kansas City Film Ad Company, supported himself and his friend, using money received monthly from his father to put up himself and Walt at the nearby Elsmere Hotel.

Walt was humbled even more when, on 18 June, he wrote a letter to Winkler to explain that the studio was behind schedule on *Alice's Wonderland*, attributing it to a number of delays, unforeseen circumstances, and the recent move into the Wirthman Building. Walt promised to complete the film as soon as possible, even going so far as to state that he would be in New York City, print in hand, sometime around 1 July to meet with her for the signing of a contract.

At the end of his tether, Walt wrote to Roy in California, explaining everything. Roy soon wrote back: "Kid, you gotta get out of there," he wrote. "I don't think there's anything else you can do to save it."

Walt was crushed. This dream that he had pursued over the course of the previous few years since first getting his job at Pesmen-Rubin had seemingly come to an end. Walt filed for bankruptcy and began to liquidate his assets, deciding to follow Roy's advice and move to California where he could start afresh. Needing enough money to purchase a train ticket to head west, Walt went door-to-door in the surrounding neighbourhoods, offering to take films of young couples' children. He soon made enough money to afford a train ticket and sold his camera, using those funds to help pay off some of his debts, including to the proprietors of the Forest Inn Café.

The night before he left Kansas City in late July 1923, Walt enjoyed dinner with Edna Francis. While he had lost everything, including his dreams, Edna noticed that he was excitedly optimistic about the opportunities Hollywood presented, talking non-stop about how he would abandon animation in favour of a job as a film director instead.

The next morning, he visited the home of Louise Rast, the mother-in-law of his brother Herbert, to prepare for his journey. Mrs Rast provided Walt with some food for the train and even gave him a set of clothes that no longer fitted one of her sons so that he was more presentable. Soon, a family friend of the Rasts arrived to take Walt to Union Station.

After a short while in the North Waiting Room, an announcement was made: "Now boarding the Santa Fe, California Limited for Los Angeles and all points in between!" Walt made his way through the doors on the west side of the hall and down the wooden steps to the platform below. As he boarded the train and made his way into first class – he had decided to begin the next phase of his life on a confident note – he likely drew furtive glances as he was wearing a worn-down outfit consisting of black-and-white checkered trousers, a matching jacket, and a brown cardigan sweater. The nicer outfit Mrs Rast had given him was packed in a well-used cardboard suitcase at his side, along with the few pairs of socks and underwear he still owned and a tinned print of *Alice's Wonderland*. A wad of cash, totalling $40, was stuffed in his pocket, which was enough, he hoped, to help him get by.

Walt looked out the window at the platform below from the window of his upper berth of the first-class car. It had always reminded him of the loss he had experienced with the departure of his parents and sister, but he felt no sadness this time.

Only excitement for the things that lay ahead.

Part VII

The first animated cartoon studio in Hollywood

Los Angeles, California, 1923–1928

Chapter Nineteen

Alice

Arriving in Los Angeles a few days later presented a fresh start for the young Walt Disney. With 1 August coming to pass as he rode the train west, a new month had begun putting the events of the previous month behind him. He didn't owe money to anyone in town and had nothing but opportunities for work in the film industry. And perhaps most important of all, he was near family once again. Roy, who had moved to Glendale three years earlier, had worked for a time as a door-to-door vacuum salesman. However, when he experienced a relapse of tuberculosis, he checked himself into the VA hospital in Sawtelle, a suburb west of Los Angeles. Walt also finally had a place to live: shortly after the death of Aunt Margaret, Uncle Robert had moved to a small bungalow at 4406 Kingswell Avenue in the town of Los Feliz, located a few kilometres north of Los Angeles, and he invited his newly-arrived nephew to move in with him.

Almost immediately, Walt, the aspiring director, began to visit the large studio lots throughout Hollywood, not only enamoured by the film culture but also looking for work. To appear more professional, he ordered business cards listing himself as the Kansas City representative of Universal and Selznick Newsreels. Donning the outfit he'd received from Mrs Rast, Walt confidently marched up to the front gates of Universal Studios, thrusting his business card at the attendant and asking for a pass to enter the studio. Walt seemed so official that he immediately received a pass unchallenged and spent many days, from morning to night, wandering the lot, entering sound stages, and watching productions. Over the next few weeks, he made his way into other studio lots, including Vitagraph, Paramount, and Metro-Goldwyn. Among the many films he saw being made were *The Hunchback of Notre Dame* starring Lon Cheney, and Cecile B. DeMille's *The Ten Commandments*, and he also rubbed shoulders with the likes of Gloria Swanson and Rudolph Valentino. While each personnel department at the respective studios rejected the enthusiastic young man as a director, he was lucky to land a rare part as a film extra, riding a horse in a western film. Unfortunately, even that didn't work out for him, as the shoot he was scheduled for got rained off and his role was quickly replaced. He somehow even ended up in the offices of film producers, his reel of *Alice's Wonderland* tucked under his arm, petitioning them to distribute his animated short, but to no avail.

After several weeks of this, Uncle Robert was beginning to get frustrated with Walt's idleness. While Roy usually defended his kid brother from adults' unwarranted scolding, this time he agreed with his uncle: enough of wandering Hollywood chasing dreams, he wrote from his hospital bed in Sawtelle, "It's time to find a job."

The bankruptcy proceedings for Laugh-O-gram Films continued in Walt's absence. With the folding of the Tennessee branch of Pictorial Clubs, Walt had been unable to pay off creditors or investors. Luckily for them, a law firm that had been hired by his creditors was able to extract some money from the New York branch, enough to restore investments by about 45 per cent. Lienholders sold off the remaining assets from the defunct Laugh-O-gram studio, and on 30 October 1923, Walt's Kansas City studio ceased to exist.

Walt recognised that he hadn't had much success with creating the animated fairy tales for Pictorial Clubs and didn't have the manpower to make another short like *Alice's Wonderland*. Instead, he decided to pursue in Hollywood what he'd found success with in Kansas City: creating gag reels like he'd done for Frank Newman's theatres. Carrying some samples with him, Walt made his way to the office of Alexander Pantages, the owner of a chain of movie and vaudeville theatres throughout Los Angeles. Not wanting to be rejected outright by a secretary, he waited until he could waylay Pantages himself. However, after waiting a while, he resorted to stopping one of the executive's assistants and began to pitch his idea.

"I'm sorry," the assistant stated with exasperation, feeling like his time was being wasted. "I'm afraid Mr Pantages isn't interested."

"Who says I'm not interested?" roared a voice from a nearby open door. Suddenly, a towering figure filled the doorway. The assistant seemed to shrink back, colour draining from his face at the appearance of Pantages himself. The executive exuded authority with a serious look always showing on his face due to his heavy dark eyebrows and thick lips. The power he had was magnified by his obvious wealth, highlighted by his slicked hair parted down the middle and his expensive suit, the buttons of the pinstriped waistcoat straining behind the man's girth.

"I'm interested in your idea," Pantages explained as he stepped between his assistant and Walt. "Work up a sample reel and I'll take a look. If it ends up being as good as you say, you've got yourself a deal."

Walt held his composure, but inside he was brimming with excitement: this could finally be his door into the Hollywood film business! Within a few days, he had persuaded Uncle Robert to allow him to create a makeshift studio in the small garage on the property, paying a fee each week to use the space.

Walt purchased a Pathé camera and set up a camera stand using wooden fruit boxes and spare lumber that he found lying around the garage. He also set to work on animating the sample gag reel using simple stick figures with emoted faces. The characters in the reel told each other jokes, represented by text in speech bubbles above their heads.

In the meantime, Walt decided to reach out to Margaret Winkler one final time to update her on recent events. In a letter at the beginning of October 1923, Walt apologised for his lack of contact since June, explaining that he was no longer affiliated with Laugh-O-gram Films, instead establishing a new studio in Los Angeles in an attempt to create a series based on *Alice's Wonderland*. She quickly wrote back saying that they had been corresponding over the film since May but was frustrated that Walt was all talk and no action: "It seems to me that [your letters] are all that this has amounted to." Unbeknownst to Walt, Winkler was experiencing friction with Pat Sullivan over the distribution of his Felix cartoons and was desperate to secure a new series.

Walt, who was terrified at losing this opportunity, decided to send Winkler his print of the Alice film. He first had to acquire permission from the sheriff of Kansas City due to the fact he didn't officially own the print: it was still technically owned by the lienholder of Laugh-O-gram's assets.

When Margaret Winkler screened *Alice's Wonderland* for the first time, she was fascinated by what she saw. The opening scene featured little Alice, knocking on an open door marked 'STUDIO'. The shot changes to show an animator hard at work, drawing a doghouse on a blank white board. Alice knocks again and the animator turns to look at her, revealing the artist to be Walt Disney, who motions to the girl to join him at his desk. Suddenly, the drawing comes alive as the doghouse begins to quiver and jump while a dog and cat fight with each other. Walt then shows the curious girl around the studio, where a number of Disney artists are hard at work at their drawing boards. One artist notices that the animated dog and cat from the previous scene have started a boxing match and rallies the other artists to his side where they begin to cheer on the match. Later that evening, as Alice dreams, the film changes to be fully animated. A cartoon train rushes through the countryside before arriving at a small town populated by a number of animals, all prepared to welcome the live-action Alice. The girl is whisked away to a parade in her honour atop the back of an elephant before attending a concert where she entertains her new friends by performing a dance. However, because the town's citizens are at the girl's celebration, they are unaware that a pack of lions has escaped from the Cartoonland Zoo. When they spot the little girl, they begin to drool and start chasing her into a tree, a cave, and a rabbit's den. Unable to escape, Alice decides to jump off a cliff before the film fades to black.

Walt received an enthusiastic reply from Winkler on 15 October via telegram: Winkler accepted Walt's proposal, ordering a six-film series with a payment of $1,500 for each film upon receipt. The contract also offered the option to renew the series for an additional six Alice films at an increased rate of $1,800 apiece. Walt only had two months to shoot his first film, which was due on 15 December. The biggest stipulation to accepting the contract, however, was that Winkler expected Virginia Davis to star in the film as Alice.

After receiving the telegram, Walt immediately left Uncle Robert's house and boarded a bus for Sawtelle, one of the only passengers because it was a late hour. Walt walked from the bus stop to the VA hospital and crept across the grounds to the screened-in porches where the tuberculosis patients slept. He let himself into one of the porches and tip-toed around the beds until he found Roy. Gently sitting down on the corner of his brother's bed, he shook him awake.

"What're you doing here, Walt?" Roy asked, blinking and sitting up to make room. He noticed a piece of paper gripped in his younger brother's hand and assumed the worst. "What's the matter?"

"We did it, Roy! We got a deal!" Walt practically shouted his whisper.

Roy shushed his brother: not only did he not want to wake up those sleeping nearby, but he also knew they would both get in trouble if Walt was caught there. After a few minutes, Roy was able to calm Walt down enough to get him to explain his news.

"I can't do this without you," Walt explained. "Let's go, Roy."

Roy knew about Walt's previous attempts in the animation business and how difficult it was to get into the film industry in Hollywood. He also recognised that it would be almost impossible for his little brother to become a successful animator in California with the entire industry located on the other side of the country in New York. After getting assurances from Walt as to how he could be successful in producing the Alice films, Roy agreed; he would check out from the hospital the next morning.

He would never return to the hospital with a relapse of tuberculosis again.

The signed contract with Winkler meant there was a necessity for capital, new equipment, and the establishment of a new studio. Unfortunately for the Disney brothers, none of the people Walt had borrowed money from to finance his pursuits in the past would be thrilled about the prospect of providing funds now that Laugh-O-gram had collapsed. Roy, who had ample experience in financial matters due to his previous employment at the First National Bank of Kansas City, visited local banks requesting loans. The answer was the same over and over: animation wasn't terribly popular and as a result, the financing of animated films was too risky for the established financial institutions.

Instead, Roy resorted to phase two: requesting money from family. Taking advantage of the kindness he'd repeatedly shown the family, Roy went to Uncle Robert, asking for a loan of $500. The boys' uncle, however, was reluctant, explaining that Walt had a history of not repaying creditors. "The boy is an irresponsible dreamer," Uncle Robert argued. Roy, standing up for his brother, angrily retorted that they didn't really need Uncle 'Gold Bug's' money anyway and stormed out. Eventually, however, Robert relented, and his $500 was added to the coffers, joining the pension Roy received as a disabled veteran, which provided the brothers with enough capital to begin production of their first official Alice film.

One of the first things Walt did after signing his contract with Winkler was reach out to Mr and Mrs Davis in Kansas City to inform them of the distributor's requirement. As part of his note, Walt offered the Davises a one-year contract for Virginia to star in twelve episodes of what would become the 'Alice Comedies', offering the family $100 per month with an escalating salary of up to $200 per month by the end of the contract year. Virginia's parents quickly accepted the film-maker's offer: Mr Davis was a travelling salesman and could conduct his work anywhere. Young Virginia had also had a few bouts of double pneumonia from which she almost died; as a treatment plan, her doctor suggested that the family move to a dry climate. As a result, Los Angeles was the perfect place for the young family who had hopes for their daughter in the film industry. Within a few weeks, the Davises gathered up their things and rode the train west from Kansas City to Los Angeles to join the Disneys in California.

Walt and Roy immediately began working on their first Alice Comedy for Winkler, titled *Alice's Day at Sea*, with Walt completing all the animation and Roy operating the camera. Recognising that the small garage alongside Uncle Robert's house was insufficient for the work they needed to accomplish, the brothers decided to rent an office at the rear of the Holly-Vermont Realty Company building at 4651 Kingswell Avenue, just a short distance from Uncle Robert's home. Walt soon hired two additional staff to help produce the film: Kathleen Dollard and Ann Loomis, both of whom inked and painted Walt's sketches onto cels.

Not only did the brothers move their studio down the street, but with Roy recently released from the VA hospital, he now needed a place to live. Walt decided it would be better to move in with his older brother rather than continuing to live with his uncle, especially after some recent disagreements. The two young men found an apartment at 4409 Kingswell, across the street from Uncle Robert's and close enough for Roy to leave the studio in the afternoons while Walt was working on the animation to take a nap: Roy was still fairly weak from his bouts of tuberculosis. By the time Walt arrived at home, Roy had dinner ready before Walt got back to work.

In addition to singlehandedly doing the animation for *Alice's Day at Sea*, Walt also directed the live-action, paying children in the surrounding neighbourhood 50 cents per day for work as extras. One of these children was Ruthie Thompson, who often spent her afternoons watching Walt and Roy pose Virginia and give her direction until they were ready to use her as an extra. *What's so special about her?* young Thompson wondered, her arms crossed over her chest. *Why did they pick her to be Alice and not me? So what if she has pretty blue eyes and naturally curly hair.* However, all of this jealousy disappeared when Roy Disney arrived and began giving her directions. She enjoyed the man's company and often spent time in the small office behind the realty company, watching Walt draw and Roy photograph. The process didn't look very magical to her, but the whole operation seemed fascinating.

While *Alice's Day at Sea* was his first film completed for Margaret Winkler, Walt had already missed his deadline, sending the print to her eleven days later than contractually agreed on 26 December 1923. Winkler was so pressed to get the film turned around in time for release to theatres that she requested he send all the raw footage he had so they could conduct the editing at their end.

Winkler was less than impressed by the film the Disney brothers produced. "You focus too much on story and not enough on gags," she explained to Walt via telegram. "Try to include as much humour as you can in future films."

Undeterred by Winkler's criticism, Walt quickly began production on the second film in the Alice series, *Alice Hunting in Africa*, which was also submitted late to Winkler in January 1924. Once again, Winkler explained upon receipt of the film that it lacked humour and was too focused on plot. "I feel I have greatly improved on this film since *Alice's Day at Sea*," Walt wrote back to Winkler. "I assure you that I will do my best to inject humorous situations and as many humorous gags as possible in future productions."

Walt recognised that in order to give the distributor what she wanted, he needed to expand his staff and resources. Using the money received from the first two Alice films, Roy and Walt moved to a storefront located just down the street at 4649 Kingswell Avenue to accommodate a larger team of staff. They also began paying rent on a vacant lot on the corner of Hollywood Boulevard and Rodney Drive, less than half a kilometre southeast from the studio. To make themselves more reputable as an animation studio in a city based on the film industry, the name of the new organisation, THE DISNEY BROS. STUDIO, was engraved on the front window.

With more space, the two film-makers were ready to welcome more staff. In addition to Dollard and Loomis, Walt hired another animator, Rollin 'Ham' Hamilton, to help carry the load of creating Alice's cartoon world. With the recognition that animation quality and 'humorous situations' needed to increase, Walt determined that another ink-and-paint girl was needed on staff. He asked Loomis and Dollard if they knew of any girls looking for work, and Dollard reached out to Lillian Bounds, the younger sister of her friend, Hazel Sewell. Bounds had been interested in the production of the animated films, as she often watched the live-action production of *Alice Hunting in Africa* at the vacant lot across the street from her home located at 4618 Hollywood Boulevard. After speaking with Walt, she decided to take the job receiving a wage of $15 per week, officially coming on the staff on 14 January 1924.

With the larger staff and workspace, the studio began working on its next film, *Alice's Spooky Adventure*. While this film also experienced a delayed submission to Winkler due to unfavourable weather conditions, she was very happy with the final product, explaining that the quality of the humour was what she had been waiting for. Winkler was so pleased with the quality of *Alice's Spooky Adventure* that it became the first of the series she released to theatres in New Jersey, Pennsylvania, Delaware, Maryland and Washington, D.C. on 24 March. It was agreed that Virginia Davis herself would be flown to the east coast for appearances to draw audiences into theatres. After performing a little dance and bowing to the audience, she would introduce the film as the title card flashed onto the screen.

This new-found confidence began to embolden the young Walt Disney. As he moved into the next three Alice films in his first contract, he strayed away from the slapstick humour typical of animation at the time, turning instead to a more 'dignified' form of humour, which included puns, cultural references, and mischief that aligned to the overarching plots of the films. Upon submitting the films to Winkler, Walt included short notes defending his decision to focus more on incorporating comedy-driven plot rather than just a routine string of gags. Winkler was too focused on the accolades of *Alice's Spooky Adventure* to care: as long as the Disney Bros. continued turning out films of the same quality, she felt confident in the decisions Walt was making.

Not only was Walt flying high on the success of his Alice Comedies, he'd found love. Every day after work, he would offer to drive the ink-and-paint girls home in his Ford runabout, going out of his way to stop at the Sewells' last. As he pulled up at Lillian's door one evening, he got out of the car and walked around to open the door for her.

"So I'm thinking about buying myself a new suit," he explained. "When it comes in, would it be okay if I called on you?" The girl, who had found her boss handsome, creative, and enthusiastically outgoing, agreed that this would be alright.

A few days later, Walt purchased his new suit, a grey and green double-breasted deal, complete with a hat. He hopped in his car and drove down Hollywood Boulevard to the Sewells'. When he knocked on the door, Lillian's brother-in-law answered and welcomed the dapper young man inside, where the two men conversed in the foyer, the former introducing Walt to his wife. Soon Lillian appeared and, taken aback by her beauty, Walt awkwardly asked her how she liked his new suit. Everyone laughed, thinking that he was making a joke, but he had simply not known what to say in front of her sister and brother-in-law. The couple bid the Sewells a good night and climbed into Walt's car before making their way to a nearby theatre for a showing of the stage musical, *No, No, Nannette*.

With more expenses, such as increased rent and more staff members on the payroll, finances began to become strapped. Roy, who acted as bookkeeper in addition to operating the camera, explained to his brother that something needed to change if the studio was to afford to continue. Walt suggested that they reach out to their friends and family for loans, which Roy, knowing his brother's history of repaying such loans, was against. Behind Roy's back, Walt wrote to Carl Stalling and Edna Francis in Kansas City for funds, receiving $275 and $25 from them, respectively.

Roy wasn't happy when he learned of his younger brother pressuring his fiancée for finances. This was one instance in a string of recent disagreements between the two young men who were spending almost all of their time together, including living in tight proximity in their shared apartment. Things came to a head one night when, exhausted after a long day at the studio, Walt returned to the apartment to find dinner prepared by Roy on the table.

"How was the rest of the day?" Roy asked.

"Fine," Walt explained, stabbing at the food on his plate. "No thanks to you."

"What is that supposed to mean?"

"We ran into a jam and you weren't there to help out. You were here sleeping and cooking this mush instead. Speaking of work," the frustrated Walt ejaculated, pushing the plate away and standing up from the table, "there's more to do. I'll see you later."

"The hell with you!" Roy yelled, standing up as well. "If you don't like the effort I put into dinner every night, then we can quit this business of living together!"

Walt stormed out of the apartment, the sound of his shoes clunking down the stairs to the street below. Roy carried the plates over to the sink and threw on a light jacket before making his way down to the telegram exchange. In a heated moment of frustration, he jotted out a telegram to Edna Francis, suggesting that she come to Los Angeles as quickly as possible – he was ready to get married. Edna, who had been waiting for Roy to commit to marriage since before he'd gone off to fight in the First World War, immediately accepted.

The wedding was held at Uncle Robert's home in Los Angeles on 11 April and both Roy and Edna's parents were in attendance. Roy and Walt had patched things up by the day of the wedding, with the groom's younger brother serving as his best man. Because Edna didn't know anyone in Los Angeles, Lillian was her maid of honour, much to Walt's delight.

Lillian and Walt spent much of the wedding festivities draped over each other, with Walt even going as far as planting a kiss on the girl's lips in front of the rest of the family. It had quickly become apparent that the couple were more than just co-workers and that Walt had begun courting his latest employee. As their relationship progressed, Lillian quickly learned to love her boyfriend's quirky sense of humour and the way his mind worked. Never at any point did her boss take advantage of her through unwanted advances, as their relationship evolved in a healthy, organic way.

One evening, while Lillian sat next to him at the drawing board watching him work, she leaned close to him. Sensing her, Walt turned to his inker and kissed her. Their relationship moved quickly after that, with the young film-maker teasing her playfully as the main form of courting. Knowing that she preferred to work at the ink-and-paint table on animation cels, Walt would often ask her to fill in as the receptionist, not only because he knew she hated it, but also because it would give him a chance to work closer to her. When she playfully disagreed with his decision to have her work as the receptionist, Walt explained that the only way to relieve the studio of the terrible job she'd do as receptionist was to marry him. While it was not uncommon for the studio to miss pay checks for the staff due to low funds, Walt also joked that he would have to marry Lillian in order to pay off his debt to her. However, it soon became obvious that he was becoming more serious in progressing their relationship to the next level. Walt, who often lacked tact in stressful situations, explained to his steady girlfriend that "I really enjoy your sister's fried chicken and eat there with you often, so we might as well get married" and presented her with an engagement ring with a small diamond. Little time was wasted as Lillian, her sister and her mother began planning the wedding, which was set for July.

The last film of the first series of Alice Comedies was completed and sent to Winkler for distribution on 24 May 1924. Negotiations quickly began to renew the contract with the Disney Bros. Studio for the next six shorts in the initial series of Alice Comedies. However, rather than sign a deal with Margaret Winkler, Walt had to negotiate with her new husband, Charles Mintz, whom she had married in the late autumn of 1923 and who had taken over the duties of distributor. Mintz was critical of what the Disney brothers had sent thus far with the first six Alice films, complaining that the animation was 'jumpy' and lacked gags, focusing too much on story. For the remaining six films of the first series, Mintz wrote that he would only be paying the studio $900 rather than the agreed-upon payment of $1,800, citing that the first six Alice Comedies hadn't made enough in theatres to justify a full payment.

It was clear to Walt that he once again needed to produce higher-quality shorts to justify Mintz paying him full price. While he had felt that the quality of the animation, plot and gags of his films were great, no one would see them without the distributor's approval. Recognising that he needed to step back from animating to focus instead on developing stories, scenarios, and humorous situations, Walt turned to the one person he trusted to replace him by providing quality animation: Ubbe Iwwerks.

When he received the note from Walt on 1 June, Ubbe was at first hesitant to join his friend and former business partner in California, recollecting how both Iwwerks-Disney and Laugh-O-gram had gone under. However, with enough persistence and an offer of a salary of $40 per week, Walt was able to convince his friend to move west. Not wanting to leave his mother alone in Kansas City, Ubbe convinced her to join him, and the two began to pack their things up for their new life in Los Angeles. Before long, Walt had another favour to ask his friend: when the Davises moved to California, they were so eager to get Virginia to work that they'd taken the train, leaving the family car in Missouri. Would Ubbe be willing, Walt wondered, to drive their car to California? He agreed, and together Ubbe and Mrs Iwwerks took seven days to drive the Davises' Cadillac west to California.

While Mrs Iwwerks began to unpack and settle things in the small house she and her son rented near the Disney Bros. Studio, Ubbe quickly got to work producing the animated sequences for the latest Alice Comedies. One of the first things he decided was to anglicise his name as much as possible to make himself more acceptable to the American film crowd, changing the spelling of his name to Ub Iwerks.

Walt and Mintz immediately saw a change in the animation and content of the Alice Comedies as Ub came on board. With Walt more able to focus on coming up with scenarios for the films, Ub and Hamilton focused on lengthening the animated sequences so that the films were only bookended by live-action. Ub also came up with an improvement on taping Virginia in front of a white backdrop. Instead, he chose to place a Virginia-shaped matte cut-out over the camera lens so that only the girl was photographed for live-action, allowing more mobility through different settings rather than being confined to the white sheet hung in the vacant lot. Iwerks also developed a new character that accompanied Alice through the cartoon world and eventually eclipsed the girl's role: Julius the Cat. As the Alice Comedies continued to be released, the live girl began to be seen less often as Julius started to become the star of the shorts, popularised due to his ability to use his body parts for gags, such as turn his tail into a unicycle, much in the same way the Fleischers did with Felix.

Luckily Walt's plan panned out: the improved animation that resulted from Ub's work appealed to more audiences, which pleased Mintz enough to begin paying the studio the agreed-upon price of $1,800 per film. With the initial run of twelve films drawing to a close, Mintz agreed to renew the series with the Disney Bros. for twenty-six films with a new instalment to be delivered to the distributor approximately every two weeks. With this new contract, the studio actually lost money per film submitted, with Mintz reducing the per film price to $1,500 rather than the $1,800 agreed upon during the previous series. Financial difficulties would be increased even more for the studio when the contract stipulated that they would only receive a payment of $900 upon receipt of the print, with the remaining $600 to be paid within three months.

With the larger contract and the expectation from Mintz that films be delivered bi-weekly, Walt had more work than artists and decided to once again hire his best from his Laugh-O-gram days. Shortly after sending word to Kansas City to Hugh Harman and Rudy Ising, the two young men accepted their friend's offer due to the lack of opportunities in the medium in Missouri. A new cameraman was also hired, allowing Roy the opportunity to focus instead on the business side of the enterprise, as well as picking up odd jobs around the studio to help facilitate the ease of creating the films. Two new ink-and-paint girls were brought in to assist the animation process: Ham Hamilton's sister Irene and Ruth Disney, the younger sister of Walt and Roy, newly arrived from Portland.

It was also around this time that the studio developed a technical innovation which at first seemed insignificant. While many in the industry had a series of pegs across the top of the artists' tables to hold the drawings in place, someone at the Disney Bros. Studio came up with the idea of putting the pegs across the bottom of the board. This made it easier for the artists to check their drawings for accurate and lifelike movement of their drawings by putting the papers between each finger and 'rolling' them back and forth to check the animation. While the standard top pegs allowed artists to flip between two or three drawings at a time, the bottom peg system allowed for flipping between four and five drawings, saving precious time and making the animation process easier and more advanced.

Within a month of Ub joining his pal in Los Angeles, the studio released its most popular entry to the series of Alice Comedies, *Alice Gets in Dutch*. After he was able to preview the film at the Bard's Hollywood Theater, Walt ordered a few minor changes and improvements be made to the film before enthusiastically sending the print to Mintz at the end of the month. Evidently, Mintz shared Walt's excitement for the film as a few months later, he wrote to the young studio executive that the film had premiered on 20 October at Broadway's Piccadilly Theater in New York alongside the Warner Bros. feature film *This Woman*.

Mintz soon recognised the promise that the Disney Bros. had in producing quality animation. In addition to the remaining five Alice shorts, he charged the studio with reworking the first two Alice Comedies, *Alice's Day at Sea* and *Alice Hunting in Africa*, claiming that they had served as a financial liability to Winkler. He also complained that the films were too plot-driven and while Walt used extended and complex gags, the shorts lacked the slapstick gags that audiences craved. Ub quickly got down to business, reanimating some of the scenes from the initial prints in an effort to get increased payment from the distributor.

With less money immediately coming into the studio due to the new contract stipulations, Walt and Roy began to look at ways to cut costs. Walt, who had greatly expanded his art staff, petitioned the ending of the live-action portions of his films that occurred at the beginning and end of the shorts. Mintz, however, argued that the live-action sequences provided context to audiences.

With the distributor not allowing him to save money by eliminating live-action and refusing to cut costs to his animation department, Walt decided to issue a new deal to Virginia Davis. Rather than placing the girl under contract and paying her a salary as he'd done in the past, he explained to her parents that he would only pay her for the days she was shooting. Mr and Mrs Davis read between the lines to discern what was really being said: Virginia's shooting schedule would likely decrease and Walt was unwilling to pay the girl the same amount for less footage. The young film executive went on to explain that all of the live-action would be shot over a total of eighteen days during the next year, meaning that the Davises would only receive payment and their daughter would only work for two and a half weeks. After petitioning Charles Mintz in vain to pressure Walt to change his mind, Virginia's parents decided to withdraw her as the headlining character of the Alice Comedies, leaving the Disney Bros. Studio without a star.

Walt quickly found a new young girl named Dawn O'Day to replace the original Alice. However, when it became obvious to the girl's parents that Walt was unable to pay their daughter what they desired, they withdrew her services from the studio at the completion of filming *Alice's Egg Plant*.

With one last shot at solving his problems with the live-action character that drew audiences to his Alice Comedies, Walt reached out to the parents of 4-year-old Margie Gay, who had filled in for Davis in *Alice Solves the Puzzle* when the studio was negotiating with Virginia's parents. Gay's parents immediately accepted Walt's proposal, providing the studio with its new face beginning with April's *Alice Loses Out* and lasting until December 1926. While these contract negotiations over the character of Alice were a struggle for the studio, it did allow Walt to cut back on the length and number of the live-action sequences, as well as give him an opportunity to expand the quality and complexity of the animation. Julius the Cat became more of a central character, with Alice in a mere supporting role, joining other increasingly regular characters including a police dog, a skinny dachshund, and a villain named Bootleg Pete.

An expanded staff and a larger focus on animated sequences in the Alice films led to a greater emphasis on technical improvements. While earlier animated films produced by the Disney Bros. used tracing of characters, especially by less experienced animators, this often left the movement of the characters jerky and less lifelike. Walt soon asked Ub to develop character model sheets, which depicted the various characters from different angles and with different expressions, that served as reference points for those animating the characters. Almost immediately, the quality of animation improved as the lack of tracing and the increase of free-handed drawing allowed for more lifelike and fluid movement on screen.

With more artists producing the animation, Walt was finally able to focus on scenario work, including the development of stories and gags. Gathering his artists together, the young creative held story meetings where they discussed the plot of the story being told. Everyone was welcome to contribute, and often gags suggested by the various artists made it into the final cut of the film. As the story developed, Walt would often stand before his staff and act out the scenes, demonstrating the movements and expressions that he wanted shown in the films, much to the delight of the artists.

With the staff once again increasing and producing films for Mintz more often, the small studio space on Kingswell quickly became too small for day-to-day operation. Walt and Roy found space available at 2719 Hyperion Avenue, a little less than 2.5 kilometres west of the current studio. On 6 July 1925, the brothers paid $400 as a deposit on the lot.

Things had begun to move very quickly for Walt Disney, not only professionally, but personally as well. Less than a week after purchasing the land for the Hyperion studio, Walt and Lillian married on 13 July 1925. The bride wore a lavender dress as the two became man and wife in the living room of Lillian's uncle in Lewiston, Idaho, her hometown. After the small ceremony, the newlyweds boarded a train and headed north. Poor Walt found himself unable to enjoy his wedding night: he had developed toothache, which prevented him from sleeping. Rather than wake his bride, he went to the back of the train and stayed up all night, helping the sleeping car porter polish shoes before returning to wake Lillian as the sun rose. After getting his tooth pulled upon disembarkation at a dentist in Seattle, Washington, the couple was able to enjoy their honeymoon exploring the city before moving on to Mount Rainier, Washington, and stopping to see Flora and Elias in Portland before returning home to Los Angeles.

Once back in the city, Walt secured a small apartment for which he paid $40 per month. True to his word, upon marrying Lillian, Walt requested that she no longer work at the studio in an attempt to keep his private and professional life separate. However, not wanting to confine his new bride to the small apartment, Walt suggested to Roy that they purchase adjoining lots to build homes somewhere near the new studio. Roy agreed, and the brothers paid $16,000 to build neighbouring homes on Lyric Avenue, a mere 10-minute walk from the Hyperion lot. The houses were identical and were prefabricated, measuring approximately 185 square metres. Walt quickly gave Lillian a budget to fit out the house, a task she absolutely adored, while her husband was hard at work at the studio.

While things were looking up for Walt's studio as 1925 progressed, contractual relations with Charles Mintz had once again begun to break down. Rather than send the payments for the Alice Comedies directly to Walt, Mintz had started sending the cheques to George Winkler, the brother of his wife who lived in Los Angeles, to deliver to the studio. This gave the distributor the opportunity to receive insider information and keep an eye on production, as well as the chance to influence money-saving measures. This new procedure prevented royalty cheques from arriving at the studio as often as Walt would like, leading to a series of angry exchanges between the young film executive and his distributor in New York.

"I have lived up to my end of the contract," Walt explained. "It is my expectation that you do likewise. I will continue to deliver the pictures to you every sixteen days as agreed upon in our contract and expect immediate remittance in return. Your failure to do this will result in a breach of contract and will result in me looking for another distributor."

"Don't you have a grateful bone in your body?" Mintz retorted a few days later. "The first seven pictures you sent to us were a failure, a total loss to us, even though we paid you the agreed-upon amount. You should be ashamed of yourself asking for more money when we haven't made a single dollar off any picture we have received from you."

Quickly realising that he was at the mercy of the distributor and that he wouldn't make any money from his films without Mintz, Walt began to negotiate a new contract. Once again, it decreased the amount of money he would receive from the distributor, offering $1,500 per film, but also extending the offer of a 50 per cent share in all movie theatre rentals of the Alice films after the distributor had made the first $3,000 from rentals. Mintz explained to Walt that he was distributing the Alice Comedies on what was called a 'states-rights basis' for the Film Booking Office. Essentially, this meant that a distributor was renting film reels to individual theatre chains, who had the option to screen the film as many times as they liked to make as much money as possible, paying a portion of sales back to the distributor. At the end of a film's run, or in the case of a film that didn't draw audiences, the theatre owner would return the reel to the distributor, who would look for another theatre to rent the films to. If the distributor was unable to find a theatre interested in the film, it often meant that the film was a financial loss to the distributor as the fee paid to the studio had already been issued. As a result, because, Mintz argued, the previous Alice Comedies hadn't made him enough money on rentals, he was unable to justify paying Walt more per film, as it didn't guarantee a good return for himself. After much negotiating, a version of the contract was signed in February 1926 and the next series of Alice Comedies began production.

In mid-February, shortly after signing the new contract with Mintz, Walt moved his artists into their new studio home at 2719 Hyperion Avenue. Roy quickly suggested that the new studio be named the Walt Disney Studio, explaining to his little brother that it would be less confusing for audiences if they could associate the films with a single name. Roy also secretly recognised the passion that Walt had for the films and wanted his brother to revel in the success he'd finally achieved after his numerous previous failures.

Finally having a studio complex of their own, the staff began to embrace a familial lifestyle as professionalism and camaraderie became intertwined. The artists were constantly playing jokes on each other and spent time together outside of work. Athletic fields were installed on the studio campus, allowing the staff to not only exhibit friendly competition, but also giving them a chance to exercise after working a job that required them to sit hunched over an artist's desk for hours. Walt often participated in these athletic events, acting as a formidable opponent on the polo and baseball fields and badminton courts.

Throughout 1926 and 1927, it became obvious that the occasional successes the studio had experienced with the Alice Comedies had begun to wane. Walt spent late nights at the studio in an attempt to meet Charles Mintz's ever-increasing demands for more gags; not wanting to spend the night at home alone, Lillian often sat with her husband, falling asleep on the couch in his office while he worked, often until 2.00 am.

Not only was it difficult to create quality films that met the distributor's expectations in the allotted timeline, it was difficult to do so with the limited finances Mintz provided. Walt once again reached out to Dr McCrum in Kansas City, offering to make another film similar to *Tommy Tucker's Tooth*. McCrum agreed, working with the studio to write a story that would educate youngsters in how to practise good dental hygiene. The result, *Clara Cleans Her Teeth*, starred Walt and Lillian's niece, Marjorie Sewell, in the starring role, who in a dream is chased by animated dental tools which scares her into practising improved brushing techniques. While Walt didn't make much money from this contract compared to the Alice films, it was enough to help for the moment.

The stress of financial constraints and the constant barrage of insults by Mintz began to wear on the staff at the Walt Disney Studio. In late 1926, Ham Hamilton left the studio after experiencing disagreements with Walt, and was replaced by another artist from Kansas City, Isadore 'Friz' Freleng. Hamilton's departure and replacement resulted in a souring relationship between Walt and his artists, including Hugh Harman and Rudy Ising.

Mintz soon began to realize that the Alice Comedies had started losing their steam, as well. In January 1927, Margie Gay's contract as Alice ended and Walt hired a new actress, Lois Hardwick. He immediately received an angry note from the distributor, demanding to know why the star of the series had been replaced. Walt calmly explained that George Winkler had done a screen test with Hardwick and liked her in the role better than Gay, authorising her replacement. While this answer seemed to satisfy Mintz, it soon became obvious that moviegoers were less than satisfied. Mintz began to demand that the length of the films be shorter to compensate for lower returns, decreasing the length from 183 metres to 169 metres. In a panic, he soon began to threaten to not release some of the shorts at all, including *Alice Chops the Suey* and *Alice's Circus Daze*, placing blame for the lack of success on the studio.

After an examination of the declining interest in the Alice Comedies, Walt, Roy, Mintz, and George Winkler decided that the current season, which ended with *Alice in the Big League* on 22 August 1927, would be Alice's last. The blending of live-action and animation was no longer considered 'fresh' or 'new', mainly due to the success of the Fleischers' *Out of the Inkwell* series. New animated series had begun to be popular, including those developed by Paul Terry and Pat Sullivan. As a result, Walt, Roy and their distributor began to look for new ideas.

Luckily for the Walt Disney Studio, Mintz already had something lined up. In early 1927, he received word from Carl Laemmle that Universal was interested in distributing a new cartoon series. Laemmle suggested that the new series feature any kind of creature except a cat as the animation world seemed to have an overabundance of cat characters, including Felix and Julius, but left the development of the character up to Mintz.

Mintz soon reached out to Walt, suggesting that his team develop some sketches of a rabbit character as a proposal for Universal, but with one of the Big Five studios interested in distributing a series created by Walt Disney, he included an important caveat in his note.

You're in the big leagues now, the tone of his note suggested. *Don't screw this up.*

Chapter Twenty

Oswald

Over the next couple of weeks, Walt and Ub worked together on developing the new rabbit character for Universal. It was decided that it would be taller than Julius the Cat and would feature long ears and big feet, not only to characterise him as a rabbit, but also to differentiate him from the other cartoon characters seen in theatres. Ub also explained that the rabbit's rounder shapes made him easier to animate than the sharper angles of Julius. When Walt submitted the sketches to Mintz, he was non-committal, simply forwarding the concepts on to Universal.

After reviewing the drawings, Laemmle himself responded enthusiastically to them and sent a contract to Mintz to act as the go-between. The agreement, which was signed on 4 March 1927, called for twenty-six animated shorts featuring the rabbit character to be paid for by Mintz at $2,250 per film.

The name of the new character still needed to be decided. Together, Walt and his staff came up with a number of different ideas and sent them to Universal to make the final decision. Upon reaching Laemmle's office, the names were thrown into a hat and the winning name was pulled out by P.D. Cochrane, Universal's vice president of advertising. The new character finally had a name: Oswald the Lucky Rabbit.

Meanwhile, as the Walt Disney Studio finished its last Alice Comedy, Walt had Ub hard at work on producing the first Oswald film. Within two weeks, Ub and his team of animators, including Harman, Ising, and Freleng, had completed the film, *Poor Papa*. Walt provided some suggestions and criticisms, and the animators got back to work to make corrections before the final film was printed and shipped to Mintz in New York on 10 April. The short featured Oswald as a new father, overwhelmed by the sheer number of baby rabbits that his wife delivered. Over the next few minutes, Oswald finds himself becoming more and more angry as he chases his new sons and daughters around, many of whom are getting into mischief or causing destruction. At his wits' end, he climbs up onto his roof, shotgun in hand, and begins firing at a fleet of storks preparing to drop more babies down the chimney. As the cartoon ends, the new father collapses against a wall, hand on forehead, resigned to the fact that he is now provider for dozens of children.

Charles Mintz was furious by what he saw. He jotted a frustrated note to Walt, explaining that Oswald was not being portrayed as a hero that audiences could get behind and was lost in the scores of characters in the film including a doctor, Oswald's wife, the children, and an army of storks. He was also embarrassed by what Disney came up with because, he explained, the character of Oswald wasn't much different than the other animated characters on the market. Instead, he suggested, Oswald should be "young, snappy-looking and wearing a monocle". Universal agreed with Mintz's assessment, explaining to Walt that Oswald was fat and old-looking. In a letter dated 15 April, Hal Hodes, the sales director of Universal's Short Product & Complete Service Departments, explained that the animation was jerky and too repetitive, that Oswald wasn't a humorous character, and that the gags in the film were unrelated and didn't drive the story forward. As a result, it was decided that Universal wouldn't release *Poor Papa* to theatres.

Walt was crushed. He responded to Mintz's letter by explaining that he was accepting of the points made by Hodes, calling them "constructive criticism". He went on to apologise to Mintz and Universal that *Poor Papa* was so disappointing, explaining that he himself was unhappy with the finished product and assuring Mintz that his team would revisit the character and method of storytelling in the next instalment.

It was literally back to the drawing board for Ub and Walt as they sat together and looked at the character. *What is it that is distinct about Oswald the Lucky Rabbit from other cartoons on the market?* they asked themselves. It was determined that they intended for Oswald to have his own personality on-screen, one that was grouchy, highly energetic, whose emotions were obvious and who solved problems in a distinctly creative manner. To capture this personality, they slightly changed the look of the character, making him appear more youthful and thinner than he did in *Poor Papa*. They also determined that Oswald himself wouldn't cause gags through mischief, but rather *respond* to events unfolding around him in a creative way which would lead to a gag.

Taking this new philosophy towards the character, Ub quickly got to work on the second Oswald film, *Trolley Troubles*, completing it within two weeks for shipment to Mintz on 1 May. Universal was much happier with the second Oswald film, deciding to premiere the film on 4 July at Los Angeles' Criterion Theater and on 9 July at New York's Roxy Theater, going into general circulation throughout the nation on 5 September. Reviewers loved Oswald the Lucky Rabbit too, explaining that audiences erupted in laughter at the on-screen action, while Universal's in-house newsletter called the short film a 'sensation'. Throughout America, theatre marquees began to advertise 'Oswald the Lucky Rabbit', which drew just as many crowds to the theatres as the feature films. Jealous that Walt Disney was getting all the credit, Charles Mintz explained to him that the real credit should go to George Winkler, who had begun hanging out around the studio, delivering notes from his brother-in-law, and even occasionally consulting on the films.

Walt had finally found the success he'd been looking for since his entry into the world of film in 1921. With the success of *Trolley Troubles*, the Walt Disney Studio began to turn out new animated shorts every two weeks, receiving the agreed-upon amount of $2,250 per film from Mintz. To meet their schedule, Walt began hiring more animators and ink-and-painters, increasing the size of his staff from ten to twenty-two by the end of 1927. During this time, Walt drew extensively from his Kansas City crowd, hiring back Ham Hamilton and Carman Maxwell, as well as Les Clark, a young artist looking for an entry into the industry. With the added pressure of producing a popular and successful series, Walt's expectations for his staff increased, to the chagrin of his artists. As a result, he had little mercy for Rudy Ising, firing the young man he'd worked with for years, when Rudy fell asleep while photographing one of the films.

Recognising the short timeline that delivering a film every two weeks necessitated, Walt made some changes to the structure of his studio. Production was divided into two separate units, putting his best animators, Ub Iwerks and Hugh Harman, in charge of each respective unit. He also instituted a more formalised process of developing the animated shorts. After the script of each one was typed out, Ub and Harman developed rough sketches of the action in each scene so that the animators assigned to a sequence knew how it would progress.

As the series continued, more characters were developed to accompany Oswald on his adventures. Some of the characters were recycled from the Alice Comedies, including the dachshund, police dog, and recurring villain, renamed Putrid Pete instead of Bootleg Pete. Recognising that Oswald needed a love interest, a female rabbit named Fanny was developed, which added a whole new layer of humour as the films' protagonist was constantly vying for her attention, leading to scores of gags. After the sixth Oswald film, *All Wet*, Fanny was replaced by an unnamed female cat who would serve as his love interest until the end of the series.

The situations of the Oswald films varied. While the characters and personality of Oswald stayed consistent throughout the shorts, the roles of the cartoon rabbit changed from film to film. For example, in July's *Oh Teacher*, Oswald played a schoolboy defending his sweetheart from the playground bully. In December's *Harem Scarem*, Oswald was a tourist visiting a Moroccan café who fell in love with a belly-dancer. While the films were often situational comedies, the gags and details often came from the news and current events. For example, in September's *Rickety Gin*, Oswald plays a cop who goes head-to-head against Putrid Pete, the head of a bootleg liquor gang in prohibition-era America.

With increased popularity, Universal began to actively advertise Oswald through an extensive marketing campaign. Merchandise featuring the Lucky Rabbit began to be offered to consumers, including a milk chocolate candy bar produced by Portland's Vogan Candy Company. The bar became incredibly popular and itself was advertised in the windows of drug stores and in newspapers, only adding to the popularity of Walt Disney's character.

As the studio staff increased and the papers continued to sing his praises, the executive of Walt Disney Studios began to feel like his work was worth more than what Mintz was paying him. In addition to the constant criticism of his films, the distributor became frustrated as Walt had begun playing hardball, requesting that the price per film be increased to $2,500.

Unbeknownst to Walt, Mintz instructed George Winkler to begin holding secret meetings with Walt's animators in the evenings, planting ideas in their heads that their boss was creating a foul working environment. Citing the recent firing of Rudy Ising, Winkler suggested that Oswald's recent success was making Walt paranoid and abusive, willing to stoop to whatever means possible to ensure his own success at the expense of his staff.

As the top artist working at the Walt Disney Studio, Ub was one of the first approached by Winkler to turn against his boss. However, Ub's devotion to his friend, which extended back to their time together at Pesmen-Rubin, overcame the lies being told by the distributor. He mentioned the clandestine meetings to Walt who, in his pride, refused to believe what his friend told him and feigned unconcern.

Married life continued to be good for both Walt and Lillian. Their house felt even more like a home when, on Christmas Day 1927, he presented her with a wrapped hatbox. As Walt handed Lillian the gift, it shifted and moved in her hands, feeling much heavier than she expected a hat to be. A small scratching and whimpering noise came from inside the box as she began to untie the ribbon that held the top on. When she lifted the top, she gasped as she discovered a small puppy inside the box. Lillian was immediately smitten with the small Chow and named the new addition to the family Sunnee.

Meanwhile, as the first series of twenty-six Oswald films came to a close, Walt decided it was time to negotiate the subsequent series with Mintz: if Universal expected the Walt Disney Studios to continue producing Oswald the Lucky Rabbit at the same high quality, the price delivered per film would need to increase. Walt determined that the best way to conduct what he assumed would be difficult negotiations was to visit Mintz in person rather than send telegrams. Thus, in February 1928, Walt and Lillian Disney boarded a train to New York City, leaving Roy in charge of the studio.

Without Walt's knowledge, Winkler had made the decision to move forward with producing Oswald shorts without Walt's leadership. As Walt was heading east by locomotive, Charles Mintz signed a new three-year contract with Universal to produce Oswald shorts. Tired of the constant begging for money and control over creative license that Walt demanded, Mintz determined that George Winkler would become the new head of animation over the Oswald films and ordered Winkler to sign new contracts with all the Disney artists in Walt's absence. Only Ub Iwerks and Les Clark refused to turn on their friend, choosing instead to resign rather than become employees of Mintz.

As Walt entered Charles Mintz's office in New York, unaware of what was transpiring in Los Angeles, he could perceive that something was awry. Sitting down at the negotiating table, Walt made his request that his studio be paid an additional $250 per film than the previous season. Mintz countered with an offer of $1,800 per film.

Walt was incredulous. He was having a hard-enough time producing a film on $2,250 using the staff he already had, he explained. How could he possibly produce a high-quality film for $450 less?

Mintz explained that the offer of $1,800 per film stood. Not only that, he went on, but Walt would no longer be in charge of the studio but rather a subcontractor who would submit to George Winkler, the new head of production.

As Walt left Charles Mintz's studio that afternoon, he wandered out in a daze. What had happened? What would he do? He realised that he needed to get word back to Roy in California to secure his artists before Mintz's plan went into action.

"There's a break with Charlie looming," Walt explained in a telegram to his brother. "Write a new contract with the boys before we're undermined. Offer them a 10 per cent pay increase with the option for bonuses, too. Don't worry – everything is okay." Unfortunately, Walt was too late.

The next day, when Walt returned to Mintz's office, he began to make threats that he would find a new distributor for the Oswald films through unless he received the $2,500 per film he asked for. Mintz laughed in his face. Walt couldn't legally negotiate with another studio without ole' Charlie Mintz, he explained. Walt Disney Studios didn't own Oswald the Lucky Rabbit: Mintz did.

There was little Walt Disney could do. While he had created Oswald the Lucky Rabbit with Ub Iwerks and his name was on the studio that produced the shorts, film distributors in the early part of the twentieth century owned the rights to the character. This meant that legally, since *Poor Papa* debuted in 1927, Oswald and his twenty-six animated shorts *never* belonged to Walt but to Mintz the entire time.

Walt recognised that in his naivety, Mintz had won. Standing in the doorway of the distributor's office, he conceded defeat and told Mintz he could have Oswald. The young artist had one more thing to offer his devious previous distributor: a strong word of advice.

"Watch your back, Charlie," he explained. "If the boys abandoned me, they'll do the same to you." Walt's prophecy to Mintz ended up coming true: in 1929, Universal decided to part ways with Charles Mintz when they gave the series to Walter Lantz, whom Mintz had hired to direct the Oswald shorts after stealing the character from Walt Disney. Lantz and Universal would go on to create new Oswald the Lucky Rabbit cartoons until 1938.

Returning to the hotel to find Lillian, Walt didn't need to tell his wife anything: she knew by his mannerism that the fight was over.

"Let's get out of this hell hole," he suggested. Stopping by the Western Union office at a New York train station, he sent word back to Roy: LEAVING TONIGHT, STOPPING OVER IN KANSAS CITY. EVERYTHING OK.

Together, Walt and Lillian boarded the New York Central Cannonball to return to Los Angeles. Walt's final conversation with Charles Mintz had left him a changed man. Feeling like the richest man in the world when he arrived in New York City not two weeks before due to the success he'd experienced with Oswald, he was returning home impoverished, realising that he'd owned nothing. He recognised that in this world, the only person one could truly trust was oneself. He vowed he would never work for another person the rest of his life.

As the New York Central Cannonball followed the sun westward towards Los Angeles on 13 March 1928, Walt Disney felt like he was leaving his dreams behind.

The 26-year-old artist had five days to stew about the injustice that had been done to him by the artists he'd trusted most and Charles Mintz. He had decided that, while he had been betrayed, finishing the current season of Oswald cartoons would be the right thing to do. If all went according to schedule, the final animated film, *Hot Dog*, would be completed and submitted to Universal on 3 August.

As the train sped through Missouri a few evenings after Walt and Lillian left New York, the conductor stepped into the first-class cabin and announced that they would be stopping in a little town called Marceline to refuel; passengers were welcome to step off the train to stretch on the platform, even though it was the middle of the night.

Walt contemplated whether to get off the train or not. Marceline had been so special to him. It had taught him about hard work, discipline, and community. *Some good those lessons did me*, he scoffed to himself. Even though he had been disciplined and worked hard to follow his dreams, they'd never been his for the taking. And not only that, but the community he'd built over the years at Laugh-O-gram and the Walt Disney Studios had abandoned him.

He realised that living in Marceline had also taught him to never give up, primarily through watching his father do everything he could to maintain the family farm and attempt to convince his neighbours to better their lots against the banks and railroad companies. In the end, his fondness for his Marceline years won him over and he decided he would give this animation business one more shot. Reaching over, he gently shook Lillian awake and told her he wanted to get off the train in his Marceline during their one-hour stop-over to show off the small town he was so proud of.

After their short stop in Marceline, the train continued on to Kansas City, where the young couple disembarked to spend a day touring to help break up the monotony of the journey. As they wandered around the city, Walt showed Lillian the Bellefontaine house that served as the hub for Elias's paper route. He recounted the years getting up hours before dawn, sometimes in the freezing cold, to deliver newspapers, explaining that it had taught him to work hard simply because it was the right thing to do, even in the face of adversity. They passed the Scottish Rite temple where Walt had been inducted as a DeMolay in 1920, where Dad Land instilled in him the importance of fidelity, courtesy, comradeship, and creativity. Walt even took the time to show his wife where he worked for Pesmen-Rubin, the Kansas City Film Ad Company, and finally the Laugh-O-gram studio, explaining how he'd started as a simple lettering artist and had worked his way up to become one of the premier producers of animated shorts in Kansas City.

As their time in Kansas City came to an end, the couple made their way through the Grand Hall and into the North Waiting Room of Union Station. Walt recalled how, for years, he had visited Union Station every week to bathe because in his homelessness, he didn't have running water otherwise.

Standing beneath the large glowing clock, Walt realised he had a major decision to make and little time to do it in. His decision had two options, but only one terminus could be chosen: should he simply give up following his dream and potentially lead Lillian and himself into financial ruin as he did when he had been living in the Laugh-O-gram studio, or would he choose to work hard, overcome adversity, and use his creativity to press forward and change the route to achieving his dream?

As the couple made their way through the west doors of the North Waiting Room, down the wooden staircase to the platforms below, and stepped onto the train that would lead them home to Los Angeles, Walt had made his decision.

But how to get to his dream? How would he restart and rise from the ashes to once again become a somebody in the world of animation?

As the train began moving and headed west out of Kansas City, it passed a small forest of trees. He remembered goofing around at Swope Park with his artists while he operated Laugh-O-gram and how he had released his pet mice into the park when he decided to move to California.

Mice. Nobody had created an animated mouse before.

"I'm thinking about making a new character," Walt suggested to Lillian. "A mouse. I'll call him Mortimer."

"Mortimer? That doesn't sound quite right," Lillian said.

Walt raised his eyebrow. His wife sat quietly, watching the trees fly past the windows. Turning to look at Walt, she made another suggestion.

"What about Mickey?"

A Word from the Author

When I write my books, I want to make them as historically accurate as possible. As a result, I rely on a number of different methods.

First and foremost is the research. Extensive research is conducted. This takes place through electronic databases, newspaper articles, historical journals, monographs, local histories, and with the assistance of local researchers. In the case of this biography, I also drew upon a number of well-known and lesser-known biographies and bibliographies about the life of Walt Disney, all of which are listed in the bibliography at the end of this book.

While *some* liberties have been taken in dialogue that occurs in this book, nothing that was said was historically inaccurate. At times, I have combined or slightly modified quotes by important individuals found in other biographies, have pulled things from speeches or interviews given by Walt Disney himself, or have even hypothesised about conversations that Walt, his friends and family may have had surrounding specific events. However, everything that was said by any of the players in this book *is* historically accurate, if not verbatim, then what may have been said.

In order to really get into the stories that I tell, I especially like to travel and experience what my main characters would have experienced. For example, when I wrote my *A Historical Tour of Walt Disney World* book series, I wandered around Walt Disney World and made first-hand observations. In researching for the series *Walt Disney and the 1964–1965 New York World's Fair* I visited Springfield, Illinois and Dearborn, Michigan in order to see where the Illinois Commission to the New York World's Fair met, as well as the headquarters for the Ford Automotive Company that planned the Magic Skyway Pavilion for the World's Fair.

In researching for this book, I was personally able to travel to Chicago and step *inside* the home where Walt Disney was born and spent his first few years on Tripp Avenue. I was able to admire the designs that were birthed in Flora Disney's mind and the work crafted by Elias's hands. I was also able to visit St. Paul's Congregational Church a few blocks away, which Elias helped to build and where he served as a deacon and guest pastor. Those interested in the excellent restoration process that has been occurring at the Disney home on Tripp Avenue should check out www.TheWaltDisneyBirthplace.org to see the amazing work being done, as well as to find out when the venue is holding Disney-themed events and tours.

The research process is not just visual and auditory, but can also tap into the other senses as well. As I researched, I came across the information that rights to the O-Zell Soda Company had been purchased and the company had been restored. The new owners of O-Zell have produced a half-dozen sodas, not only mimicking the recipes of those created when Elias and Walt worked for the factory in Chicago, but also new and innovative flavours, such as Pineapple Whip, which tastes *exactly* like the Dole Whip treats sold at Disneyland and Walt Disney World resorts. For more information about this great company, visit www.O-Zell.com.

I originally had plans to make a pilgrimage to Missouri in April 2020, but due to the Coronavirus pandemic, I had to cancel. I was devastated: as a historian, I have always found it easier to convey a story by walking in the footsteps of my individuals of study. Unfortunately, I found it more prudent to stay home and quarantine to keep myself, wife, and boys safe and healthy. It also quickly became obvious that even if I did travel to Missouri, nothing would be open due to the extended closures of businesses, restaurants, and museums throughout the nation.

As the country began to reopen in the late spring and early summer, my wife suggested that I once again pursue a trip to Walt's homeland. As a teacher who was conducting distance learning from home, it didn't matter *when* I travelled. My wife, who was sick of staring at the interior walls of our home, decided she and the boys would join me, conducting their own distance learning from the backseat of our minivan.

Through email communication, I was able to line up tours of the Walt Disney Hometown Museum in Marceline, which led to mind-blowing opportunities, including a one-on-one tour of Marceline with Kaye Malins, the director of the museum, spending the night on Don Taylor's farm, and enjoying an evening being entertained at Walt Disney's childhood farmhouse, now a private residence.

I was also able to connect with Dan Viets, author and co-owner of the Laugh-O-gram Studios, who gave an afternoon talking to me about Walt's life in Kansas City, as well as an automobile tour of the city and important Disney locations, culminating in a few minutes conversing on the front porch of the Bellefontaine house, also currently owned by a private individual.

When I found out that Union Station wasn't open like I had originally thought, I was crushed. Out of all the things in Kansas City that I'd been looking forward to seeing and touring, Union Station was it. My wife suggested that I send an email to the station leadership explaining the purpose of my visit, which I reluctantly did. Within a few hours, I received a call from the office of Union Station's marketing department, who was excited to give me a private tour the next day of the magnificent Beaux-Arts structure. Later that afternoon, we enjoyed a picnic across the street from Union Station in Penn Valley Park in the shadows of the Liberty Memorial, whose ground-breaking and dedication ceremony Walt had attempted to film for theatre newsreels.

Ironically, I didn't plan on having first-hand research on the 1918 Spanish influenza epidemic. Along with everyone else on our planet, I was impacted by the novel Coronavirus, also known as COVID-19, which emerged during the latter part of 2019 before it became a global pandemic in the first quarter of 2020. As I was researching and writing the chapter about the spread of the Spanish flu around Chicago and Walt taking ill, schools around North Carolina, including the one I teach at, were closed, and my city was put under a shelter-in-place ordinance, preventing my family from leaving home. While horrified by the number of deaths globally from the Coronavirus, and feeling great empathy with those whose families, jobs and bank accounts were impacted by the virus, it was fascinating for me as a historian and researcher to see the way that the United States reacted to the illness, almost identically to how it responded to the Spanish flu over 100 years ago.

While I have written and published four books on Walt Disney World and events significant to the history of the Walt Disney Company, this book left me with a new experience: upon completing the book in July 2020, I found myself saddened as I typed out the last few lines of the story. Yes, Walt and Lillian were incredibly discouraged at their misfortune of losing Oswald and most of the artists to Charles Mintz, but the story ended on a high note with the 'birth' of Mickey Mouse. Rather, I found myself saddened as I finished telling the story of the early life of Walt Disney.

As an avid reader over the past three decades, I have heard authors time and again talk about how the end of a book brings similar feelings, as though they have got to know the subjects of their books as family. I never really understood that sentiment until now. Over the past year, I have visited three separate homes that the Disney family lived in, two schools attended by Walt, his first official studio in Kansas City, and have even walked a portion of the paper route that Walt and Roy delivered on. I feel like I have got to know the mischievous and creative young man who was born in Chicago, experienced Marceline, and came of age in Kansas City. And now, as I tap out the last few keystrokes of the book, I feel as though this is a goodbye.

Walt Disney was the ultimate dreamer, achieving his dreams to become an animator, to create the first full-length animated film, to create a presence as a film icon on television, and to create a place that families can enjoy together. He has also inspired millions of others to dream.

So maybe this isn't goodbye.

I have a dream that this is only the beginning.

Appendix

A Tour of the Walt Disney Birthplace

30 December 2019

Rey Colón, a former alderman for the Hermosa neighbourhood of Chicago, now partners with the Walt Disney Birthplace by performing a number of jobs for the organisation, headquartered in California.

As Rey leads my family and I around the right side of the Disney home, he begins by explaining the rear exterior of the structure.

Rey: Kind of like the yellow tone of the house, that's the original house. When the house was built, it ended where the light green is. Where that board is. Like I said, the house would not have had the foundation. It would have been at-grade [on the same level]. So, they just would have had a one-step stoop that they could walk out of to come outside of the house. So, the restoration that's taken place really only reflects the older part of the house. What you're going to see inside is going to be kind of like the house as it was at that time at that size.

Andrew: Okay.

Rey: The extra space we're using as a back office, a venue for events and things like that. Also the bays [windows] in the front, that's been recreated. There are two more houses on the block that Elias Disney built and one of them is not intact but is mostly intact and the other one is totally remodelled, so we took basically the influence of that bay over there on this one here.

Andrew: Do you by any chance know what those addresses are so that we can drive by them later?

Rey: One of them is 2114. I wanna say one of them is 2018 and maybe the other one is 2116 but I'm not 100 per cent sure.

We have now entered the house and are looking at photographs in the parlour.

Rey: This is kind of the way the house looked. We have two pictures of the house. This is more or less how it looked. We have a picture of the house after it was renovated. The other thing is that they made it into two flats so we had to convert it back to a single family home.

Rey: As I mentioned, that's a colorised picture – the only picture we have of Walt at the house, and Ruth his younger sister. So, after the house was renovated and converted into two flats, this is a photograph of the way it looked like. Which is kind of like the era we would like to replicate. Because we had no plans to go by, we had to do a forensic demolition. This floor was totally replaced, so we couldn't really use the floor as a guideline. We had to kind of go into the walls. There were a lot more windows here but they were not in the original place so we had to find where the original windows were and put them back. So that's basically what we did.

Rey: That's the end of the house right there as it was then. That square there is where there was a window. So, this would have been the living room. In those days they called it the parlour. I guess when people passed away and they had their visitation, they used to do it in the parlour but after they did away with that practice, they changed the name to the living room. Thus, not the dead room. (Laughter) The other thing is that all these mouldings are a recreation of what was there. There was one closet under the stairs that still had the original mouldings, so we replicated those and put them throughout the house.

Rey: This floor is not original to the house but on the second floor, we peeled off a layer of flooring and found the original floor so it was a lot easier to figure out where the bedrooms were. We kind of divided them up accordingly and really reconstructed the second floor based on what was on the floor. Over here, we had to look at what was in the ceiling and what was on the walls in order to find out where everything was.

Rey: This area over here would have been a dining room. This little corner here, that's a chimney stack. All of the stoves would have been connected to that, both upstairs and downstairs and also in the kitchen. Most likely all the stoves were pretty much connected to that stack. They would have burned coal or wood back in that time. According to the city's water records, the Disneys were the first on the block to have running water and a sewer, and that's probably the reason why Elias was building houses on the block because it was a place where he could do that. So, we believe that this was kind of his model home, and in addition to living in it, one that he could show people, 'You know, this is what you could get.' And they built this house for $800 at the time.

Andrew: And Flora designed everything.

Rey: Flora designed it. Flora was the architect of the house and Elias built the house.

Rey: Elias was also a deacon at a local church around the corner. And Pastor Walter Barr [sic] and Elias were very good friends. The reverend named one of his children Elias, and Elias named one of his children Walter, which was Walt. It's interesting because a lot of people in the neighbourhood don't realise the extensive history that the Disneys have here in the neighbourhood. We even have some old clippings from the *Chicago Tribune* ground-breaking ceremony for the church. They didn't use photography, they just did renderings, but there's a rendering of Elias Disney there.

Rey: We had Mickey Mouse here last year [2018] for Walt's birthday. On 5 December every year we have some type of a birthday celebration, so that year the Disney Company sent us the real Mickey Mouse from Florida, so it was very nice.

Rey: The house is like 99 per cent complete, but not 100 per cent, so we're just in the fundraising stage. We're still trying to get the electronics figured out. You'll see some of these speakers that are being installed throughout the house for different effects. And this window will be a large LED screen so it will look like a window but when you look outside, you'll see how things were in 1893 when the house was built. So that's the plan. Both upstairs and downstairs you'll see these cut-outs and those are where the original windows were.

Rey: This is the kitchen. Throughout the house you can see we have these little renderings like the one of the living room. They're concepts of how it might look once we furnish it. We had those renderings done with kind of like period furniture, stoves and appliances and that type of thing. And you'll see here that we still have this cut-out there. We did find that this was the doorway, but it took us a long time to figure that out because we didn't want to disrupt any of the original plaster that was in the house. We had to kind of mismatch, where's their drywall, where's their plaster and kind of figure out. The owners did take it with them but right over the doorway was a huge horseshoe. And they had it, so we think that was original to the house as well.

Andrew: So, this door would go into the backyard?

Rey: Correct. Back in that time, it would have gone into the yard. We don't really have any plans of that garage, but most of the neighbours, according to the plans, all had barns at that time.

Andrew: So then in 1905–1906 there was the break-in in the car barn and Elias was upset because the two boys that supposedly killed the police officer were the same age as Ray and Herb. Is that around here? Or was that somewhere else?

Rey: Right. It was around here. It was his kind of like reasoning for wanting to leave Chicago because of the crime in the area. So yeah, that would be been in this area.

Andrew: And that would have been a car barn, kind of like the garage?

Rey: Yes. The other thing I guess that I wanted to point out is it took us a long time to figure out if there was a washroom in the house. But one of the city water inspectors did a tour of the house and pretty much pointed out that the ventilation plumbing which goes up the side of the house, so the washroom would have been under the stairs. They didn't have a bathtub but they had a toilet and a hand sink. We have a farm sink in the back that has not gotten installed yet, but that's going to go over on this wall here. And then there will be a stove here which will connect to this chimney stack.

Rey: All the doors were purchased from an old farmhouse in Indiana from that same period. A lot of the oak woodwork and the doors are not original to the house, but we did try to find the wood from that time.

Rey: The railings are not original, but the stairs are. And you'll see upstairs where the floor looks kind of scratched up, those are original and we didn't want to alter them. We just scrubbed them down with some Murphy soap and kept things as is.

Rey: Actually in addition to getting the doors donated we also had someone who actually designed that transom from the one at Disneyland and sent it to us. So, we are going to have a light installed in the back of that. But that's kind of like the Disney crest that you'll find at Disneyland.

Andrew: That's cool.

Andrea (Andrew's wife): That's really fun.

Rey: It is fun.

Andrea: So, the stairs are original.

Rey: Yeah, the stairs are but the railings are not. (sounds of walking upstairs)

Rey: As you see up here, we had a little more to go by. Some of the floor has been repaired but what you see here is original. So, once we lifted the other floor, we kinda knew where the doorways were and so we just filled it in accordingly. We've got three bedrooms up here. One of them would have been the boys' bedroom and one of them would have been Ruth's bedroom. And again, that's the end of the house.

Rey: Our plan here is to keep that doorway but to make it look like a window. So, it will still function as a door so we can still utilise the rest of the house and the emergency exit. They were kind of packed into this house.

Rey: This floor was redone. It's new. But the reason is because this was a washroom and the original floor was pretty much rotted out. And as I mentioned there was a floor on top of this.

Rey: This would have been another bedroom. Again, the same concept with the magic window.

Andrea: So, these are original floors?

Rey: These are all original except for these boards here. Throughout the house we saw the piping for gas lighting so these boards would have been directly over the light fixture downstairs and this would have been the light fixture that would have been in the dining room.

Andrew: Have you guys been able to identify based on records which room Walt would have been born in?

Rey: Yes. Well, the master bedroom is the most likely room that he was conceived and born in. And it's the only room that has a closet that's actually big – a big closet which would lead us to believe that it was most likely kind of a nursery of sorts, 'cuz Ruth was also born here so they had some of the kids here. We'll go there now.

Rey: And these again are the vents from the little wash closet downstairs. And those vents go up to the ceiling.

Rey: While there was nothing written to confirm it, we believe that this is the room that Walt would have been born in. And again, there is that closet over there that I spoke about. In those days they really didn't have closets. They would use an armoire. They wouldn't have that much clothes. So, these windows, again we had to move them to their original location. And you probably see these little name tags around the house – they are part of our fundraising efforts to help get the project done. While Disney has donated to the project this is a non-profit effort and so we are always raising money [in] different ways – finding ways to raise money to keep the project going.

Rey: We also found on our little search there's this compartment here [points to a square hole in the floor]. When we were sweeping up some linoleum there was this little kind of squared off area here. When I gave the people from Disney Archives a tour, a woman says she has a box that fits this compartment here. [It] would have had all the important papers of the house: birth certificates, marriage certificate, deeds, all that type of stuff. They would have had their bed here and would have had their important stuff hidden under the bed there. It was kind of like their safe.

Andrea: That's neat.

Rey: Yeah, it is kind of neat. We found a newspaper stuffed in there from 1913, a German newspaper, and the family that bought the house after the Disneys were German, so we think it was something that got left behind when they redid the house and like I said, there was a floor on top of this. They left newspapers throughout the house in the walls. It was kind of like markers of time when they did these different changes. It's not a very big house, so it's not a very big tour.

Andrea: The windows were decorated like that? That was the look that they had?

Rey: We put the windows where they originally were. These are Marvin windows so the windows cost more than what they spent to build the house. But we put them in their location and based on the cut-outs that were in the wall, that's the correct size. The ones downstairs are actually pretty long. They had a lot of sunlight – natural light – in the house.

Andrew: Elias came here in 1893 for the World's Fair. The World's Fair was done so he started building houses. What did he do? Was that all he did when he lived here at the house before they moved to Marceline, build houses? Or…

Rey: Well no, he built the houses but I believe he was working on the World's Fair as well. He was doing both.

Andrew: And that was out at the lakeshore. Did he take a trolley to get out there?

Rey: That's a good question. I don't know how he commuted back and forth. You know, when they came back to Chicago they didn't live in this area. They were closer to the University of Illinois area.

Andrew: And they came back around the First World War, right?

Rey: Yes.

Andrea: So how did you get involved in this?

Rey: I was actually on the Chicago City Council at the time [the house began being restored] and this was my district. They came to see me a few times and after getting off the council, they approached me about becoming part of this project. I'm kind of like the Chicago person on the ground, doing events, getting permits, fundraisers, tours, overseeing the construction and the project management of the restoration of the house. Or to give somebody a tour. I'm the person that's here. They come a couple of times a year. Eventually we hope to have a full-swing of events and tours happening in the house. There are some events getting planned right now so there will be more fundraising efforts for us to complete the house.

Andrew: So, do you guys have a projected time of when you plan on having it open?

Rey: We do and every time we do, it changes. I'm thinking in another year because everything has taken a year. You know, building the porch… it's kind of been a pay-as-you-go project so we raise funds, we do another phase. You know we've gotten really far on the place. If you would have seen it five years ago it looks nothing like it did back then. I don't know if you've gone on our website, but there are lots of pictures there of what the house used to look like and what it looks like now. Again, we had to de-convert it from a two-flat to a single family home and figure all that out so this was a living room over here, that was a dining room back there, where you saw the bedroom was a washroom, behind the wall was a kitchen in the addition of the house.

Andrew: So, they had a stairway to get up the back or something?

Rey: Yeah, there was a porch – there's an enclosed porch but it was not part of that period. So that was added on. There was a door downstairs separating that apartment from this apartment. So, when they bought the house there were two families living here.

Maxwell (Andrew's son): Where's the beds? Like the beds that used to be here?

Rey: Right now we don't have any furniture. Part of what we're doing is we're raising some money and we're getting some antique furniture back from that time period. But there's been a lot of families that have lived here and a lot of different beds that have been here. So, the Disneys took their beds with them when they left.

Andrea: Are you charging a fee to tour it, do you think?

Rey: Yeah, I think the plan is, so as not to disrupt the parking of the neighbours, to have an off-site visitors centre and just kind of be able to tell the story, not just of the house but just the neighbourhood and the church, what the Disneys did and to be able to tell their story. Because the house itself is not a big tour. It's like really small. But you know, how the house got built, the whole story with the church, Elias being [a] carpenter, and building houses for sale, all of his different business ventures. So, when they came back and Walt was a teenager, he worked at Elias's – he had some interest in a soda pop company called O-Zell and so the owners of the house bought the rights to O-Zell so they are selling O-Zell soda online. They're having it made. They have O-Zell coffee. Elias was a religious guy who didn't like alcohol so the soda business was his thing.

Andrea: We're glad you could show us.

Rey: We're glad that the house is here. I live just a couple of doors away from where Frank Baum wrote *The Wizard of Oz*. And you know, there's only a marker – there's a sign on the parkway that says that there was a house here but the house is not there. It's like public housing there. The one thing that they did that was nice is they replaced the sidewalk with yellow bricks. And they have a big kind of corner marker that says "There's no place like home". So that's something that they just did a few months ago. But you know it makes you grateful [for] an important structure like this, and that we're able to kind of bring it back to what it would have looked like and pretty much have it intact.

Andrew: Yeah. So, were a lot of the houses that are on this street built the same time as this one?

Rey: Yes, the ones that you see are wood and they would have been the same thing. The houses would have been lifted. There was a lot of flooding that happened in the houses that were at-grade so it just became a thing to start building basements and foundations which is what happened here.

Andrew: Okay. So, they just lifted the entire house then up to a—

Rey: They lifted the entire house. That's why we lost the floor on the first floor. You probably saw that we have the Honorary Disney Family Avenue street sign. We were able to do that a few years ago. Like I said, because I was on the city council, I was able to write that ordinance and just have the alderman sign off on it. There are street signs between two blocks in both directions.

Andrew: Okay. And then I had talked to the guys that are kind of heading up this project on the phone and they said there's a school that Roy went to. Is it that big school back there?

Rey: Yes, that school there. That's Nixon Elementary School, so yeah, Roy would have gone there. Walt was 4 when they moved, so he never got a chance to go there. But that would have been like a state-of-the-art school back in that time period. We have a really good partnership with that school and so whenever we have our events here, their choir, we give them access to the house if they ever want to do storytelling or that stuff. So, we do work with local neighbourhood organisations. That little community library [Rey indicates a small box on a post in the front yard] – this neighbourhood is called Hermosa, so the Hermosa Neighbourhood Association – we worked with them on putting that library together. And we just dedicated that on the fifth of this month.

Andrew: So, then the road – was it a dirt road? Was it blocks like a brick road?

Rey: I'm not sure what they would have used. I know a lot of times they just threw down wood planks and I know a lot of the roads were like that. But when they put in the sewer system, I'm not sure. We're still replacing a lot of sewers that are 100 years old. Some of them were made out of wood. I'm not sure what they had here. They were replaced—they've been replaced since then.

Maxwell: What are those pipes, mommy?

Rey: Those pipes are for air. When you would have flushed the toilet, they needed ventilation and that's what those pipes are. Having a toilet was a big deal in those days.

Rey: We would love it if you guys signed our guest book.

Andrew: Oh absolutely.

Rey: Whenever I give a tour we like to kind of memorialise who came through.

Andrew: Did this photograph come out of the newspaper? Or was this a photograph that somebody took in the family?

Rey: I'm not sure where they got it. I guess photography was relatively expensive back then so there's not a lot of it. It looks like they made Walt sit a long time for it. (laughter)

Maxwell: And Ruth.

Rey: And Ruth.

Andrew: So, Flora, she just stayed home with the kids.

Rey: Yes.

Andrew: And Walt and Ruth and the boys just kind of ran around the neighbourhood?

Rey: It looks that way. This part of the city would have been newly incorporated into Chicago. This was a very rural part of the area, so… probably a lot of farmland over here at that time.

Andrew: So, lots of migrants?

Rey: Yes.

Andrew: So, was there a large immigrant population that was moving out to this area? The Europeans?

Rey: Probably German. A lot of German. It was very European back then. I mean, very close to here is Humboldt Park. And like I said, we found the German newspaper, so a German family moved into this. This was primarily German [with] lots of different European ethnicities here.

Andrew: Okay, and how far away were the slaughter yards from here? The stockyards?

Rey: Oh, they were quite a distance from here. They're very southeast from this location. They would have been nearby – closer to where the Disneys lived when they moved back to Chicago. But even still a little distance from there. It was that far east but further south.

At the end of the tour, we signed the guest book, thanked Rey for his time and parted ways.

Bibliography

Abbott, Karen, *Sin and the Second City: Madams, Ministers, Playboys, and the Battle for America's Soul*, (Random House Trade Paperbacks, New York, 2007)

American Red Cross, 'The American National Red Cross Annual Report for the Year Ended June 30, 1918', (The American Red Cross, Washington, D.C., 1919)

American Red Cross, 'Annual Report of the American Red Cross', (The American Red Cross, Washington, D.C., 1919)

American Red Cross, 'The Work of the American Red Cross During the War: A Statement of Finances and Accomplishments for the Period July 1, 1917 to February 28, 1919', (The American Red Cross, Washington, D.C., 1919)

Ankeney, Chris Taylor, 'A Narrative of the Taylor Family in Marceline, MO' (undated)

Ankeney, Chris Taylor, 'Erastus Taylor' (undated)

Beadle, Muriel and the Centennial History Committee, *The Fortnightly of Chicago: The City and its Women: 1873–1973*, (Henry Regnery Company, Chicago, 1973)

Bossert, David A., *Oswald the Lucky Rabbit: The Search for the Lost Disney Cartoons*, (Disney Editions: Los Angeles, 2017)

Broggie, Michael, *Walt Disney's Railroad Story*, (Pentrex, Pasadena, 1997)

Brown, Dee, *Hear That Lonesome Whistle Blow: The Epic Story of the Transcontinental Railroads*, (Holt, Rhinehart and Winston, New York, 1977)

Bryant Jr., Keith L., *History of the Atchison, Topeka & Santa Fe Railway*, (University of Nebraska Press, Lincoln, Nebraska, 1974)

Burnes, Brian, et. al, *Walt Disney's Missouri: The Roots of a Creative Genius*, (Kansas City Star Books, Kansas City, 2002)

'Centennial Celebration Special Edition', *Union Station On Track*, Fall 2014

Chicago Federal Building Bombed', *Morning Oregonian*, 5 September 1918

Chicago Gang History, 'Hermosa', https://chicagoganghistory.com/neighborhood/hermosa/

Chowell, Gerardo and Viboud, Cecile, 'Pandemic Influenza and Socioeconomic Disparities: Lessons from 1918 Chicago', (Proceedings of the National Academy of Sciences of the United States of America, 2016)

Christensen, Lawrence O. and Kremer, Gary R., *A History of Missouri: Volume IV, 1875–1919*, (University of Missouri Press, Columbia, Missouri, 1997)

Cullen, Niall, 'Walt Disney's Irish Ancestors', *Irish Central*, 20 February 2015

Dedmon, Emmett, *Fabulous Chicago*, (Random House, New York, 1953)

'DeMolay', Freemason Hall, www.freemasonhall.com/appendant_bodies/demolay/

Diner, Steven J., *A Very Different Age: Americans of the Progressive Era*, (Hill and Wang, New York, 1998)

Disney, Elias, 'Biography of the Disney Family in Canada', 1957

Dulles, Foster Rhea, *The American Red Cross: A History*, (Harper and Bros., New York, 1950)

Fargey, Kathleen M., 'The Deadliest Enemy: The U.S. Army and Influenza, 1918–1919', *Army History* (U.S. Army Center of Military History, 2019)

Finch, Christopher, *The Art of Walt Disney: From Mickey Mouse to the Magic Kingdom*, (Harry N. Abrams, Inc., New York, 1975)

Gabler, Neal, *Walt Disney: The Triumph of the American Imagination*, (Vintage Books, New York, 2006)

Grantz, Kyra H., Rane, Madhura S., et. al, 'Disparities in influenza mortality and transmission related to sociodemographic factors within Chicago in the pandemic of 1918', (*Proceedings of the National Academy of Sciences of the United States of America*, 2016)

Green, Amy Boothe and Green, Howard E., *Remembering Walt: Favorite Memories of Walt Disney*, (Disney Editions, New York, 1999)

Hatch, Darwin S., 'Making Ambulance Drivers', (*Motor Age*, 1918)

Havig, Alan, 'Mass Commercial Amusements in Kansas City Before World War I', *Missouri Historical Review*, vol. 75, no. 3, April 1981

'Here's a Merry War', *The Inter-Ocean*, 14 May 1899

History.com Editors, 'Homestead Act', (HISTORY, A&E Television Networks, 9 November 2009, www.history.com/topics/american-civil-war/homestead-act)

'How Gangs of Boy Bandits Terrorize Chicago', *The Chicago Tribune*, 28 January 1906

Hurd, Charles, *The Compact History of the American Red Cross*, (Hawthorn Books, New York, 1959)

The Influenza and Pneumonia Pandemic of 1918, (U.S. Army Medical Department Office of Medical History)

Iwerks, Don, *Walt Disney's Ultimate Inventor: The Genius of Ub Iwerks*, (Disney Editions, Los Angeles, 2019)

Jackson, Kathy Merlock, *Walt Disney: A Bio-Bibliography* (Greenwood Press, West Port, Connecticut, 1993)

Johnson, Mindy, *Ink & Paint: The Women of Walt Disney's Animation*, (Disney Editions, Los Angeles, 2017)

Jones, Marian Moser, 'The American Red Cross and Local Response to the 1918 Influenza Pandemic: A Four-City Case Study', *Public Health Reports* (Sage Publications, Inc., 2010)

Jordan, Edwin O., Reed, Dudley B. and Fink, E. B., 'Influenza in Three Chicago Groups', *Public Health Reports*, (Sage Publications, Inc., 1919)

'Kansas Pacific Railroad', *Kansas Heritage Group*, http://www.kansasheritage.org/research/rr/kp.html

Keogh, Grenville T., 'With the American Ambulance in France,' *Red Cross Magazine*, 1917

Korkis, Jim, 'The Story of Walt's Garage', MousePlanet, https://www.mouseplanet.com/10843/The_Story_of_Walts_Garage

Korkis, Jim, 'Walt's Canadian Connections', MousePlanet, https://www.mouseplanet.com/11799/Walts_Canadian_Connections

'Lamport and Holt's SS *Vauban*', Blue Star on the Web, www.BlueStarLine.org

Larson, Erik, *The Devil in the White City: Murder, Magic, and Madness at the Fair that Changed America*, (Vintage Books, New York, 2003)

Lemesh, Nicholas, 'From the Archives – Walt Disney, World War I Driver', (American Red Cross, 2015), https://redcrosschat.org/2015/09/17/archives-walt-disney-world-war-driver/

Lesjak, David, *In the Service of the Red Cross: Walt Disney's Early Adventures 1918–1919*, (Theme Park Press, 2015)

Lincoln, Abraham, 'July 4th Message to Congress', (4 July 1861)

Maltin, Leonard, *Of Mice and Magic: A History of American Animated Cartoons*, (McGraw Hill, New York, 1980)

Mayer, Harold M. and Wade, Richard C., *Chicago: Growth of a Metropolis*, (The University of Chicago Press, Chicago, 1969)

'Members to Pull the Plow', *Chicago Daily Tribune*, 19 May 1900

Merritt, Russell and Kauffman, J.B., *Walt in Wonderland: The Silent Films of Walt Disney*, (Le Giornate del Cinema Muto, Pordenone, Italy, 1993)

Miller, Diane Disney, *The Story of Walt Disney*, (Dell Publishing Co., New York, 1957)

Missouri State Highway Department, *Missouri: A Guide to the Show-Me State*, (Duell, Sloan and Pearce, New York, 1941)

Morens, David M. and Taubenberger, Jeffery K., '1918 Influenza, a Puzzle with Missing Pieces', *Emerging Infectious Diseases* (National Institutes of Health, Bethesda, Maryland, 2012)

Mosley, Leonard, *Disney's World*, (Scarborough House, Lanham, 1985)

'The Most Famous DeMolay of All: Walt Disney', DeMolay International, 2018, www.demolay.org/the-most-famous-demolay-of-all-walt-disney

Nasaw, David, *Children of the City: At Work & At Play*, (Oxford University Press, New York, 1985)

O'Brien, Carolyn, 'A Look at Cook', www.ALookAtCook.info

Pacyga, Dominic A., *Chicago: A Biography*, (The University of Chicago Press, Chicago, 2009)

'Pastor Guides the Plow', *Chicago Daily Tribune*, 20 May 1900

Perisco, Joseph E, 'The Great Swine Flu Epidemic of 1918', *American Heritage: The Magazine of History*, (American Heritage Publishing Co., New York, 1976)

'Plan of Re-Numbering City of Chicago: Table Showing New and Old House Numbers' (August 1909) http://www.chsmedia.org/househistory/1909snc/start.pdf

Ralph, Julian, 'Chicago – the Main Exhibit', *Harper's Magazine*, February 1892

Reid, Ann H., Janczewski, Thomas A., et. al, '1918 Influenza Pandemic and Highly Conserved Viruses with Two Receptor-Binding Variants', (Centers for Disease Control and Prevention, 2003)

Sanborn Maps of Marceline, Missouri, August 1911

Sayford, Irving S., 'Chicago Sets a Record', *Red Cross Magazine*, 1917

Schroeder, Russell, *Walt Disney: His Life in Pictures*, (Disney Press, New York, 1996)

Scully, Simone M. and Bonaccorso, Nicole, 'The Pandemic that Killed 50 Million', (The Weather Channel, 2019)

Shidler, Derek, 'A Tale of Two Cities: The 1918 Influenza Epidemic', *Historia* (Eastern Illinois University, 2009)

Silvester, William, *The Adventures of Young Walt Disney*, (Theme Park Press, 2014)

Simpson, Wade, 'Happy New Year, Virginia Davis', MousePlanet, https://www.mouseplanet.com/8604/Happy_New_Year_Virginia_Davis

Sklar, Robert, *Movie-Made America: A Cultural History of American Movies*, (Vintage Books, New York, 1994)

Spears, Timothy B., *Chicago Dreaming: Midwesterners and the City, 1871–1919*, (The University of Chicago Press, Chicago, 2005)

'Studies of the Great West – Chicago (Parts 1 and 2)', *The Midwest: A Collection from Harper's Magazine*, (Gallery Books, New York, 1991)

Taubenberger, Jeffery K. and Morens, David M., '1918 Influenza: The mother of all pandemics', *Emerging Infectious Diseases* (National Institutes of Health, Bethesda, Maryland, 2006)

Taylor, Lisa, 'Pull Over! It's an Emergency!: World War I Ambulance Drivers', *Library of Congress*, 2014

'The Ancient Graffiti That Proves Mickey Mouse Almost Never Existed', *DailyMail. com*, 15 April 2014

'The O-Zell Story', The O-Zell Soda Company, www.O-Zell.com/the-o-zell-story

Thomas, Bob, *Building a Company: Roy O. Disney and the Creation of an Entertainment Empire*, (Hyperion, New York, 1998)

Thomas, Bob, *Walt Disney: An American Original*, (Simon and Schuster, New York, 1976)

Thomas, Frank and Johnston, Ollie, *The Illusion of Life: Disney Animation*, (Disney Editions, New York, 1995)

Thompson, Kristin and Bordwell, David, *Film History: An Introduction*, (McGraw Hill, New York, 1994)

Tomes, Nancy, '"Destroyer and Teacher": Managing the Masses During the 1918–1919 Influenza Pandemic', *Public Health Reports*, (Sage Publications, Inc., 2010)

'Tripping the Light Fantastic…and Then Some!', KC History, https://kchistory.org/week-kansas-city-history/tripping-light-fantasticand-then-some

U.S. Army Medical Department Office of Medical History, 'Annual Reports, War Department, Fiscal Year Ended June 30, 1919, Report of the Surgeon General, U.S. Army to the Secretary of War, 1919 in Two Volumes', *Excerpts on the Influenza and Pneumonia Pandemic of 1918* (U.S. Army Medical Department, 1919)

U.S. Army Medical Department Office of Medical History, 'Evacuation Hospitals, Mobile Hospitals, Mobile Surgical Units, Professional Teams, Convalescent Depots, Evacuation Ambulance Companies, Mobile Laboratories', *The Medical Department of the U.S. Army in the World War: Field Operations* (U.S. Army Medical Department, 1925)

U.S. Army Medical Department Office of Medical History, 'World War I: The Ambulance Service', *The United States Army Medical Service Corps*, (U.S. Army Medical Department)

Union Pacific Railroad Company, 'Timeline', https://www.up.com/timeline/index.cfm/

United States Bureau of Labor, 'Wages and Cost of Living', in *Bulletin of the United States Bureau of Labor*, (No. 53, Volume IX, July 1904)

Van Dine, Sophia, 'How Boys Are Made Criminals', *Chicago Tribune*, 18 February 1906

Walsh, Jane, 'Celebrating Walt Disney's Birthday and His Irish Roots', *Irish Central*, 13 January 2012

Walt Disney Hometown Museum, *Tour Guide of Marceline, Missouri: Walt Disney's Home Town*, (Eisterhold Associates Inc., Kansas City, MO, 2001)

Weisberger, Bernard A., *The New Industrial Society*, (Wiley, New York, 1968)

Weiss, Werner, 'The Demise of the O-Zell Company', Yesterland, https://yesterland.com/ozell.html

Wright, Louis B., *Life on the American Frontier*, (Putnam, New York, 1968)

Index